GROUP PROCEDURES
FOR COUNSELORS
IN EDUCATIONAL
AND COMMUNITY
SETTINGS:
Original and Selected Readings

Edited by
Richard J. Malnati, Ph. D.
Temple University
Edward L. Trembley, Ed. D.
University of Delaware

MSS INFORMATION CORPORATION

Distributed by **ARNO PRESS**
3 Park Avenue, New York, N.Y. 10016

This is a custom-made book of readings prepared for the
courses taught by the editors, as well as for related courses
and for college and university libraries. For information
about our program, please write to:

MSS INFORMATION CORPORATION

MSS wishes to express its appreciation to the authors of the
articles in this collection for their cooperation in making
their work available in this format.

Library of Congress Cataloging in Publication Data

Malnati, Richard J   comp.
    Group procedures for counselors in educational and
community settings.

    1. Group counseling. I. Trembley, Edward L.,
joint comp. II. Title.
BF637.C6M3   361.4   73-22372
ISBN 0-8422-5161-8
ISBN 0-8422-0385-0 (pbk.)

CONTENTS

CHAPTER IV. GROUP PROCEDURES WITH THE CULTURALLY DIFFERENT

CHAPTER V. GROUP PROCEDURES WITH ADULTS AND SPECIAL COUNSELING PROBLEMS

CHAPTER VI. GROUP PROCEDURES: A REVIEW OF THE LITERATURE

It has been our experience as counselor educators that introductory group counseling texts have addressed themselves to standard issues such as group goals and purposes, group composition and size, leadership styles, membership considerations, clients selection, and stages of group process. Few texts have focused on providing the group counselor-in-training with strategies and procedures appropriate for clients of different ages and from diverse populations. This has been the case, even though group counselors in many settings must work with clients of varying ages and backgrounds.

The purpose of our project has been to provide the beginning group counselor with a set of readings on procedures that can be applied to groups in different settings with clients of different backgrounds and ages. Additionally, we have included two chapters to provide (1) an overview of group counseling and (2) an extensive group counseling and psychotherapy bibliography. To achieve our objective, we have selected twenty-nine articles on group procedures with children, adolescents, and adults and organized them into six chapters. Twenty-five of the articles have been published previously in fifteen journals, four of the articles were written for this collection.

The credit for this book belongs to the contributing authors. As editors, we are grateful to the authors for granting permission to use their articles.

CHAPTER I

GROUPS: AN INTRODUCTION

THE GROUP AS A UNIQUE CONTEXT FOR THERAPY[1,2]

MORTON A. LIEBERMAN   MARTIN LAKIN   DOROTHY STOCK WHITAKER

A major impediment to the development of theory of group therapy stems from the conceptual blurring of multi-person and dyadic relationships. One need only thumb through the journals in group psychotherapy to see that the predominant effort has been to build bridges between group and individual psychotherapy. This is not surprising, since most of us have cut our eye teeth as therapists in a two-person context. Even if this were not typical training experience, the two-person relationship would still be the likely model for the beginning group therapist. In our culture the expected setting for psychic help is a private, intimate relationship with one person—be he therapist, bartender, lawyer, doctor or clergyman. Even corporate bodies like the family or the church generally tender psychic relief in a two-person context, not through the corporate body as a whole. This cultural conditioning mediates the behavior of patients as well as therapists, and often obviates the employment group properties for therapeutic objectives. Most of us who do therapy in groups are successful the hard way. We swim upstream, against the forces of the group, depending on definable charismatic dimensions of our own personalities which, together with much sweat and toil, may illuminate some insight and may generate emotionally corrective transactions. We push and pull, to produce a climate in the group that will be conducive to therapeutic interactions. This engagement often produces beneficial effects. But does it maximize the potentials unique to the group situation?

Six characteristics of groups seem to us important influences on the therapeutic experience of the patients. These are its capacities to:

1) Develop cohesiveness or sense of belonging.
2) Control, reward and punish behavior.
3) Define reality for the individual.
4) Induce and release powerful feelings.
5) Distribute power and influence among individuals.
6) Provide a context for social comparison and feedback.

THE RELEVANCE OF GROUP PROPERTIES FOR THERAPY

1) The capacity to develop cohesiveness. The fundamental ambivalence of the neurotic requires a force of some kind for keeping him in the treatment situation. In a dyadic relationship we think of positive transference as the force enabling the patient to undergo the anxiety associated with the therapeutic process. In a two-person context, the therapist may offer the patient exclusive attention and unconditional acceptance. He is always able to take the patient's side against his real or imagined protagonists. In the patient's fantasy, if he abides by the rules, the therapist can offer him deliverance.

The group therapy patient, whom we see as little different from the individual patient, also enters the treatment situation with expectations of deliverance conducive to feelings of positive transference, but the group context vitiates many of the preconditions for positive transference. The group therapist cannot offer exclusive attention to each patient. He is un-

An earlier draft was presented in a paper, "The Therapist Versus the Group," at the Tri-State Psychotherapy Society, Cincinnati, Ohio, October, 1966, and the Illinois Group Psychotherapy Society, December, 1966, by Morton A. Lieberman.
Some of the ideas presented here first appeared in a paper, "The Implications of a Total Group Phenomena Analysis for Patients and Therapist," presented at the 23rd Annual Conference, American Group Psychotherapy Association, Philadelphia, January, 1966, by Morton A. Lieberman. In press, *International Journal of Group Psychotherapy*.

PSYCHOTHERAPY: THEORY, RESEARCH AND PRACTICE, 1968, Vol. 5, pp. 29-36.

7

likely to express unconditional acceptance at all times, for his feelings inevitably will shift as first one patient and then another supports or sabotages the therapeutic effort or behaves constructively or destructively toward the others. He cannot be each patient's ally uniformly, because the protagonists are not all outside but right there in the group, and share an equal right to his protection. The competing demands, shifting alliances and complex emotional structure present in the group context do not allow the patient to feel protected by the therapist as totally as in a two-person relationship. The therapist cannot be a fantasied deliverer in a group in the same personal sense that he can in a two-person relationship. What, then, binds the individual to the group? We suggest that the cohesive forces created in groups serve the same fundamental purpose as positive transference in the dyadic relationship. Feelings of belongingness motivate the patient to stay with the group and work with it and mitigate the pains associated with therapeutic exploration.

This is not to say that strong positive transference cannot take place in a group situation. The group therapist can, by considerable effort and charisma, establish and maintain attitudes and sets necessary for positive transference, but the style necessary to maintain such a stance in a group may interfere with strategies for inducing a therapeutic climate. Moreover, the likelihood of a charismatic therapist establishing such a relationship with all his patients is exceedingly small. Failures frequently drop out in the early sessions. On the other hand, for those patients with whom he succeeds in forming such a relationship, the therapist has restricted the range of interpersonal strategies available to him. Later changes are frequently achieved at the expense of patients experiencing profound disappointment and undue anxiety.

This does not imply that cohesiveness is entirely a productive quality in a therapy group. High cohesion lowers the willingness of patients to risk the disapproval of others—a fundamental condition in psychotherapy for discovery of new ways of behavior. Patients may come to value the group and membership in it above the gains potential in self-exploration and self-exposure. Thus it becomes important for the therapist to pay attention to the degree of cohesiveness in the group, to evaluate its relationship to the therapeutic process and to take responsibility for its management.

2) The capacity of the group to control behavior and to provide a system of rewards and punishments. In our previous work on focal conflict theory (Whitaker and Lieberman 1965) we discussed the capacity of the group to establish norms and standards (and its tendency to pressure and punish those who violate or challenge these norms). The process of working out solutions to focal conflicts was seen as the dynamic mechanism through which norms and standards are built up in the group. It is evident that in a therapeutic context which includes such group-generated influences, the therapist cannot have the same degree of influence over the meting out of reward and punishment that he would in a dyadic relationship.

Groups have powerful means of enforcing the norms and standards they establish, making conformity an issue for both therapist and patient. The group therapy patient is almost inevitably confronted with pressure from others to change his behavior or views. For some neurotics, being open to influence is a frightening, overwhelming possibility. These people "dare not conform" and, therefore, resist any kind of influence. At the same time they feel they cannot influence their environment. The power of the group to control behavior, however, also implies that each member has a greater opportunity to shape the environment than the patient in individual therapy. Thus one can recognize two kinds of conformity: the passive, inflexible conformity of the individual who does not attempt to influence his environment, and the active, functional conformity of a person who recognizes that others can influence and be influenced by him.

The normative need to be in step, to abide by the rules, is a powerful factor inducing conformity in a group. Disregard for the rules brings the potentiality of punishment. The ultimate punishment available to a group is the power of exclusion—either psychological or physical. In a dyadic relationship it is not exclusion the patient fears if he does not go along with the therapist, but loss of love. We are dealing, then, with two very different ps

-hological experiences leading to similar be-
-avior—conformity.

Pulling equally toward conformity is the
-roup's most-prized reward—its power to offer
-he authenticating affirmation of one's peers.
They are the ones whose acceptance, in the
-inal analysis, is desired. The experience of
-onsensual validation by persons who are im-
-ortant in a real and present world appears to
-e much more gratifying to the group therapy
-atient than the affirmation of the therapist.

This is not to deny that, as in individual
-herapy, the group patient wants acceptance
-rom the therapist and fears the loss of his
-ove. However, conformity to the *group's*
-values and standards and the influences of ex-
-lusion and peer affirmation are paramount.

3) The capacity of the group to define real-
ty for its members. The group exerts consid-
-rable influence on how each patient views
-imself, the group as a whole and others in the
-roup. A salient example of this influence was
-ontributed in a group therapy course in
-vhich psychiatric residents observed two of
-heir members working as therapists with an
-ngoing group:

The observers watched from a darkened observation
-om and discussed the proceedings afterwards with
-e two therapists. Before the eighth session began,
-e found that the window blinds had been removed
-or cleaning, so that the patients would be able to see
-e observers through the one-way mirror. The two
-udent therapists felt that since all the patients knew
-ey were being observed there was no need to call off
-e observation. As the patients arrived one by one
-ch looked particularly closely at the large observa-
-on mirror and then took his seat. The meeting began
-ith members talking about how difficult it was to
-mmunicate with people, "Particularly when you
-uldn't see them—in telephone conversations, etc."
-hey referred to the observers (which they had not
-one in previous sessions) with statements like "It's
-ncomfortable." "I don't like being observed because
-'s one-sided. The observers can see the patients but
-e patients cannot see the observers." The meeting
-ent on in this vein for about a half hour and then
-e topic shifted to other material. When the two
-sident therapists joined the rest of the students for
-discussion of the session, the observers asked them
-hy they had not intervened and brought some sense
-f "reality" to the group by pointing out that the
-bservers could be seen for the first time. They an-
-vered that the light had shifted and the observers
-uldn't really be seen. Their belief was so strong that
-veral of us had to accompany them into the therapy
-om and demonstrate that obviously the group could
-e the observers—perhaps not every facial gesture,
-ut clearly at least their outlines.

This to us was a dramatic instance of a
group's capacity to define its own, special reality. The two therapists, who had gone into the
meeting knowing the observers could be seen,
and the patients collectively upheld as "reality" the illusion that the observers could not
be seen.

In this case the group defined an illusion as
reality. In other instances the group-generated
reality destroys or challenges illusions of individual patients—as for example, convictions
about one's own unattractiveness, or the un-
trustworthiness of others, or about the facts of
any given matter.

In dyadic therapy a major task of the therapist is to define reality for the patient. The
therapist's view of reality is often accepted
rather readily by the patient—perhaps because
of the therapist's status as an expert or perhaps because the process of identification
forms so strong an element in the patient's
relationship to him. In the group, reality
grows out of the multitude of interactions and
counteractions, and frequently one can see a
struggle between the group and the therapist
over who is the arbiter of reality. This is particularly true of therapists who have a highly
developed model, because these more articulate
theories emphasize "rules" for translating patient productions into more abstract categories. Therapists who employ a theory that emphasizes primitive, unconscious feelings frequently engage the group in struggles over the
"real meaning" of a particular event. Similarly
therapists who emphasize particular transactions will often engage the group in a struggle
to "correctly" label a particular interaction,
for example, as "game playing." Labelling such
occurrences as "therapeutic resistance" all too
frequently obfuscates a detailed examination of
the phenomenon and its potential therapeutic
possibilities.

The group therapist can, of course, attempt
to impose his version of reality on the group,
but the price may be to create a gross dependency state or to generate unexpressed reservations or rebellion. Another pitfall for the therapist is to participate in the consensus about a
perceived "reality" that is in fact an illusion.
Groups frequently establish dangerous illusions as in scapegoating, where an individual
in the group becomes the focus of particular

9

feelings. Some of the group's "realities" are illusions that need to be dealt with therapeutically. We believe the error of attempting to be the sole definer of reality is made more frequently by therapists than the error of taking too little responsibility for this process. The most appropriate stance is that of monitor of the group's realities, challenging consensus when it seems necessary, but also recognizing that most group definitions of reality are useful.

4) The capacity of the group to induce, stimulate and release powerful feelings. Historically, emotional contagion was the first phenomenon to interest investigators of groups. LeBon, MacDougall and Freud pointed out that powerful primitive affect can be released in groups. Individuals may be carried away, may experience feelings which they later believe are uncharacteristic of themselves, and may act on feelings without displaying their typical controls. This potential in groups can have either positive or negative effects on therapy. An individual may experience previously-denied feelings not with enduring terror but with growth—the corrective emotional experience of finding that the feelings are not overwhelming or that the feared consequences do not occur. Negative effects may occur when an individual is overwhelmed by affect and must defend against the group situation by literal or psychological withdrawal, or by the invocation of undesirable defenses.

Since contagion occurs in groups, but not in individual therapy, the process of circumventing defenses may be quite different in the two settings. In individual therapy the sequence involves first analyzing the resistance in order to release the feared affect. In group therapy, participation in group-generated affect may allow the patient to by-pass defenses so that the feared affect may be experienced first, thus rendering the resistance less necessary.

It is also possible that the kinds of affect are rather different. Feelings of solidarity with others, empathy toward peers, ganging up against a common enemy are not experienced in individual therapy. Moreover, a particular affect may have a different quality in the two therapies. For example, the patient in individual therapy who intimates his innermost feelings to a benign professional person undoubtedly risks far less than the group therapy patient, who may undergo feelings of extreme exhilaration or fear as he reveals himself "in public."

The managing of group affect becomes one of the essential skills of the therapist. This skill involves tamping down contagion where necessary, protecting individuals who need to be exempted from participation in group affect, breaking up group resistance in order for affect to emerge, sensing when to let the affect run on and develop and when to introduce cognitive reflection about the affect.

5) The distribution of power and influence in the group. Power is distributed unevenly in groups. Some members have great influence over the course of group events, standards, the way the group defines reality; others have not. Power is fluid—it does not consistently remain in the same hands, but fluctuates with the state of the group.

The power of the therapist, for example, is rarely discussed perhaps because it is not a problem in the interpersonal setting of two-person therapy. The individual therapist has considerable influence on what is talked about and how it is talked about. The group therapist, on the other hand, senses differences at times in his degree of control or influence. His power vascillates because, singly, he cannot effect the "therapeutic contract." The therapist in a group setting must pay attention to the area of power and influence and realize that, no matter how sensitive or skillful he is, he cannot have the same degree of influence on the interpersonal situation that he would in a two-person relationship.

Associated with the group therapist's experience of power are attitudes he may hold towards his patients. He may feel less personal responsibility for his charges in the group setting. The amount of influence we have with another human being is related to the amount of responsibility we feel for him; groups, no matter what their purpose, tend to blur the lines of individual responsibility, making it more difficult for any single person, no matter what his role, to feel that what happens to the group or to individuals in a group is directly related to his own behavior.

The group therapist, for example, has difficulty seeing any one-to-one correspondence etween his interventions and therapeutic benefit to a particular patient. Group therapists indicate that they have difficulty perceiving what they have done to help a particular person in a group; that is, they find it difficult to rticulate the relationship of a specific intervention to a particular response in an individual patient. The group therapist can point to ffective interventions, but he sees them as art of a long chain of events in which they re interwoven with the interactions of a roup of patients. The fate of a particular patient in a group depends upon many factors nd, although the therapist influences all of hese factors, he cannot experience the direct ausal relationship between his behavior and he patient's therapeutic gains that he does in ndividual therapy. Others have put it that in a roup there are "multiple therapists"; whether r not one agrees with this formulation, it illustrates how the group therapist experiences is role.

What are the consequences of giving help in situation where it is difficult to relate one's wn efforts directly to the help received by he patient? Does it limit the types of gratification the group therapist can experience in he role of the help-giver? His inability to articulate a direct connection between his intervention and the ultimate therapeutic benefits o individual patients would seem to mean that e cannot experience the same kinds of legitimate gratifications that are possible in a dyadic elationship. Expecting rewards similar to hose experienced in the individual setting is a requent cause for the neophyte's sense of frustration in a group.

6) *The capacity of the group to provide a ontext for social comparison and feedback.* During group therapy patients frequently ompare their attitudes toward parents, husbands, wives, children; their feelings about mmediate events in the group; the things that nake them sad, happy, guilty, angry; the ways hat each typically deals with and expresses nger, affection, and so on. Such comparisons ccur naturally and facilitate revisions of the atient's identity by confronting him with new ossibilities in feeling, perceiving and behaving.

Another kind of interaction which is possible in groups is commonly called feedback.

One patient says to another, "When you went on and on just now I felt like giving up," or "You just said something sarcastic to me and I felt hurt and resentful." Such comments allow the recipient of the feedback to understand better the impact of his behavior on others. Feedback contributes quite directly to the therapeutic goal of helping each person to recognize and accept responsibility for the interpersonal consequences of his behavior.

Asking for and providing feedback does not come naturally; or rather, it may be imbedded in potentially destructive behavior. Patients sometimes try to "help" one another by offering interpretations: "You dominate the group because . . .," or "you are sarcastic because you are afraid to be angry in any more direct way." Sometimes interpretations are apropos, useable, and offered in a helpful spirit, but often they are heavily invested with projection, or function as a personal defense or a safe way of expressing hostility. The group therapist must teach the group to utilize feedback appropriately. Social comparison and feedback occur in individual therapy only occasionally as deliberate tactics, never as major avenues toward therapy.

SOME IMPLICATIONS
For Therapeutic Outcomes

These six group properties create conditions that engage the group therapy patient in a number of activities and concerns which differ from those of the patient in dyadic treatment. In comparison with the latter, the group patient gets little practice in reflecting about himself and his interactions with others, in associating about his own feelings, in analyzing dreams, in linking present and past experiences or penetrating covert meanings; he is too busy actually interacting and finding a viable place for himself in the group. But he gets greater practice in expressing his feelings to peers, in noting the consequences of such expressions, in attempting to understand and empathize with others, in hearing from others about his impact on them and in comparing himself with others.

Does this differing balance in experience lead to differences in outcome? It is commonly assumed that the group patient should end up getting help of much the same order as he

11

would have obtained in a dyadic relationship. It is perhaps helpful to test this assumption against, first, the end-state of the patient at the close of therapy (symptoms, conflicts, defenses, interpersonal patterns and the like); and second, the meta-learning achieved (learning how to approach problems, how to confront and resolve conflicts and how to cope with anxiety).

Three aspects of the patient's end-state are relevant: (1) the symptoms or presenting complaint; (2) the revision of maladaptive patterns, the relinquishment of neurotic defenses or the resolution of neurotic conflict; and (3) the unsought, ancillary gains. Symptom relief, for example, may be achieved at different rates. (The "placebo" effect, critical in many instances of rapid symptom relief, seems to us unique to the dyad). Particular behavior changes or conflict resolutions may be accomplished better by one of the two settings depending on the nature of the problem, the composition of the therapy group, and so on. For example, a therapy group whose composition encourages a patient to maintain an established neurotic pattern may be less effective for that patient than individual therapy. On the other hand, a group which, say through emotional contagion, led a patient to experience a previously-feared affect may be more effective than individual therapy.

Finally, the two treatment situations may be conducive to rather different ancillary benefits. For example, difficulty in giving to others may be only peripherally related to the patient's presenting complaint or core conflicts, but nevertheless an issue. Since giving to others is often a focal concern in a group, many opportunities appear for each patient to note the nature of his anxieties about giving and to try out giving behavior. Thus, changes in giving behavior may occur sooner or more directly than in individual therapy. The two therapies may also call attention to different aspects of man—in group therapy, for example, patients are likely to be struck by the basic kinship, the sharing in the human condition, of persons who may appear quite different. They may be impressed both by the difficulties in communicating meaningfully to others and by the profound rewards experienced when such communi-

nication proves possible. The dyad, in contrast, does not directly facilitate such experiences.

The differences for meta-learning may be even greater than the differences in end-state outcomes. In any form of therapy the patient often adopts a style of approaching problems which reflects the characteristic processes of the therapy. It is not unusual for a patient to emerge from a psychoanalysis with an increased tendency to pay attention to his dreams, to deduce emotional meaning from forgetting, to search out unrecognized feelings when he notes inconsistencies in his behavior. A patient who has undergone group treatment may be more likely to seek out feedback from others, to make social comparisons, to test out behaviors interpersonally.

For Selection of Patients

Patients may vary in their aptitude for therapeutic gains within the two environments. Some patients may "take to" the processes characteristic of individual therapy readily. They may be highly reflective, more investigatively inclined, interested in searching out their own feelings and in speculating about links with past life. Similarly, some patients may enter more readily into the fluid round of interactions characteristic of group therapy. They may need a present arena for trying out new behavior, comparing themselves with peers, asking for and receiving feedback. Patients who may be comparable in terms of diagnostic category, severity of impairment, conflict area, and so on, may not be comparable in aptitude for the two therapeutic situations.

For the Therapist

May not the same reasoning apply to therapists? If the two settings involve quite different processes, the therapist's task, the potential stresses upon him, even his way of understanding the patient may all be different. A therapist may be unevenly suited for the two roles. The person of the therapist is important in the dyad because he is the instrument that creates or induces the climate in which psychotherapy will take place. His warmth, his understanding and his strength are paramount. Conditions of intimacy and non-judgmentalness are required to create the therapeutic milieu. Trust and faith in the person of the therapist permits the patient to undergo the risks and pain of the process. The patient's wish to be like the therapist is an important element of the dyadic process.

These personal qualities are less important for the group therapist, whose central role is to manage the group conditions to effect a climate for therapeutic encounters. Warmth, understanding, symbolization of strength are not paramount. They are not totally unimportant, for group therapy must include some aspects of charisma. Nevertheless, the group is ultimately the salient psychological body for the patient; in the long run the personal qualities of the therapist are not critical in shaping the therapeutic climate, or inducing appropriate identifications.

Self-understanding also may play a different role in the two therapies and different kinds may be required. The dyadic therapist must know his own vulnerabilities, conflicts, biases and predispositions, so that his responses are less likely to be insensitive, destructive, or inappropriate. Self-understanding is also expected to sharpen his perception of "what is going on."

The group therapist, too, must be aware of "what is going on," but this includes group and interpersonal phenomena which are not present in individual therapy. Self-knowledge does not take the group therapist as far as it does the individual therapist since he is not a direct participant in all that is going on. The kind of self-knowledge he needs concerns how vulnerable he is to various kinds of group contagion, how threatened he is by unanimous attack and what defenses he is likely to invoke against it, what it means to him to maintain a deviant position in a group and much else that is irrelevant for the individual therapist.

A therapist must come to know his patients. For some, understanding of another human being comes from knowing what he has experienced, what he thinks and what he feels. Others understand another human being through seeing how he behaves and what he does. The first type of person may make a poor group

therapist or may find the role distasteful because the kind of information he needs about others may not be available in a group—at least not without fighting against the character of the group itself.

Finally, the special characteristics of the group as a context for therapy may generate differing views of human nature. The moral pessimism associated with the psychoanalytic tradition may be generated by the analyst's experience of the patient in the analytic setting, which emphasizes such features of the personality as the primitive character of impulses, the intractable nature of defenses and the like. In contrast, the group therapeutic process emphasizes capacity to settle differences, interpersonal sensitivity and communication, which may lead to an image of man cast in terms of competence.

For Training

What has all this to do with training the group therapist? In our view, the special qualities of the group context suggest that a critical training need is to help the group therapist adopt the perspective of a "social engineer," a term that perhaps seems cold and manipulative, but is meant rather to underscore the management of social forces and the mining of group resources as the essential skills which the group therapist must develop. Most training relies on an apprenticeship relationship which utilizes the process of identification—a tool of the charismatic leader—to teach the novice how to become a group therapist. The trainer points out what is "really occurring" in the group, thereby relating to the student therapist in the same fashion as he relates to his patients—incorrectly. The training tradition, in other words, duplicates with the student the very errors he is to correct as a group therapist. But are there any ways out of this quandary? Part of the answer may lie in our paying closer attention to certain aspects of the personality of the trainee. If it is true that people differ in how they acquire understanding of their fellow men, then some people may have less aptitude as group therapists than others. There are other personal qualities that may make considerable difference in how well a person can function as a group therapist. The model of social engineer, which we suggest is appropriate to the group therapist, is alien to the tradition from which most therapists stem. The medical model, which all the helping professions share, is a cure model in which the patient is seen as sick and needing something to be done for him; there is also a "hothouse model" in which psychotherapy is seen as an artificial situation designed to stimulate growth and, finally, a "powerhouse model" wherein positive persuasion is used to deal with the patients' problems. All three, or any combination of them, involve the therapist in certain psychological relationships to the patient. They involve forms of deliverance and intimacy which are external to the natural processes that occur in groups. Training programs must take into account the impact of these traditional conceptions about the role of the help-giver and the needs of the help-giver. Otherwise they will create therapists who unwittingly align themselves against the inherent forces in the group setting which can contribute most to therapeutic gain.

REFERENCE

WHITAKER, D. S. & LIEBERMAN, M. A. *Psychotherapy through the Group Process.* New York: Atherton Press, 1965.

Group counseling

CLARENCE A. MAHLER

This article reviews the major concerns of group counseling and differentiates among group guidance, group counseling, and group therapy. It also evaluates the research status of group counseling. Finally, the author presents implications for the future of this approach.

THE DEVELOPMENT of group counseling has a short history of 30 to 40 years. It was slow in gaining acceptance. In the last 10 years, however, group counseling has expanded rapidly in both school and nonschool settings. Its location as a helping procedure between education on one hand and group therapy on the other has been confusing. Perhaps the most supporting evidence for a legitimate place for group counseling has come from the broad acceptance of encounter and sensitivity groups. This acceptance has been a mixed blessing, since the weaknesses of sensitivity training are often focused upon group counseling programs.

Two other areas that have contributed much to the growth of group counseling have been the steady development of group psychotherapy in the past 30 years and the rapid expansion of research in group dynamics. So while there is still a lack of adequate theoretical views and definitive research, there is increased sophistication in the design of programs and in the research with groups.

CONCERNS ABOUT THE PRESENT STATUS

Many of the leaders in group counseling, myself included, have concerns with the growth process of this area. It appears that our favorite child, group counseling, has attained the adolescent stage of development, with all the anxiety and confusion accompanying it.

One major concern is the too frequent, naive view that the mere placing of individuals in a group will be good for them. This view holds that anyone trained in individual counseling would be able to do group counseling. Further, individuals, particularly teachers, who have experienced the exhilaration and all too often temporary intimacy of encounter weekends, endeavor to apply the encounter experience to their subject matter area.

Perhaps the most naive example of misapplication I have ever known was a young sociology instructor who attended an encounter weekend in the summer. Then, in September he began all four of his sociology courses with nonverbal methods. The students responded well, and they did feel the emotional forces, both personal and group, that emanate from closer personal contact with others. But the main problem, from my position, was that the young instructor had no idea how to move from the deeply satisfying mood of being personally involved to the broader goals of his classes. I am personally very concerned that emotional experiences, long neglected in our whole educational system, should not merely *replace* cognitive experiences. The cog-

CLARENCE A. MAHLER is Professor of Psychology at Chico State College in Chico, California.

PERSONNEL AND GUIDANCE JOURNAL, 1971, Vol. 49, pp. 601-608.

15

nitive side of man needs to be deeply integrated with his emotional nature. This integration is not, however, accomplished by superficial group experiences.

Another facet of the superficial view of group work is a belief that "groups" have an "innate" capacity to become groups without the leader's having a frame of reference or an adequate repertoire of techniques. Some of the recent research at Chico State College on the impact that the leader has on group functioning indicates that poor leaders do indeed leave college freshmen confused and lost, whereas skilled group counselors facilitate school progress as well as personal growth (Fox, 1970). I feel that a superficial approach to group counseling, both in group process and leader functioning, is worse than having no groups at all.

My second major area of concern relates to the position group counseling has in the school setting or in other agencies. We must guard against expecting it to make up for gross deficiencies in the way individuals are treated in an agency. Group counseling, like individual counseling, is of major value in an agency that deeply respects its members and wants to further their individual growth.

Group methods have been used effectively in a number of school districts to manage deep, conflicting issues, such as racial tensions. But the primary value of group counseling does not lie in the management of behavior. Thus, group counseling should be seen as complementing the basic goals of an agency. It is possible to delineate clearly where and how group counseling fits in the elementary school, the secondary school, the state employment office, the welfare office, the probation office, and juvenile hall. In fact, it is highly desirable that this process of integrating the potentiality of group counseling with the major purposes of a given agency be accomplished clearly before the program begins.

My third major concern is related to the frequent lack of a theoretical rationale for the group effort. Some counselors have very limited conceptual ideas of what counseling may accomplish. Gradually we are seeing that a theoretical point of view is essential for a counselor, whether he is working with individuals or groups.

Some group workers, particularly the encounter type, assume that learning derives from experience. These leaders often feel that catharsis and exhilarating responses will lead to changed behavior. Transfer of learning experiments have produced too much evidence that change of behavior is not easy enough to leave it to chance.

Some group counselor trainers have followed an Adlerian or behavioral view of counseling. In respect to theoretical rationale, behavioral counseling has had a clear awareness of its rationale and the procedures that may attain the desired change of behavior.

It has been my experience that many counselors and counselor trainers who claim to be eclectic are deficient in formulating their own theoretical views and integrating them with their counseling behavior. A sound conceptual frame of reference undergirding one's group efforts seems desirable and necessary before we even begin programs in group counseling.

GROUP COUNSELING DEFINED

Counseling can be viewed as a helping process aimed at aiding individuals to understand better their own and other people's behavior. The process may be concerned with a problem, with life patterns, and/or with identity-seeking. Progress in counseling has been found to be closely related to the development of mutual respect, trust, and acceptance. Thus, it is important that, in aiding the client's growth and development, the counselor learns to be congruent, open, understanding, and accepting. In group as well as in individual counseling, it is important that the client feels he is being understood, which means that the counselor and group members must learn to listen perceptively and with understanding. Clients may not be able to explain themselves clearly, but they know immediately when they feel understood by the leader and group members.

One definition of group counseling is:

Group counseling is a dynamic, interpersonal process focusing on conscious thought and behavior and involving the therapy functions of permissiveness, orientation to reality, catharsis, and mutual trust, caring, understanding, acceptance and support. The therapy functions are created and nurtured in a small group through the sharing of personal concerns with one's peers and the counselors. The group counselees are basically normal individuals with various concerns which are not debilitating to the extent of requiring extensive personality change. The group counselees may utilize the group interaction to increase understanding and acceptance of values and goals and to learn and/or unlearn certain attitudes and behaviors [Gazda, Duncan, & Meadows, 1967, p. 306].

In group counseling the major concerns that individuals bring up center on the socialization process. The main questions that they ask are: How do I maintain a close relationship with my family and yet establish my own individuality? Who am I, anyway? How do people really see me? What are my abilities and talents and where can I use them? Do men's and women's world views differ?

With this background I have defined group counseling as:

. . . the process of using group interaction to facilitate deeper self-understanding and self-acceptance. There is a need for a climate of mutual respect and acceptance, so that individuals can loosen their defenses sufficiently to explore both the meaning of behavior and new ways of behaving. The concerns and problems encountered are centered in the developmental tasks of each member rather than on pathological blocks and distortions of reality [Mahler, 1969, p. 11].

GROUP COUNSELING VERSUS GROUP GUIDANCE AND GROUP THERAPY

Group counseling, group guidance, and group therapy can be clearly differentiated even though they overlap considerably.

Group guidance is primarily a class or education experience, mainly involved with giving out information. In schools, it is usually oriented toward encouraging students to know what the adults think the participants should know. Although the same topics discussed in group counseling may also be discussed in group guidance, the major responsibility in guidance remains with the teacher. In group counseling the focus is upon each member, not the topic being discussed, and upon changing his behavior, not changing behavior in general.

Group therapy is more concerned with unconscious motivation. Because of the depth of the growth problems faced by the clients, it is not unusual for the process to last months and even years. It is aimed at the more disturbed individuals.

Group counseling is a social experience that deals with the developmental problems and attitudes of individuals in a secure setting. Sensitivity training and encounter groups can best be classified as variations of group counseling. While many encounter-sensitivity groups have structured experiences planned as part of the session, they clearly do not fit under group guidance.

How do these three approaches differ? We can establish clear distinctions in six major areas—size of group, the way content is managed, the length of group life, the responsibilities of the leader, the severity of problems, and the competencies of the leader.

Size

On the basis of size, I prefer to divide group counseling into large group and small group counseling. A large group may be designated as one having from 10 to 20 members, a small group from 2 to 10 members. The group dynamics, the role of the leader, the selection of techniques, the responsibilities of members all vary considerably according to the size of the group.

Group guidance in a school or agency setting is usually of class size or larger. In a few cases the size of a group has been over 20 and has still attained the objectives sufficiently enough to be considered group counseling.

The size of groups from 2 to 10 fits both small group counseling and group therapy. Therefore, additional distinguishing features are needed to differentiate between small group counseling and group therapy.

In one NDEA (National Defense Education Act) Institute at New York University, we utilized size of group to help get group counseling into the high schools. There was a reluctance to have counseling groups of 7 or 8 students because that might be considered group therapy, and the school system was very definitely against group therapy there. So, groups of 15 members were established and thus could the program fit the desired goal—that group counseling must be a part of the education program.

Management of Content

Considerable difference exists among the three approaches in ways that subject matter or content of discussion is dealt with. There is also variation within each area as to how content is managed; but, by and large, the differentiation is greater between areas than within areas.

In group guidance the topics of experiences are usually selected by the leader or are part of a regular program of instruction. For example, in a "How To Study" unit the content and procedures are often ready to use regardless of the particular class and the readiness of members for the topic. Secondly, the content is often handled in an "academic" manner. That is, the topic is talked about or the discussion is about the topic rather than the members of the class being responsible for establishing their own views on the topic or evaluating for themselves what the class experience means personally. The danger lies in the result that something is done to a class rather than the members themselves being involved meaningfully in the learning experience.

In group counseling the topic is derived from the immediate or stated concerns of the group members. Many of the same topics covered in a group guidance unit come up in group counseling. But the real issue is that the choice is up to the members: They select the topic or specific group they wish to participate in. Thus, from the counseling point of view the member selects the topic or area he wishes to work on. The prior selection of a topic is much less the issue than the way in which it is managed.

Behavioral counseling, as a form of group counseling, selects an area of concern and programs procedures to accomplish the specific goals. But there is a real concern for the personal involvement of the participants. In fact, even more than in "laissez faire" or "I hope we go somewhere" group counseling, there is an aim to change specific behavior of the participants.

In group therapy the content derives from the problems presented by the members. Regardless of the variation in leader role, from very nondirective and noninterpretative to confrontative and directive, the content grows out of the life experiences of the group members.

Length of Group Life

In group guidance or orientation-type programs, the life of the group is determined mainly by organizational aspects. A semester or a three-week unit or other variations set the time limits. In group counseling there has been experimentation in setting a specified number of sessions for a group versus allowing a group to go as long as the members desire. The experience of behavioral counseling and Adlerian counseling programs in setting the number of sessions in advance holds on sound theoretical grounds. More research is needed to help practitioners in this important area. The goals set by group members will often suggest the length of time that might be appropriate.

In group therapy the most frequent pattern seems to be to allow groups to go on without limiting the number of sessions. At the present time it is not possible to prescribe so many sessions for a certain group or a specific problem area. The main weakness, particularly in doctoral dissertations, is expecting extensive behavioral change in too few sessions. For example, underachievement, regardless of whether at the elementary, high school, or college level, is not easily reversed by 5, 10, or 15 group sessions. Group participation is much more closely related to the socialization process than is individual counseling. Therefore the change process is more gradual, and often comes about by identification and modeling of group members and the leader. The best recommendation that can be made at present is to set a specific number of sessions when one starts a group. Then the leader can make provisions to have a second series of sessions with the same group members or to reconstitute the group with different members or new goals.

There is a strong tendency for all well-functioning groups to want to continue. In fact, the tendency for exclusiveness of groups within a larger program, such as school or church, can be partly controlled by the design of the group program, i.e., by the number of sessions and by mixing group members in subsequent time blocks.

Responsibility of Leader

In group guidance the leader is usually responsible for the structure and conduct of the session. Imparting information is often one of his major functions. Good discussion techniques and creative teaching methods can indeed make a meaningful group guidance program. The fact that many group guidance programs are poorly conducted, in the same manner that a subject matter class may be well or poorly taught, does not mean that group guidance is bad. A clear statement of goals for a total guidance program will go a long way in establishing the kind of guidance experiences most likely to help members. So, in group guidance the leader is seen as being mainly responsible for content and letting the personal meaning of the experiences be the member's responsibility.

In group counseling the role is largely reversed. A skilled group counselor can take almost any topic or concern and help the individual members work through their own personal meanings. Here again, it is not so much who selects the topic, member or leader, but how the topic is managed that differentiates group counseling from group guidance.

In group counseling and group therapy the basic responsibility of the leader is very similar. The difference between the two approaches lies more in the composition of the groups.

The group counselor learns that he should not deal with problems that will take extensive time to understand and solve. A student may, for instance, mention in a group counseling session that his parents have "grounded him" as a penalty for poor grades. The counselor may be aware of severe emotional problems in the family—for example, that deep neurotic conflicts and attachments of the son to his mother are helping to immobilize the youth and preventing him from doing better work. However, the counselor will recognize his need to guide the discussion toward those aspects of the problem which the student and members of the group are capable of handling. Thus, it is not that a counselor is unaware of deeper problems or afraid of deep disturbance, but more that he is realistic about what it takes to change behavior. One of the prime reasons for proposing group counseling programs is that group guidance efforts do not sufficiently change behavior; but, on the other hand, we should not expect group counseling to change deep-seated emotional problems.

Severity of Problems

One of the main differences between members in group therapy and participants in group counseling lies in the severity of the presenting problem. Excessive acting out, deep emotional disturbance, and delinquency are considered to place the members in need of therapy (group and individual). In group counseling it is assumed that almost all members of the institution, such as a school or church, are potential members. The emphasis is more on factors of socialization than on deep emotional disturbance. Often a topic of concern can be proposed as the central reason for joining a group. For example, in a college dorm all students who feel lonely and unskilled in making friends might be invited to sign up for group counseling. A recent extensive study on the content of individual therapy sessions with young adult women indicated a primary focus upon the "outer" or interpersonal sphere of their lives and the least focus upon the "inner" or intrapersonal aspect (Howard, Orlinsky, & Hill, 1969). The specific topics discussed most frequently were heterosexual involvements, occupational concerns, and hopes or fears for the future.

There is some evidence that topics in group counseling are very similar. Such evidence suggests that rather than having jurisdictional disputes over who helps whom, we need to focus on how best to help individuals with the concerns they bring to counseling or therapy. This leads to the last area for differentiating among approaches.

Competency of the Leader

Let us assume that leaders in all three approaches — group guidance, group counseling, and group therapy—are competent. What, then, is the difference in competency suggested? The difference lies in the depth of psychological understanding of individual behavior and group dynamics. What difference in competencies would we like to see in leaders discussing with young adults their heterosexual involvements, occupational concerns, and hopes or fears for the future? Not only should the leader be versed in individual dynamics of behavior but he also needs a sound background in social psychology and group dynamics. So rather than highly different training, the leader needs increasing depth of training in essentially the same areas.

In a group guidance class centered on family relations, it is desirable that the leader be well versed in the theoretical and research literature on the topic. We need not expect that he would have the skills to translate theoretical knowledge into a new learning opportunity for group members. Theoretical and conceptual knowledge in depth is essential for all group leaders; where the leaders differ is in their skill in utilizing the knowledge for personal growth.

RESEARCH ON GROUP COUNSELING

Group counseling programs have expanded rapidly in the last 10 years. However, the research and evaluative efforts, as in group psychotherapy, have lagged far behind. Gazda and Larsen (1968) conducted a comprehensive appraisal of group counseling research. Approximately 100 studies, dating from 1938 to 1968 and relating directly to group counseling, were reviewed. The main weaknesses found in the studies were: (a) theoretical orientations vague or poorly stated; (b) the nature of treatment process not clearly presented; (c) qualification of the group counselor not clearly identified; (d) because outcome variables too global to be tied down to ways treatment may affect them, specific goals needed that can be stated in precise measurable terms; (e) tendency not to have specific outcome goals for each group member; (f) many evaluation instruments unsuitable for evaluating outcome variables (Grade point average, as the most popular means of evaluating the outcome of group counseling, indicates a low degree of sophistication. Tests of function much closer to awareness of actual performance in interpersonal relations would be much better.); (g) difficulty in obtaining adequate control groups.

The past research efforts in group counseling have had generally inconclusive results. In describing the present state of evaluative efforts, it is notable that one of the most promising trends is to indicate specific measurable outcome objectives. Behavioral counseling research has been particularly helpful in showing that if one focuses upon one or two precise behaviors, it is possible to ascertain much more clearly the treatment effects. The practices of using global adjustments as an outcome variable will continue to decrease. We need to explore a wider variety of significant behaviors than were studied in early work in behavioral counseling. The trend to study deeper and more significant problems is evident. The work of Krumboltz at Stanford University on loneliness from a behavioral modification approach is indeed promising. In fact, it has been discouraging to some of the behavioral modification critics who have tried to tag the method as being too mechanistic.

The future of research on methods, processes, and outcomes will undoubtedly be greatly influenced by the outstanding work of Carkhuff (1969). Carkhuff not only tackles the whole process of counseling and counseling outcomes but he also derives a method of training to go along with the theoretical basis and procedures for those who want to be helpers. He has submitted a much-needed challenge to all trainers of professionals to validate their training methods in terms of change in client behavior. Carkhuff feels that it may be more feasible to train lay personnel to help than to make real helpers out of students in our present "academically" oriented training programs. He presents extensive research evidence to show that the functioning level of the leader in interpersonal relations is the most influential aspect of the treatment effort. Of particular relevance to group counseling is his insistence upon group training as the preferred mode of working with difficulties in interpersonal functioning.

The major contribution that Carkhuff makes to the present state of group counseling training is his emphasis on assessing the interpersonal functioning of each member as the group begins and then providing specific treatment efforts to facilitate improved functioning. Group members are helped by one another to assess their own level of interpersonal functioning, and varied remedial action efforts are planned. The counselor is not left with a hazy idea of what his role is, but instead with a clear picture of his own relationship to the helping process. The approach of Carkhuff is in harmony with behavioral counseling efforts.

These trends suggest much more promising days for the helping professions. The main criticisms leveled at group work will no longer hold. Research efforts will be closely related to counseling practice, and counseling practice will be much more clearly based upon research efforts. Theories of behavior and behavior modification will be related more closely to specific treatment efforts. The skills used in helping to change behavior will be taught to group members as well as to group leaders. The benefits of these present trends will hold not only for group therapy and encounter groups but for group guidance as well. Since we will be concerned with changing behavior, there will be experiments on ways in which behavior might be changed in large group (i.e., class size) instruction.

Group therapy research has had much the same weaknesses as group counseling. The research in encounter groups has been even less sophisticated. From now on, however, it can be expected that all helping efforts will have improved statements of theoretical assumptions, treatment efforts, and specific outcomes. The exuberant and somewhat irresponsible adolescent period of group counseling (all of group work, for that matter) seems to be approaching a more responsible, adult position. I hope that we can better contain the "bandwagon" rush to implement group work in every possible helping agency. In schools, employment agencies, probation offices, welfare services, and church settings we must strengthen our in-service efforts to train group leaders more adequately. For readers whose backgrounds in group counseling are limited, I recommend that two recent texts on group counseling, Mahler (1969) and Ohlsen (1970), be considered.

REFERENCES

Carkhuff, R. R. *Helping and human relations,* Vol. I and II. New York: Holt, Rinehart, and Winston, 1969.

Carkhuff, R. R., & Berenson, B. G. *Beyond counseling and therapy.* New York: Holt, Rinehart, and Winston, 1967.

Fox, W. T. The relationship between group counselor functioning and the counseling group's perception of the campus environment. Unpublished master's thesis, Chico State College, 1970.

Gazda, G. M., Duncan, J. A., & Meadows, M. E. Group counseling and group procedures—Report of a survey. *Counselor Education and Supervision,* 1967, *6,* 305–310.

Gazda, G. M., & Larsen, M. J. A comprehensive appraisal of group and multiple counseling. *Journal of Research and Development in Education,* 1968, *1,* 57–132.

Howard, K. I., Orlinsky, D. E., & Hill, J. A. Content of dialogue in psychotherapy. *Journal of Counseling Psychology,* 1969, *16,* 396–404.

Mahler, C. A. *Group counseling in the schools.* Boston: Houghton Mifflin, 1969.

Ohlsen, M. M. *Group counseling.* New York: Holt, Rinehart, and Winston, 1970.

A SEQUENTIAL MODEL FOR VIEWING BEHAVIOR

AND

GUIDELINES FOR COUNSELING PRACTICES

by

Edward L. Trembley
Director
Center for Counseling and Student Development
University of Delaware
1974

This paper presents a summary description of a
sequential model for viewing behavior as we try to
understand it and help to modify it through counseling. The model is a perceptual-learning one and
the writer has drawn on the work of Ford and Urban
(1963) and Combs and Snygg (1959). First, the model
will be presented and then several implications for
counseling will be suggested.

THE MODEL

Behavior Classifications

Behavior falls into two very broad classifica-
tions: covert behavior and overt behavior. Overt
behavior is muscular and glandular action such as
talking, body movements, emotional displays, breathing rate, skin changes, and perspiring. Overt behavior is observable to others and is the basis for
human transactions. We come to know another person
by the actions we see him direct toward us and the
world. In the model, overt behavior is labelled as
large R.

Covert behavior is that response pattern of
which we are subjectively aware, but which is not

ORIGINAL MANUSCRIPT, 1974.

directly observable by another person. Covert behavior includes body sensations, sensory attending, perceptions, thinking and feeling. Other subclasses of covert behavior and other concepts may be used; however, these are sufficient for our discussion. These behavior patterns which occur inside of our skin are not directly observable by others, but others do make inferences. When we try to understand another person, we are making inferences about his covert behavior. Our level of understanding about a person's covert behavior depends on the quality and type of overt behavior available on which to base our inferences. We may "know" something about another person through his actions, but our knowledge is always inferential and imperfect. In the model, covert behavior is labelled as small $\underline{r}$.

Antecedents of Behavior

This model describes behavior as occurring within an ongoing environment of stimulus patterns, which is called the <u>situational context</u>. Behavior is caused; that is, it has antecedents, and does not occur randomly and spontaneously. The model treats the antecedents of behavior in two ways.

Stimulus patterns occurring in a person's situational context (S_1) may be attended to by the person and elicit sensory, thinking and feeling response patterns (covert behaviors or $\underline{r}$), as in the following diagram:

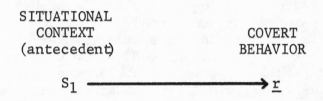

$$\text{SITUATIONAL} \atop \text{CONTEXT}$$

SITUATIONAL
   CONTEXT   COVERT
(antecedent)   BEHAVIOR

$$S_1 \longrightarrow \underline{r}$$

The model further specifies that overt behavior (R) or action is the result of the attending, thinking, feeling, and other sensory behavior in which

24

one engages in his situational context. Actions are elicited by antecedent covert behavior, which in turn, is elicited by the situational context. The following diagram depicts this sequence of antecedent - behavior relationships:

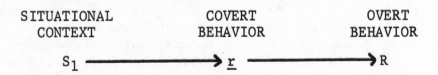

| SITUATIONAL CONTEXT | COVERT BEHAVIOR | OVERT BEHAVIOR |

$$S_1 \longrightarrow \underline{r} \longrightarrow R$$

This diagram shows that S_1 is a stimulus pattern antecedent to $\underline{r}$ and R, sequentially, while S_1 and $\underline{r}$ serve as antecedents to R. This brings us to a most important aspect of the model, the pivotal role of $\underline{r}$ in the sequence of behavior.

Situational contexts (S_1) exist at all times for a person, but have differential effects on one's behavior, not only because of the nature of the stimulus elements which compose S_1, but also because attention is selective. We attend to only a segment of the situational contexts in which we find ourselves. Since people may attend to different stimulus elements in the same situational context, we might expect their covert and overt behavior to vary accordingly.

Mediating Responses (Behavior)

Mediating behavior is a covert response pattern which has the function of serving as a stimulus for other covert or overt behavior. Dollard and Miller (1950) describe this type of covert response as "...one whose main function is to produce a cue that is part of the stimulus pattern leading to another response" (p.98). In the present model, covert behavior ($\underline{r}$) occurs as a response to S_1, but then comes to serve as a stimulus for other covert responses and for overt responses. Covert behavior ($\underline{r}_s$) which serves this role is called mediating be-

25

havior and, in a sense, bridges the gap between S_1 and R in a given situational context.

Covert, mediating behavior is primarily thinking behavior based on language. Two people may experience an identical situational context (S_1) and yet act in very different ways. For example, two students both receive an "A" grade on an exam paper; one student smiles, states that he is happy, and looks over his paper at length, while the other student glances at the grade, acts distressed and begins to sob. We might wonder about the differences in the students' actions, given a very similar situational context. The model would explain that, although the two students were in a similar situational context, their attending, thinking, feeling, and sensing behavior ($\underline{r}$) was quite different and so elicited the different actions (R). The smiling student, for example, may have thought about the value and pride he attached to an "A", that it would help him achieve an academic honor, and have felt very good about the situation. The sobbing student may have felt guilty since he cheated on the exam, thought about his inappropriate behavior, the reactions of his friends if they knew, and generally what a stupid person he was for having cheated.

The differences between the two students would be due to differences in covert, mediating behavior. The concept of mediating behavior helps us to hypothesize sensibly about the antecedents of different actions shown by people in similar situational contexts. The following diagram shows the general role of mediating behavior:

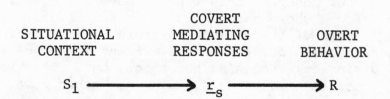

SITUATIONAL CONTEXT	COVERT MEDIATING RESPONSES	OVERT BEHAVIOR
$S_1 \longrightarrow$	$\underline{r}_s \longrightarrow$	R

Covert mediating responses can elicit other covert
mediating responses. One thought can lead to another
thought, feeling or sensation; feelings can lead to
other feelings, thoughts, and sensations, etc. The
following diagram shows these relationships:

SITUATIONAL CONTEXT	COVERT MEDIATING BEHAVIOR	OVERT BEHAVIOR

$$S_1 \longrightarrow \underline{r}_s \longrightarrow \underline{r}_s \longrightarrow \underline{r}_s \longrightarrow R$$

The above diagram implies that a person's behavior
is occurring in a situational context, to only a
part of which he attends, and that his actions (R)
in that context (S_1) are a function of antecedent
covert mediating behavior ($\underline{r}_s$), which links up
actions with situational context.

Consequences of Behavior

A fourth and final major variable in the sequential model of behavior is the consequences of
behavior. The actions (R) in which a person engages
have consequences of two types: private consequences and interpersonal consequences. The private
consequences (labelled PC in the following diagram)
are those personal and covert thoughts and feelings
one has about his own actions. While we do not
always attend carefully to our own actions, very
often we have feeling and evaluative responses to
how we act. Private consequences are the intrapersonal self-evaluations with their attendant feelings that we have about our overt behavior. We can
consider private consequences to be a covert "feedback" system by which we monitor our own actions.

Interpersonal consequences of a person's actions (labelled IC) are the reactions elicited from

other people who notice one's actions. Interpersonal consequences of one's actions are important modifiers of subsequent actions, as we know from the
principles of reinforcement. The notion of consequences is complex. For example, IC can be both
covert and overt behavior as in this situation: B's
reactions to the actions of A can be in the form of
covert thinking and feeling responses, such as B
feeling hurt by A's actions, or thinking them stupid.
B may also react to the actions of A at the overt
level by saying that he likes what A did, by smiling
at A, or by giving A a congratulatory handshake.
Another possible interpersonal consequence could be
that B does not even notice or attend to A.

The complete model can now be diagramed as
below:

SITUATIONAL CONTEXT	COVERT MEDIATING BEHAVIOR	OVERT BEHAVIOR	CONSEQUENCES, PRIVATE & INTERPERSONAL

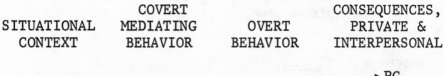

We have mentioned above that private consequences (PC) and interpersonal consequences (IC) may
modify a person's actions. Since counseling is concerned with the modification of problem behavior or
the inducement of more mature behavior, the importance of consequences in understanding behavior can
be appreciated. The PC functions as a private, internal monitoring and feedback system, while the IC
functions as a social feedback and monitoring system.
Furthermore, private consequences of actions alter
the covert behavior ($\underline{r}_s$) antecedent to those actions,
and interpersonal consequences alter the situational
context (S_1) in which the actions occurred. This
set of feedback relationships may be added to our
basic model as shown on page 7. The diagram indi-

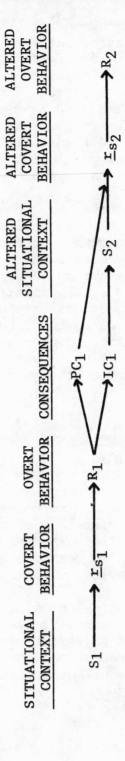

cates that private consequences modify (alter) the person's covert behavior patterns and that inter-personal consequences modify (alter) the person's situational context. The altered situational context is labelled S_2 and the altered covert behavior pattern $\underline{r}_{s2}$. The diagram also is meant to suggest that behavior continues to flow on, sequentially, with one $S \rightarrow \underline{r}_s \rightarrow R \rightarrow PC/IC$ transaction blending into the next. The sequential model of behavior may now be written out as shown on page 9.

The sequential behavior model starts with the birth and ends with the death of the individual, and is continuously occurring. Once a person acts in a situational context, he has changed that context in some way because his actions have generated conse-quences. Furthermore, the private and interpersonal consequences of his actions have altered the situa-tional context and the covert behavior that led to his actions. The controlling effect of the conse-quences of one's behavior cannot be overemphasized, whether they be private consequences or interperson-al consequences.

IMPLICATIONS FOR COUNSELING

In counseling we try to understand our clients' behavior and then assist them to modify the behavior they see as problematic. The sequential model of behavior just presented suggests a complex inter-action of four variables:

> the situational context,
> the client's covert, mediating behavior,
> the client's overt behavior,
> the private and interpersonal consequences
> of the client's behavior.

30

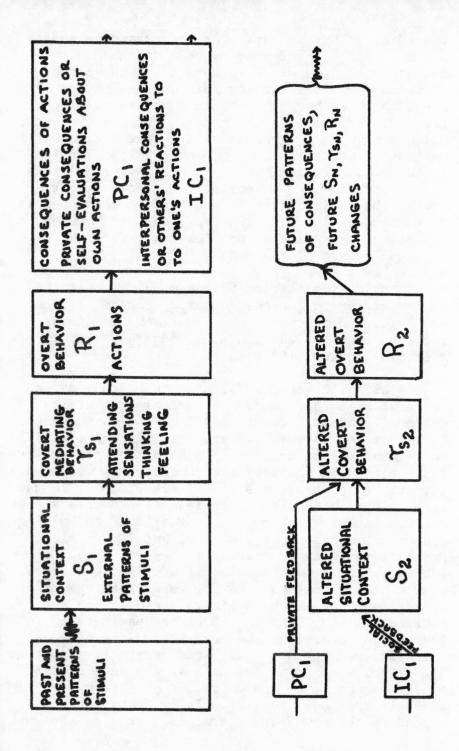

PAST AND PRESENT PATTERNS OF STIMULI

SITUATIONAL CONTEXT S_1
EXTERNAL PATTERNS OF STIMULI

COVERT MEDIATING BEHAVIOR γ_{S_1}
ATTENDING SENSATIONS THINKING FEELING

OVERT BEHAVIOR R_1
ACTIONS

CONSEQUENCES OF ACTIONS
PRIVATE CONSEQUENCES OR SELF-EVALUATIONS ABOUT OWN ACTIONS PC_1
INTERPERSONAL CONSEQUENCES OR OTHERS' REACTIONS TO ONE'S ACTIONS IC_1

PC_1
PRIVATE FEEDBACK

IC_1
SOCIAL FEEDBACK

ALTERED SITUATIONAL CONTEXT S_2

ALTERED COVERT BEHAVIOR γ_{S_2}

ALTERED OVERT BEHAVIOR R_2

FUTURE PATTERNS OF CONSEQUENCES, FUTURE S_N, γ_{S_N}, R_N CHANGES

Depending on our criteria for understanding and on our theoretical preferences, we understand our clients better as we learn more about these four elements. Our clients may seek our assistance because they are having problems with one or more of the four variables in the model. For example, some clients have real problems with a destructive situational context, some with problems in attending, thinking, or feeling, some who act inappropriately or not at all when appropriate, and some of our clients have discomfort because of the consequences of their behavior. More often than not, however, clients present us with problems in several or all of the elements of the model.

A major implication of the model is that the counselor, or in the case of group counseling, the counselor and group members, must make inquiries into the four variables of the model, or they are operating on too little data.

A client's actions (R) need to be considered in terms of three classes of variables, the situational context, covert behavior, and consequences. If any of these variables are changed, there will be alterations in actions. To help a person modify his actions, we can help him consider changes in his situational context, his covert behavior, or in the private and interpersonal consequences of his actions. Rather than focusing our efforts on helping the client change S, r_s, R or PC and IC, we might help him to consider changes in several or all of the variables. For example, if a client's concerns center on his feeling behavior (e.g. feelings of depression), we can help him to begin to achieve modifications by learning about the parameters of the problem behavior. We need to understand its intensity, duration, vigor, what starts it and stops it. Also, we need to learn about the antecedents and consequences of the depressions. Which variables in the model seem especially important will depend on the counselor's training, skills, and work settings. Attempting to achieve situational context changes will be very important for some counselors, while others may work primarily toward helping the client achieve changes in thinking, feeling, and actions, while still others may focus on the manipulation of the consequences of the client's behavior.

The model is based on the assumption that covert behavior needs to be identified and understood if a person's actions are to make sense in relation to the situational context and the consequences of the acts. In practice, we learn about another's covert behavior through his communicative actions (both verbal and non-verbal). If a person says he is depressed, he moves slowly, he looks sad, and seems to have little energy, we begin to infer from these actions and from the absence of others (e.g., he doesn't respond to humor) something about the parameters of the feeling problem he says he is experiencing. We always need to keep our inferences open to receive new, especially contradictory, data. We also need to check the accuracy of our inferences by having the client confirm or deny them. As we become clearer about the parameters of the depression, the situational context(s) in which it occurs, what the person does about his depressions, and the consequences of what he does, we begin to understand how his depression works and how it might be modified. A word of caution: counselors must be careful not to assume that a client's feelings (or other covert behavior) are like their own and that they work and can be modified the same ways.

The process of learning about the variables influencing a person's behavior depends on what might be called the self-disclosure dynamic as discussed by Jourard (1971). If we are to learn something of another's covert experiencing, we must encourage him to disclose to us material about his covert experiencing. We need to seek data on questions like: How does the client think and feel about S_1? What mediating responses precede the onset of his problem behavior? What are the private and interpersonal consequences of his actions? What are the parameters of his problem behavior? The problem for the counselor is to help create a situational context in which the client can feel increasingly comfortable in engaging in optimal self-disclosure. By optimal self-disclosure, we do not mean complete catharsis or the popular "open and honest gut-spilling", but rather we mean self-disclosures which the client can emotionally bear, which are accurate, and which are relevant to the variables influencing the problem behavior. To achieve this sort of optimal self-disclosure is a difficult and gradual process which is influenced by (a) the client's ability to disclose accurately or relevantly, (b) the client's general fears about disclosing and (c) the counselor's skills. One of the major counseling technique implications of this model is the requirement that the counselor use trust-eliciting behavior to establish a basis for client self-disclosure. To a large degree in individual counseling, and to a lesser degree in group counseling, the counselor can control how he reacts (IC) to his client which can tend to generate a sense of trust in the client, which then permits more self-disclosures.

Trust-eliciting behavior (R) that counselors may use to help clients begin to disclose are many. For example, counselor structuring statements (R) early in counseling may assure the client that what is said in counseling is confidential. The counselor may state his expectation that in counseling clients try to share experiences (r and R) that are difficult to discuss. Counselor behavior such as responding to both the content and the style of client behavior in the interview help the client to get clear that he is important enough for the counselor to attend to him closely. Other counselor behavior which indicates concern, interest, and caring about the client lend to the development of client thoughts and feelings of trust. Clients test the trustworthiness of counselors by disclosing a little and then seeing how the counselor responds to the disclosure. Common examples include the client who informs the counselor of unusual behavior or unlawful behavior. How the counselor chooses to respond to such reports helps the client make a decision about the trustworthiness of the counselor and about what other disclosures might be ventured. Emotional displays, like rages or crying behavior, often come to represent tests of the counselor. The core of the trust question for the client is how the counselor handles these very private experiences shared gradually in counseling.

Sometimes counselors overlook the value of candidly recognizing with their clients, at appropriate times, that counseling depends on disclosures and that disclosing is difficult to do. By acknowledging this point and by calling for a verbal commitment (and doing so at various times, if required) to disclose, clients are often supported to venture out with disclosures which are then a test of the counselor and which, if managed therapeutically, will elicit further disclosures.

Many counselors believe that if they engage in progressively open self-disclosures they will help the client gain the courage to disclose and, hence, learn to trust more deeply. In part, this very popular notion is a counseling strategy based on learning by modeling, i.e., the client learns to self-disclose as he observes the counselor doing so and the consequences that follow from doing so. The strategy is a worthwhile one as long as the counselor is sensible in its use. He must recognize that he can seriously frighten a client by disclosing too much too fast and that his self-disclosure is a strategy to help the client and not to unburden himself at the expense of the client or group. Counselor self-disclosure, if used sensitively and in incremental steps of depth and intensity will help the client learn that to self-disclose about feelings, thoughts, and acts is not unusual, not a sign of personal weakness, not hard to listen to, and

35

not destructive to the counseling relationship. Furthermore, the client often reports feeling that counselor self-disclosure made him feel closer to the counselor and more trusting of him.

GROUP COUNSELING

In group counseling, each client seeks behavior change through the potentially powerful stimulation and reinforcement of the group. Group counseling is difficult to do because the counselor has much behavior to which to attend. The counselor cannot attend to each member individually if the interplay of group forces are to be generated. The group counselor also has much less control than in individual counseling in establishing situational conditions for optimal self-disclosure; this is the case simply because all group members contribute in varying degrees of significance to the situational context that exists for any one of them at any given point in the group.

An important problem faced by the group counselor is to gradually establish, and help group members contribute to the establishment of, a situational condition in the group that has a stability a high quality of acceptance of differences, and trust-eliciting qualities to it. As is the case in individual counseling, a client will gain little if he cannot begin to feel trusting of others (r_s) in the group and if he, therefore, cannot or will not engage in self-disclosures that are accurate and relevant to his concerns. The group counseling literature contains many suggested techniques for creating a situational context which will help group members learn that they can self-disclose. It needs to be emphasized that the quality of self-disclosures, and not only their quantity, needs careful attention by the group counselor and other group members. Helping group members to zero in on those aspects of their behavior which is sequentially related to their problem behavior is an essential part of the task of counseling. Group members frequently become quite helpful in this process by helping their peers focus on difficult, relevant self-disclosures and providing emotional support while doing so.

For a group member at a given point in the group process, the model may be represented as shown on the following page. By replicating the diagram as many times as there are members in a group, one can begin to get an idea of the complexity of interactions that occur in a group at any time. Each group member, and especially the group counselor, has a difficult task in trying to provide an attentive and helpful situational context with so much happening simultaneously in the group.

As a counseling group moves through various stages of existence, as described by Mahler (1969), the process of eliciting feelings and thoughts of trust in the group members must continue to be attended to by the group counselor. Both the frequency and the quality of a group member's self-disclosing behavior vary over the course of a group session, just as the frequency and quality of his trusting behavior vary. As the group member listens to the disclosures of others and to his own, he frequently asks himself how much he can afford to trust the group. Often, one of the valuable outcomes of group counseling is that members learn how to trust others more and become more realistic about the importance they assign to the consequences of their actions. The IC that follows a person's actions play a major part in both eliciting trust and in eliciting further disclosures. Group counselors need to remember that the interpersonal consequences that may be helpful and supportive for one group member may not be that for another; the reinforcement effectiveness of interpersonal consequences is idiosyncratic in large measure. Thus, another problem for the group counselor using this model is to determine what inter-

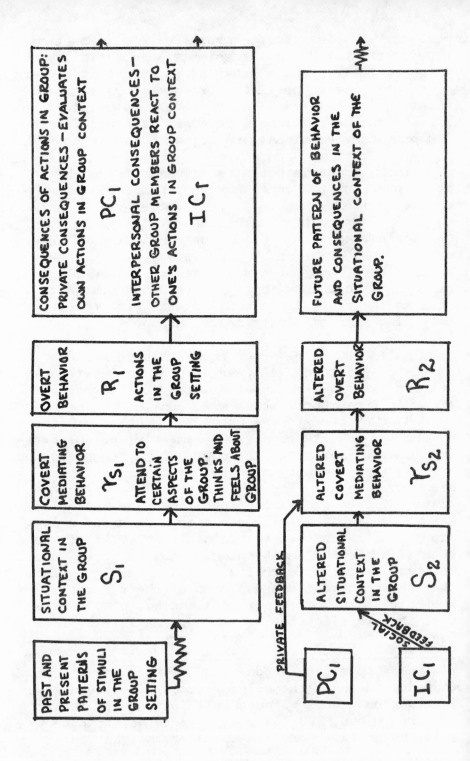

personal consequences <u>are</u> effective for each group member and then behave accordingly. Many writers, of course, would call the interpersonal consequences of our model <u>feedback</u>, about which a great deal has been written.

The model suggests that as a person acts he considers private consequent behavior which is essentially self-evaluative in nature (PC) and which is a crucial element in determining how one manages his own behavior. This behavior is often important to inquire about (if sufficient trust exists) and to ask the person to share as explicitly as he can with the group's help and support. By doing so, the group member can begin to learn how his internal assessments (PC) operate to manage his own behavior. He can then compare this to the reactions (IC) of others in the group. Discrepancies between PC and IC are common and frequently important therapeutically to reconcile. Often this process of reconciliation (Jourard and Overlade, 1966) leads to new thoughts and feelings (r_s) for the group member which are healthier and more mature than those previously maintained. This change involving new thoughts, feelings, and actions is the heart of the counseling process.

For example, one group member may be positively reinforced by verbal rewards issued by others in the group such as "I'm glad you shared that with me" or "I feel closer to you now that you've shared that" or even "That seemed hard for you to say but I'm pleased you said it." Other group members are positively reinforced by nonverbal ICs such as a smile or a nod, while others need to be verbally encouraged to start and to continue a disclosure. The point here is that what behaviors constitute positive interpersonal consequences for one group member may not be so effective for another group member.

In summary, the group counseling situation has available in it a number of powerful social behavior modifiers through which an individual group member can be assisted to achieve the behavior changes he seeks. Group members and the group counselor set up the situational context which is antecedent to both the covert and overt behavior of the individual and the group generates a great number of interpersonal consequences which can directly modify an individual's covert and overt behavior. Essentially, these modifiers are the factors which contribute to behavior change in individual or group counseling. However, in the group setting, the modifiers are greater in number and more varied in nature and strength. It is for these reasons that today many practicing counselors view group counseling as the treatment of choice for many types of problem behavior.

REFERENCES

Combs, A. W., and Snygg, D. Individual Behavior.
Harper and Row, New York, 1959.

Dollard, J., and Miller, N. E. Personality and
Psychotherapy. McGraw-Hill, New York, 1950.

Ford, D. H., and Urban, H. B. Systems of Psychotherapy. Wiley, New York, 1963.

Jourard, S. M. The Transparent Self. Van Nostrand,
New York, 1971.

Jourard, S. M., and Overlade, D. C. (Eds.). Reconciliation: A Theory of Man Transcending.
Van Nostrand, New York, 1966.

Mahler, C. A. Group Counseling in the Schools.
Houghton Mifflin, New York, 1969.

GROUP PROCEDURES IN COUNSELING: INFLUENCES AFFECTING ITS CREDIBILITY

ANGELO V. BOY

The status of group procedures in counseling can be positively or negatively affected according to which groups exert the greatest influence on the profession. Therefore, the purpose of this article is threefold: (1) to indicate the dimensions of the influence currently being exerted; (2) to indicate that the advancement and professionalization of group procedures in counseling is being hampered, to varying degrees, by the commercial communications media, reactionaries, euphoric colleagues, and gimmick-centered colleagues; and (3) to indicate that the professional status of group procedures in counseling will be sustained and improved only in proportion to our ability to separate sense from nonsense.

Commerical Communications Media

In the past few years, interest in group procedures has mounted rapidly on a national scale. Increasing numbers of Americans are being directly or vicariously exposed to the group experience. Historically, the catalysts for this interest have been the National Training Laboratories which introduced T Group work, Esalen Institute which introduced sensitivity training, and the Western Behavioral Sciences Institute, coupled with the Center for Studies of the Person, which individually introduced basic encounter group procedures.

Whenever a sufficient number of Americans develop an interest in anything (bowling, hula hoops, astrology, isometric exercises, jogging, health foods, dieting) we have a corresponding interest emerging from those whose prime motive is economic. Because of the public's fascination with the group experience, former rent-a-car magnate Warren Avis assumed ownership of Detroit's Behavioral Science Training Laboratories, while Atlanta's Human Development Institute, which grosses 1.5 million dollars a year, is a subsidiary of the Bell and Howell Corporation (Newsweek, 1969).

The profit motive has prompted some to take advantage of this peak period of interest in group work. The consuming public has been recently exposed to the following by the commercial communications media:

Life magazine published a sensational article entitled, "Inhibitions Thrown to the Gentle Winds" (Howard, 1968); *The New Yorker* gave a bizarre account of the group experience in "The Thursday Group" (Adler 1967); the *New York Times Magazine* made its contribution with "The Year of the Group: Eavesdropping on Some Highly Intelligent Neurotics"(Lamott,1968); a novel entitled, *The Lemon Eaters* depicts the participants in the group experience as an amalgamation of various kinds of deviates (Sohl, 1967); *Time* (1968) magazine produced an article about nude group therapy, "Psychotherapy: Stripping Body and Mind"; the *Boston Sunday Globe* carried the naturalistic, "T-Groups: A New Technique for Preserving Identity Amid Mass Pressures" (Dietz, 1968); *The Star Weekly* magazine produced an article which possessed a soap opera aura, "The Thousand Year Week, a Gripping—and True—Account of the Unique Kind of Group Therapy that is Bringing New Insights Into Many of the Hangups of North American Life" (Frazer, 1968); *Look* magazine mingled the experiences of natural childbirth and group therapy in "The Man and Woman Thing" (Leonard, 1968); the Associated Press wire service indicated that apartments for single persons need never be empty if the owner provides "Encounter Groups: Attracting the Singles Market" (1969); *Playboy* magazine provided its insights into the group experience with "Alternatives to Analysis" (Havemann.

PSYCHOTHERAPY: THEORY, RESEARCH AND PRACTICE, 1971, Vol. 8, pp. 333-337.

1969); and the National Broadcasting Company produced a television melodrama, "Companions in Nightmare," in which murder and intrigue were depicted as part of the group experience (1968).

The public has tended to respond by being either infatuated or negativistic. Both kinds of response are based upon ignorance since the group experience is neither a miraculous cure nor a psychological lobotomy. Such polarized responses by the public are beginning to affect the credibility and status of group experiences in professional work settings; and the source of the public's distorted and superficial information has been the commercial communications media.

Reactionaries

Because the commercial communications media have insisted on sensationalizing the group experience, the response is equally sensational. When certain elements of the commercial communications media equate the group experience with nudity, sexual promiscuity, or drugs, then the panic button is firmly pressed by those who possess diametrically opposed values. The issue becomes heated and without hope of cooling; the battle becomes joined.

An example of the degree of reactionary response to what has been promulgated by the commercial communications media is contained in the following indictment leveled at sensitivity training:

It plants conflicts, divisions and hatreds. It substitutes a mass conscience for a "right" conscience based upon the tenets of God and religion. It substitutes "choice" for "creed" because there are no absolutes. It divides children from parents. It rejects all authority; parental, civil and ecclesiastical. It substitutes humanism for deism. It tampers with sex attitudes. It tempts through prolonged erotic conversations. It encourages group confession. It fosters mutual suspicion as the result of confessing everything. It denies the doctrine of original sin and grace. It abandons inhibitions which is the control of impulse and the first principle of any civilization. It weakens the family and all society. It destroys self-confidence and the ability to make decisions. It molds youngsters into puppets. It uses Communist techniques to reduce the will to resist, as in the case of the American prisoners during the Korean war (Pope Publications, 1969).

In an article entitled "Hate Therapy," which appeared in *American Opinion,* a magazine published by the John Birch Society, Gary Allen (1968) has this to say about sensitivity training:

The group and self-criticism technique—Sensitivity Training—is used today in every Communist country in the world. Their thought-control people have learned from experience that it is an effective weapon not only for producing "mass man" or "group man," but also for locating "reactionary individualists" who may become opposition leaders.

. . . there is a sick fascination involved in sensitivity training which brings sadism or masochism. Sensitivity training attracts sadistic personalities and they tend to assume leadership because of their strength and ruthlessness. Verbal voyeurs are attracted by the prospects of vicariously running through everyone else's sex life. The process brings out the worst in everybody.

This is the essence of Sensitivity Training—substituting the will and judgment of the group for that of the individual. You exchange your personal values, convictions, and morality for those of the group. You subjugate your intellect for their emotions. Group security is substituted by individual security.

and

. . . even if Sensitivity Training were not a parallel of the Communist brainwashing tactics used in Korea—it should still be resisted by every individual who possesses any pride or self-esteem. Sensitivity Training should be resisted if only because it is emotionally and morally destructive (Allen, 1969).

The preceding reactionary responses occurred largely because of the misrepresentations of the group experience provided by commercial media which realize that the only way to compete on the economic market is to stimulate interest in the product through sensationalism.

Euphoric Colleagues

There are colleagues who are emotionally committed to group work and who become euphoric about the group experience. Such enthusiasm is refreshing, but it should be tempered with reason and objective evidence by anyone who claims to be a professional. The group experience is emotionally powerful in terms of the participant's feelings about himself and how he interacts with others. In some cases, the experience is so overwhelming that one is emotionally swept off his feet and becomes committed to developing a secular theology regarding group work—complete with an affectively based set of beliefs and rituals. Such euphoric colleagues have come to be labeled as members of a "touchy-feely" quasi-religious cult whose sole motivation for existence seems to be, "sentio ergo sum—I feel, therefore I am."

As professionals, we must go beyond the label, *sentio ergo sum,* and realize that in regard to group procedures in counseling, yes, there *are* things to be felt if man is to emerge as a person; but, at the same time, there are dimensions to be cognitively known if the art and science of group work is to be advanced and preserved as a legitimate professional endeavor. As Franklin Murphy, (1968) Chancellor of the University of California at Los Angeles has stated, in addressing himself to the problems of the larger society: "You cannot build a society on feeling alone. Only a proper blend of reason, action, and feeling will build a better world." What Chancellor Murphy has said about the larger society aptly applies to expanding our professional awareness of the rationale, process, and outcomes of group procedures in counseling.

Those colleagues who are emotionally effervescent regarding the group experience should expend an equivalent amount of energy contributing to the professional body of knowledge about group work, because such knowledge will endure long after the emotional infatuation with group work has subsided.

Gimmick-Centered Colleagues

There are professionally educated group counselors, experienced in interacting verbally with clients at an affective level, who are aware of the clinical and empirical evidence which indicates that behavioral change occurs as a result of such interactions.

But on the scene today are group leaders who are minimally educated in the art and science of verbal transactions and, because of this deficiency, they resort to nonverbal gimmicks as technique of communicating with group members and helping them to communicate with each other. The less formally educated and relatively inexperienced counselor is overwhelmed by the matrix of verbal transactions which occur in group work and is unsophisticated regarding how he should verbally respond. The only recourse, then, is to control the group by introducing nonverbal techniques which put him in command of the situation and enable the process to proceed on his

own terms—nonverbal rather than verbal because the leader is not able to respond verbally at the affective level when group members verbally express affect.

Recently, the following training exercises have been recommended for utilization by group leaders: back lift, beating, fantasy game, body positioning, doubling, humming, wordless meetings, bodily feel, no exist dyad, lost person, daydream, new names, break in, milling, pushing, break out, and roll and rock. (Schutz,1967).

The non-gimmick counselor, however, engages in, and assists group members to engage in, nonverbal modes of communication *when these modes emerge naturally, instinctively, and spontaneously from group members themselves.* In other words, he feels no need to manipulate group members toward nonverbal exercises because (1) he has no psychological need to do so, (2) he is sufficiently transparent in verbal modes of affective communication so that he has no need to rely on nonverbal supports, (3) he respects the right of group members to emerge freely as persons according to their own unique modes which could be verbal, nonverbal, or both, (4) he realizes that the most natural and revealing method of expressing the self is through personally open and honest verbal affect, and (5) he realizes that when the affective inner self of a group member emerges at the verbal level within the group, this type of emergence is more easily incorporated into one's behavior outside the group since the basic mode of communication in our daily existence is verbal.

Credible Colleagues

Credible colleagues are those who have a balanced and tempered approach when examining the theories, process, and outcomes of group procedures in counseling. They believe in the relevancy of group procedures, but they also exhibit intellectual honesty by pointing out its limitations. (Driver, 1954; Gordon, 1955; Corsini, 1957; Slavson, 1958; Dreikurs, 1960; Ohlsen and Proff, 1960; Lifton, 1961; Bradford, et al., 1964; Kemp, 1964; Mowrer, 1964; Rogers, 1968; Mahler, 1969).

I am not aware of *any* bona fide contributor to the professional literature of group procedures in counseling who has not presented both its strengths and limitations. He does this because (1) he feels professionally obligated to advance the knowledge regarding group work by looking at its limitations as well as its strengths, (2) he realizes the tentativeness of what he knows, (3) he realizes that today's truth is but a temporary stopover in his movement toward a more enlightened and encompassing truth, and (4) he realizes that no approach to working with people is without flaw, and his intellectual honesty compels him to let the flaws be known.

There are responsible colleagues who have raised some legitimate questions regarding the integrity of group work; they have made some pertinent observations and comments. If we look upon group work as a theology, then we will attempt to disregard what they say because "they are men of little faith." If we are honestly attempting to advance our knowledge about group work, we shall examine the opposite side of the coin as represented by the following: "T-Grouping: The White Collar Hippie Movement," in the *Phi Delta Kappan* (Thomas, 1968); "Group Therapy: Let the Buyer Beware," in *Psychology Today* (Shostrum, 1969); "A Little Cube of Sugar Helps the Medicine Go Down," in *Contemporary Psychology* (Hunt, 1968); "Some Ethical Issues in Sensitivity Training," in *The American Psychologist* (Lakin, 1969); "Can Sensitivity Training Be Destructive?" a letter in *The American Psychologist* (Gibbons, 1968); "The Rush to Encounter One's Self," a letter in *The School Counselor* (Rapoport, 1969); and "Encounter Groups—Seance or Sense," a panel program presented at the 1968 Convention of the American Personnel and Guidance Association (Beymer, 1968).

Group procedures in counseling *are* a professionally legitimate approach to working with people. There is ample research evidence supporting the effectiveness of group work in various reviews of the literature. (Wright, 1959) (Shaw and Wursten, 1965) (Anderson, 1969). George M. Gazda has recently summarized 107 research studies which indicate the positive outcomes of group procedures in counseling (Gazda, 1968). The professional dimensions of group work will be further advanced through scholarship which addresses itself to confronting the shibboleths about

group work which are currently being promulgated by the commercial communications media and by some colleagues.

Progress based upon scholarship is not easy, but it must occur if group work is to continue as a credible process and escape the riptide of pervasive influences. We must acknowledge the tentativeness of what we know so that we can progress. As scientist Karl Pearson (1897) stated:

No scientific investigation is final; it merely represents the most probable conclusion which can be drawn from the data at the disposal of the writer. A wider range of facts or more refined analysis, experiment, and observation will lead to new formulas and new theories. This is the essence of scientific progress.

In commenting on the same issue, Donald O. Hebb (1958) indicated that:

... theory is not an affirmation but a method of analysis that can't produce any belief. Knowledge progresses by stages, so that the theory one holds today must be provisional, as much a formulation of one's ignorance as anything else, to be used as long as it is useful and then discarded. Its function is to organize the available evidence. It is really a working assumption which the user may actively disbelieve.

The mark of a profession is to be intellectually honest, cautious, ethically responsible, and introspective regarding the services which it renders. By doing this, a profession is not only able to distinguish superficiality from substance, it is also able to improve the effectiveness of practice and fulfill its public obligation of professional integrity.

REFERENCES

ADLER, R. The Thursday group, *The New Yorker*, 43:8, April 15, 1967, 55-146.

ALLEN, G. Hate therapy. *American Opinion*, Robert Welch, Editor, John Birch Society, Belmont, Massachusetts, January, 1968, 73-86.

ANDERSON, A. R. Group counseling. *Review of Educational Research: Guidance and Counseling*, American Educational Research Association, Washington, D. C., 39:2, April, 1969, 209-226.

Associated Press Wire Service, published in the *Boulder Daily Camera*, Boulder, Colorado, July 27, 1969, 9.

BEYMER, L. Speech made at program entitled, Encounter Groups—Seance or Sense? *1968 Convention Program*, Annual Convention of the American Personnel and Guidance Association, Detroit, Michigan, April 8, 1968.

BRADFORD, L. P., GIBBS, J. R. & BENNE, K. D. *T-Group Theory and Laboratory Method: Innovation in Re-education*, New York; John Wiley and Sons, Inc., 1964.

"Companions in Nightmare" produced by Universal Studios, Hollywood, California, and presented on NBC Television, 9:00-11:00 PM, EST, November 23, 1968.

CORSINI, R. *Methods of Group Psychotherapy*. New York: McGraw-Hill 1957.

DIETZ, JEAN, T-groups: A new technique for preserving identity amid mass pressures, *Boston Sunday Globe*, Magazine Section, June 23, 1968, 28-33.

DREIKURS, R. *Group Psychotherapy and Group Approaches*. Chicago: Alfred Adler Institute, 1960.

DRIVER, H. I. *Multiple counseling: a small group discussion method for personal growth*. Madison, Wisconsin: Monona Publications, 1954.

FRAZER, S. The thousand year week, a gripping—and true—account of the unique kind of group therapy that is bringing new insights into many of the hangups of North American life. *The Star Weekly Magazine*, Toronto Star Limited, Toronto, Ontario, Canada, September 15-21, 1968, 2-25.

GAZDA, G. M., Ed. *Journal of educational research and development: Group counseling*, University of Georgia, College of Education, 1968.

GIBBONS, C. C. "Can sensitivity training be destructive?", letter appearing in *American Psychologist*, 23:4, April, 1968, 288.

GORDON, T. *Group Centered Leadership*, Boston: Houghton Mifflin Co., 1955.

HAVEMANN, E. Alternatives to analysis. *Playboy*, HMH Publishing Co., Chicago, Illinois: 16:11, November 1969, 133-134; 142; 214-216; 218; 220.

HEBB, D. O. *A Textbook of Psychology*. Philadelphia, Pennsylvania: Saunders Co., 1958.

HOWARD, J. Inhibitions thrown to the gentle winds. *Life*, Chicago, Illinois: Time-Life, Inc., July 12, 1968.

HUNT, W. A. A little cube of sugar helps the medicine go down. *Contemporary Psychology*, 13:11, November, 1968, 563.

KEMP, C. G. Ed. *Perspectives on the Group Process*. Boston: Houghton Mifflin Co., 1964.

LAKIN, M. Some ethical issues in sensitivity training, *American Psychologist*, 24:10, October, 1969, 923-928.

LAMOTT, K. "The year of the group: Eavesdropping on some highly intelligent neurotics, *The New York Times Magazine*, November 10, 1968, 29.104.

LEONARD, G. B. The man and woman thing. *Look*, Des Moines, Iowa: Cowles Communications Inc., 32:26, December 24, 1968, 55-72.

LIFTON, W. M. *Working with groups*, New York: John Wiley and Sons, Inc., 1961.

MAHLER, C. A. *Group counseling in the schools*. Boston: Houghton Mifflin Co., 1969.

MOWRER, O. H. *The new group therapy*. New York: Van Norstrand Co., 1964.

MURPHY, F. quoted in Universities: Of reason and revolution *Time*, Chicago, Illinois: Time-Life, Inc. June 21, 1968, 42.

OHLSEN, M. M. & PROFF, F. C. *The extent to which group counseling improves the academic and personal adjustment of underachieving, gifted adolescents*, Research Project No. 623, College of Education, University of Illinois, Urbana, 1960.

PEARSON, K. *The chance of death and other studies evolution*. London: E. Arnold Co., 1897.

Psychotherapy: Stripping body and mind. *Time Magazine*, Chicago, Illinois: Time-Life, Inc., February 23, 1968, 68.

RAPOPORT, D. The rush to encounter one's self, letter in *The School Counselor*, 16:3, January 1969, 228.

ROGERS, C. R. *The process of the basic encounter group*, Western Behavioral Sciences Institute, La Jolla, California, Unpublished Manuscript, 4 pages (c. 1968).

SCHUTZ, W. C., *Joy: Expanding human awareness*. New York: Grove Press, Inc., 1967.

SHAW, M. C. & WURSTEN, R. Research on group procedures in schools: a review of the literature, *The Personnel and Guidance Journal*, 44:1, September 1965, 27-34.

SHOSTRUM, E. L. Let the buyer beware. *Psychology Today*, Communications/Research/Machines, Inc. Del Mar, California, 2:12, May 1969, 36-40.

SLAVSON, S. R. *The fields of group psychotherapy* New York: International Universities Press, 1958.

SOHL, J. *The lemon eaters*. New York: Simon-Schuster, Inc., 1967.

The Group: Joy on Thursday. *Newsweek*, Newsweek Inc., New York, New York, May 12, 1969, 104-106D.

The sin of sensitivity training from the viewpoint of catholic doctrine, San Rafael, California: Pope Publications, 1:2, February 1969, 4 pages.

THOMAS, D. T-grouping: The white-collar hippie movement. *Phi Delta Kappan*, 44:8, April, 1964, 458-460.

WRIGHT, E. W. Multiple counseling: Why? when? how? *The Personnel and Guidance Journal*, 37:8, April 1959, 551-557.

Ethical standards for group leaders

LEROY C. OLSEN

A group leader is one who assumes the responsibility for a group dealing with interpersonal relationships. The leader is committed to a belief in the dignity and personal worth of each member of a group with whom he works. While demanding the freedom to function as a professional, he also accepts the responsibilities this freedom implies and defends the rights and freedom of his group members. He maintains integrity in his relationships with other professionals and the public. He does not use his specialized knowledge to take personal advantage of group members, nor does he permit himself to be used by others for purposes inconsistent with his own ethical standards. The group leader is expected to abide by and practice the ethical standards of the American Psychological Association and the American Personnel and Guidance Association. He is also expected to practice the following ethical standards that were developed for, and are more directly applicable to, working with groups.

1. The maintenance of high standards of professional competence is a responsibility shared by all leaders of groups who deal with interpersonal relationships.

2. The leader avoids misrepresentation of his own professional qualifications, affiliations, and purposes.

3. The leader must safeguard information that has been obtained in his work with groups. While the leader can vouch only for his own respect for confidentiality in the group, he must inform the members of the group of their responsibility for confidentiality and also make them aware that he cannot speak for anyone other than himself.

4. The leader respects the integrity and protects the physical and emotional welfare of the persons in the group with whom he is working.

5. The leader shall utilize adequate means for screening potential group members, and assure necessary follow-up and assistance to protect member welfare when he leaves a group or when a group is terminated.

6. The leader informs prospective group members of the important aspects of the group experience (purposes, type of leadership, techniques, duration, etc.), which will permit the prospective member to make a decision about whether or not these are acceptable to him.

7. In working with groups, the leader shows sensible regard for and helps others to respect the social codes, moral expectations, and laws that set limits on the behavior of one individual toward another.

8. The leader must protect the group member's freedom of choice, which includes his right to withdraw from any given group activity or from the group itself without being exposed to pressure from the group members or leader and without being threatened by humiliation, reprisal, rejection, or ridicule. Also, the leader must show proper respect for the convictions, sensibilities, and values of the members of the group.

9. If or when he becomes aware that a group member is receiving help from some professional person, the counselor is responsible for determining, in consultation with that professional, whether the member should or should not continue in the group.

10. The leader has a responsibility to conduct, assist, or support effective and necessary research in the area of group work.

LEROY C. OLSEN is Professor of Counseling and Guidance in the Department of Education at Washington State University in Pullman. He supervises group counseling and therapy students and wrote these standards because he believed that it was necessary to provide his students with some ethical guidelines for their work with groups.

PERSONNEL AND GUIDANCE JOURNAL, 1971, Vol. 50, p. 288.

Counseling Children In Groups

Merle M. Ohlsen

COUNSELING school children in groups has increased with recent developments in elementary school counseling. As consultants to teachers, elementary school counselors also have been encouraged to help teachers adapt group techniques for teachers' use. Though this paper is primarily concerned with introducing group counseling to children, with selection of clients, and with adapting group counseling methods for children, the writer will discuss briefly some of the possibilities for helping teachers use group techniques.

The writer assumes that the readers of this journal understand the counseling process, including the kinds of interaction that occur within a group of normal children as they talk about the problems that bother them and try to help each other learn to behave increasingly more effectively (Ohlsen, 1964, Chapter 5). Clients must learn to help others as well as obtain help for themselves. All of the competencies required of the counselor in individual counseling are required here and more, too. Besides trying to understand the client who is speaking, to capture his feelings, and to help him express his feelings and change his behavior, the counselor must help clients learn to help others and to observe how the speaker's comments, as well as the various members' nonverbal behavior, influence each of the other members. He also must select clients with care, taking account of their possible impact upon each other, and enlist their assistance in developing a therapeutic atmosphere.

The setting for group counseling meets the optimal conditions for learning described by Seeman (1963, p. 8): "It is a safe environment; it is an understanding environment; it is a caring environment; it is a participat-

THE SCHOOL COUNSELOR, 1968, Vol. 15, pp. 343-349.

ing environment; and it is an approving environment." Clients also perceive counseling as a place where it is safe to be open, honest, and frank —where it is safe to test their ideas and the solutions to their problems and where they can obtain frank evaluations of their efforts to change. As a consultant to teachers, the elementary school counselor also can use his knowledge of behavior within groups to help teachers develop Seeman's optimal conditions for learning within their classrooms.

Introducing Group Counseling

As a regular member of the school staff, rather than as a specialist functioning out of the central office, the elementary school counselor has many opportunities to get to know the pupils and the staff and to describe his services for them. When, therefore, he wishes to introduce group counseling, he will be able to describe (to teachers either in informal contacts or at a faculty meeting and to pupils in their classrooms) group counseling, to explain how pupils may be helped in groups, and to answer their questions on what will be expected of clients in groups. Such presentations encourage self referrals and help teachers to understand the nature of the treatment process.

When pupils ask to join a counseling group or are referred by their teachers they are scheduled for an individual interview. The purposes of the individual interview are: to answer any questions a prospective client has about group counseling; to help the counselor get to know the child better in order to determine how he can best be helped and with whom he would best fit in a counseling group; to give the child a chance to discuss the problems with which he

hopes to obtain assistance in the group and thereby increase his readiness to discuss these problems in the group; and to assess his readiness for group counseling and commitment to change his behavior. The counselor often supplements the information obtained in the individual interview with a teacher conference, a parent conference, and a careful examination of the child's cumulative record.

Since only a few individual sessions are required to help many school children, not all children who refer themselves or are referred by their teachers will be assigned to groups. Thus, the intake interview may become the first in a series of several individual counseling sessions. Sometimes a counselor will decide to work with a child on an individual basis and later decide to assign him to a group.

Selecting Clients for Groups

Children who seem to profit most from group counseling include shy children, children who have difficulty participating in class discussion, children who want to make friends, and children who have better ability than their performance indicates. Usually the last type needs help in accepting their ability before they actually improve their performance. Rarely is it advisable to include in a single group only one type of client, e.g., gifted underachievers. Usually such children can best be treated along with some other children who can accept their ability and are concerned about why they are not doing better than they are. Ohlsen (1964) reported that best results were obtained when, after describing group counseling to children, more children volunteered than could be included in the next group to be begun. Under these circumstances prospective clients tried harder to convince the counselor in the intake interview that they were ready for counseling and that they really had something to talk about in the group. As they tried-to convince the counselor that they should be included in the next group, they increased their own readiness for counseling.

A counselor must select clients carefully for every group. He must be permitted to accept only those clients whom he feels reasonably certain he can help and preferably only those who want to join a group after they have learned what will be expected of them and what they can expect from others in their group. Even after a group is organized the counselor must feel free to take an unproductive member from the group or reassign anyone who does not seem to fit into the group. Both Fiedler (1949) and Broedel, Ohlsen, Proff, and Southard (1960) found that even a single blocking client can sometimes take such an anti-therapeutic stance that its members never establish a therapeutic climate.

Ohlsen and Gazda (1965) concluded that for group counseling to be effective with even upper grade elementary school children, both pupils and their parents must understand what will be expected in the counseling groups and accept these conditions. Sonstegard (1961) obtained significant results with similar clients, but he also provided group counseling for the pupils' parents and teachers. Where this is not feasible, or possibly not even necessary, Ohlsen and Gazda suggested that at least regular consultations with parents and teachers are essential. Their underachieving fifth graders discussed many situations in which they felt they had been treated unfairly and felt there was nothing that they could do about it. A fifth grade boy described his feelings as follows: "We're just kids and don't count for much; even our dogs are treated nicer than we are." Whereas adolescents are able to help a peer convey to the person who has hurt him *how* he has been hurt and can help him do something about his situation to improve it, fifth-graders feel trapped. They lack the independence and the adolescent's repertoire of social skills to cope with life's problems. Hence the important adults in their lives must accept considerable responsibility for helping them cope with problems and improve their environment [Ohlsen and Gazda, 1965, p. 81]."

Adapting Group Counseling Methods for Children

The writer's counseling experiences and research with groups indicate that though the same basic principles of counseling apply to all ages, the counselor must adapt his techniques to his clients' social and emotional maturity, their previous experiences in groups, and the development of their communication skills. Work with fifth, sixth, seventh, and eighth graders clearly suggests that the discussion type of counseling that is effective with high school and college students also works well with seventh and eighth graders, but certain changes are recommended for fifth and sixth graders which probably also apply to fourth graders:

1. These younger children need more structure and more carefully defined limits. Even when they are carefully selected for a group, they have difficulty defining limits and enforcing them as the committed older children do. They must understand what is expected in group counseling and how this differs from what is expected in their classrooms.

2. Associated with the need for more structure, Ohlsen and Gazda (1965) concluded that there seemed to be a need for more active participation on the counselor's part than was required in the adolescent group. These younger children did not seem to be able to detect and reach beyond mere talk to respond to significant therapeutic material as Ackerman (1955) indicated that his adolescents were able to do. Though their ability to do this increased over the treatment period and they were able gradually to accept more responsibility for helping develop a therapeutic climate, fifth and sixth grades required more time to learn to do this than did adolescents. Furthermore, when the counselor failed to participate enough, especially during the early sessions, the clients became restless, were easily distracted, and often competed for the counselor's attention.

3. Though these children do have some ability to empathize with peers, as Lerner (1937) reported, they have difficulty maintaining a sustained interest in another's problem. Consequently, Ohlsen and Gazda (1965) concluded that these children should be treated in smaller groups (perhaps five or six instead of seven or eight) and for shorter periods of time (perhaps forty to forty-five minutes instead of an hour). They also recommended three meetings a week instead of two.

4. Ginott (1961) reported that prevailing practice in clinics is to separate boys and girls for treatment during the latency period. Ohlsen and Gazda noted that in their group girls were more mature, exhibited more interest in boys than boys did in girls, tended to threaten boys with the discussion of topics related to sex, were more verbal, and tended to dominate discussions. Hence, though they generally favor the treatment of mixed groups, they conceded that it may be wise to treat girls and boys of this age in separate groups. On the other hand, they had some strong reservations concerning this recommendation: the counseling group may be the best place for boys and girls to deal with these antagonistic feelings and to learn to relate with each other.

5. Within the group clients often need to act out as well as talk out their problems. Role playing is effective whenever a client has difficulty describing a situation or conveying to others how he feels about it; or he wants to obtain others' reactions to his way of meeting a situation; or he feels that he needs practice in meeting a situation (Ohlsen, 1964, pp. 174-178). Puppets also may be used with them effectively, especially when the group develops the skits to be portrayed by the puppets. Other play materials such as family dolls, finger paints, and sketching paper may be used with these children, but care must be taken in selecting the materials lest the children perceive use of these materials as "kid stuff."

Finally, the writer would like to consider briefly how a counselor may work with primary school age children in groups. Though this writer believes that the normal children with whom he has worked can put their feelings in words better than many authors have indicated, special attention must be given to communicating with these children. Since this is discussed in another paper it will not be discussed again here (Ohlsen, 1965). Suffice it to say that more use should be made of play materials than was suggested above for fourth, fifth, and sixth grade children. A short description of a counselor working with five first- and second-graders illustrates how children who had difficulty talking to each other can be helped in groups. All of them tended to be shy and two were having difficulty learning to read. Before they entered the rooms, the counselor had laid out sheets of brown wrapping paper, finger paints, modeling clay, and various sizes of dolls—some dressed as adults and others as children. When they came into the room, each selected the materials of his choice and sat down to play. Provision was made for the children to sit around a long table in a large office which was used as a playroom. One of the girls and two of the boys chose to play with finger paints. The third boy played with clay and the remaining girl played with dolls. As the children played, the counselor moved about, responding first to one child, then to another. As he watched a child play, he would try to determine what the child was trying to express and respond to him in the child's medium, e.g., if the child was playing with finger paints, he would respond to him with finger paints. The children were also encouraged to interact with each other. Occasionally, one would speak to the entire group—a sort of show and tell. When necessary, the counselor helped such a client get the attention of the entire group. He also tried to convey to his clients that not everyone was expected to speak to the entire group just because one wanted to do so. Although normal children do seem to express themselves verbally better than disturbed children, counselors are urged to take note of Ginott's (1958, p. 413) warning: "Many serious mistakes in child therapy are committed by adults who try to give verbal insight to children whose language is play. Forcing them to verbalize is like compelling them to converse in a foreign language."

Teacher's Use of Group Techniques

Most elementary school teachers are interested in their pupils as individuals, and many are already using group discussion techniques. They exhibit this interest in their pupils by listening to them when they bring problems to school, by encouraging them to talk about their interesting experiences in show and tell sessions, and by giving them a chance to role play situations that trouble them.

The teacher's guidance responsibility is to listen and to try to understand—to let his pupils know that he cares about them and that he will set aside time to give them a chance to discuss special topics that concern them. When his pupils begin to discuss topics that the teacher feels should not be shared with the entire group, he arranges private conferences with individuals or small groups. On the other hand, the teacher should not be expected to do counseling. It should be reserved for persons who are qualified to do it. With the help of a counselor, however, the teacher can encourage normal social, emotional, and intellectual development of children with effective use of group techniques.

Rogge (1965) did an excellent demonstration to illustrate how a teacher can use group methods to motivate learning. He set aside a time when pupils were given a chance to ask any questions they wished. Rather than to merely answer their questions, he helped them explore where they could find the answers to their questions and helped them talk about how they felt about each other's questions. In order to excite learning further when one pupil has answered a question, the teacher may ask them still further questions.

Since some teachers doubt their ability to field such questions and to deal with the embarrassment associated with some questions, they often need help in learning to apply Rogge's methods. He usually begins with a demonstration in the teacher's classroom. After they have discussed it and sometimes even critiqued his tape recording of it, he encourages the teacher to try it with him observing. Usually he encourages the teacher to make a recording of the discussion so that he will have specific responses to discuss in helping the teacher critique his own session. Teachers also can help each other critique tape recorded sessions of such discussions.

Role playing (some call it sociodrama) is another group technique that the classroom teacher can use. It differs from "playing house" or "playing school" in that it is an organized effort to teach pupils to cope with specific problems. It provides the pupil who requests assistance with an opportunity to relive a specific problem, to express his feelings about it within a safe emotional climate, to test his ideas for coping with the problem, to obtain his classmates' and teacher's ideas for solving his problems, and to practice these solutions interacting with people whose reactions he values. In fact, when a child describes a situation and the people involved in it, tells how he feels and how he thinks they feel, directs and participates in the scene role played, and answers his classmates' many and varied questions before playing the scene, he usually understands himself and the whole situation better even before he role plays the scene.

"For example, Robert, a second grader, was beaten up by Mike, a fifth grader, during the lunch period. After helping Robert clean up, Miss Pickens suggested that perhaps the class could help Robert figure out how to cope with Mike. Since Mike had been picking on several of the small boys in the neighborhood, this idea appealed to the pupils. They set the stage for the sociodrama by having Robert describe what happened during the incident. Then members of the class volunteered for the various roles; several children volunteered for their own roles. The others in the scene were briefed by Robert. Finally, Miss Pickens pointed out that though they should try to re-enact what happened, they should not worry about saying precisely what was said before—instead they should try to say and act as they felt their characters would. When Miss Pickens thought they had gone far enough into the scene to help Robert, she interrupted and asked Robert to tell what he would have done differently and suggested that he ask questions about the issues which concerned him. Then she gave the other players a chance to comment on how they felt about what happened and to make suggestions to Robert. Finally, she gave the rest of the group a chance to express their feelings about the scene and to offer Robert suggestions. Not only did Robert get many good suggestions but all of them obtained ideas for coping with bullies [Ohlsen, 1959, pp. 640-641]."

Thus, group techniques can be used effectively by teachers, too. Though there are many questions for which no one has answers at this time, much can be done to help children in groups. Lack of qualified personnel is probably the most serious problem facing school counselors who want to initiate group counseling programs. These personnel are needed to counsel pupils and to help teachers improve their competencies in working with groups.

References

Ackerman, N. W. Group psychotherapy with a mixĕd group of adolescents. *International Journal of Group Psychotherapy*, 1955, *5*, 249–260.

Broedel, J., Ohlsen, M., Proff, F., & Southard, C. The effects of group counseling on gifted underachieving adolescents. *Journal of Counseling Psychology*, 1960, *7*, 163–170.

Fiedler, F. E. An experimental approach to preventative psychotherapy. *Journal of Abnormal and Social Psychology*, 1949, *44*, 386–393.

Ginott, H. G. *Group psychotherapy with children*. New York: McGraw Hill, 1961.

Ginott, H. G. Play group therapy: A theoretical framework. *International Journal of Group Psychotherapy*, 1958, *8*, 410–418.

Lerner, E. The problem of perspective in moral reasoning. *Journal of Sociology*, 1937, *43*, 294–299.

Ohlsen, M. M. *Guidance services in the modern school*. New York: Harcourt, Brace, and World, 1964.

Ohlsen, M. M. (Ed.). *Modern methods in elementary education*. New York: Henry Holt, 1959.

Ohlsen, M. M. The elementary school counselor. A mimeographed paper, College of Education, University of Illinois, 1965.

Ohlsen, M. M. & Gazda, G. M. Counseling underachieving bright pupils. *Education*, 1965, *86*, 78–81.

Rogge, W. M. A demonstration on elementary school teachers' use of group discussion methods to motivate learning. Mt. Zion Conference, June 10, 1965.

Seeman, J. Motivations to high achievement. Guidance Summer Lecture at University of Colorado, 1963.

Sonstegard, M. Group counseling methods with parents of elementary school children as related to pupil growth and development. Mimeographed report, State College of Iowa, 1961.

Group Counseling with Children:
A Cognitive-Behavioral Approach

G. ROY MAYER, TERRENCE M. ROHEN, AND A. DAN WHITLEY

Salient factors from social learning theory and cognitive dissonance theory were applied to elementary school group counseling. Several examples were presented to illustrate how dissonance could be created in a group-counseling setting. Conditions applicable to group counseling, which would increase the probable efficacy of dissonance, were discussed in relation to probable concomitant behavioral outcomes. Group counseling, which utilizes such factors, may prove to be a powerful means for assisting and/or influencing changes in elementary school students' attitudes and behaviors.

Attempts at group counseling with elementary school children are presently being undertaken by pupil-personnel workers in elementary schools throughout the nation. However, evidence regarding the school counselor's relative effectiveness when employing various group-counseling procedures with elementary school children is almost nonexistent. The intent of the present paper is to initiate further thought, discussion, and research concerning the applicability of a cognitive-behavioral approach to group counseling with elementary school children.

Mayer and Cody (1968) and Rohen and Mayer (1968) have illustrated the apparent applicability of aspects of Festinger's theory of cognitive dissonance (Festinger, 1957) to individual counseling. Several individuals (Krumboltz, 1966; Krumboltz & Hosford, 1967) have also illustrated the applicability of aspects of social learning theory to counseling. Both approaches have implications for group counseling with children.

Festinger's (1957) theory is primarily concerned with the necessary conditions for attitudinal and, to a lesser degree, behavioral changes persisting as a consequence of a given behavior or commitment. Social learning theory (Bandura & Walters, 1963) is less concerned with attitudinal consequences. Its major concern appears to be with bringing about behavior change while usually ignoring attitudes.

The present paper presents salient segments from the two empirically oriented approaches, social learning theory and dissonance theory, and applies them to elementary school group counseling. The segments are integrated and are presented as complementary to one another along with several findings from research in group dynamics.

Research findings from both approaches suggest that the probability of an attitudinal and/or behavioral change occurring is enhanced when a counselee "sees" a model or models do something that is contrary to or different than his (the counselee's) opinion or previous behavior (Bandura, 1965a, 1965b, 1965c; Bandura & Walters, 1963; Brehm & Cohen, 1962; Brock & Blackwood, 1962; Cohen, Terry, & Jones, 1959; Elms & Janis, 1965; Festinger & Carlsmith, 1959; Hovland & Pritzker, 1957; Janis & King, 1954). A "model," for the present purposes, is a fellow group member or counselor.

A state of dissonance (Festinger, 1957) will result if an individual sees another do something that is contrary to his private opinion. Dissonance is purported to be a prerequisite if attitudinal and behavioral change is to occur. It refers to a motivated state characterized by feelings of conflict and tension during which an individual experiences contradictory perceptions either about himself or his environment. Any two items of information which psy-

JOURNAL OF COUNSELING PSYCHOLOGY, 1969, Vol. 16, pp. 142-149.

55

chologically do not fit together are said to be in a dissonant relation to each other.

Counselors, then, can foster dissonant-enhancing situations from which attitudinal and/or behavioral changes are likely to occur by providing opportunities for their clients to observe contradictory items of information. The items can relate to behaviors, feelings, opinions, or events in the environment. Several examples should serve to illustrate how dissonance could be created through observation.

1. Jim had the opinion that "adults tell me what to do." In counseling, he observed that the counselor, an adult, did not tell him what to do.

2. Mike had the opinion that "adults don't listen to kids." During group counseling he observed that the counselor did listen to children.

3. Tom constantly interrupted when others talked. (He may have had the opinion that others did not mind when he interrupted.) He later observed that the group turned their back on him when he interrupted.

Each of the above individuals experienced dissonance as a consequence of "seeing" or experiencing contradictory items of information, that is, "adults tell me what to do. This adult does not tell me what to do." Such a state would motivate each of them to change or reduce the incompatibility of their perceptions in that dissonance represents an uncomfortable state of affairs, or feelings of tension and conflict, which individuals attempt to reduce or alleviate (Brehm & Cohen, 1962; Festinger, 1957).

Research findings suggest that the probability of an attitudinal and/or behavioral change occurring is enhanced when a counselee "hears" something from a model or models that is contrary to his opinions (Brehm, 1959; Brodbeck, 1956; Hovland, 1959; Salzinger, Feldman, Cowan, & Salzinger, 1967).

A verbal expression of a group member's perception or experiencing could introduce an attitude, behavior, or some other item of information inconsistent with the opinion or attitude held by an individual or the group, thus creating dissonance. Several examples should serve to illustrate how dissonance could be created through the sense of hearing.

1. A counselee may express doubt concerning a group member's respect for him. The group member then may verbally state his personal experiencing of high respect for the counselee.

2. A third-grade client may feel no remorse relative to his stealing activities at school. However, during a group guidance or counseling session conducted by the counselor the client and the other group members are exposed to the Ojemann (1967) story "Andy Can't Play." The significant others in the story disapprove of the stealing activities which the central character performs and this position is endorsed in the ensuing discussion by the group members.

3. A client might believe that he should not discuss his difficulties at school. During group counseling he hears another group member talking about his difficulties, and also hears the counselor and other group members accepting this behavior.

In each of the above examples a dissonance-creating situation, which is conducive to attitudinal or behavioral change would have been created due to the introduction of contradictory items of information.

Research findings suggest that the probability of an attitudinal or behavioral change occurring is enhanced when the counselee "says" something that is contrary to his opinion or previous behavior (Festinger & Carlsmith, 1959; Keirsey 1965; Krumboltz & Schroeder, 1965). Counselors can foster dissonance-enhancing situations, which could result in attitudinal and/or behavioral changes, by providing opportunities for their clients to say contradictory items of information. For example, one of the authors did some counseling with a group of six children in a camp setting. One of the children was reported to be urinating on the sleeping bags of his fellow campers. The counselor asked each of the six campers their opinion about the behavior. He also asked each one if he felt that whoever was doing it should stop it or not. The suspected camper's opinion was not asked for first, a procedure likely to create dissonance and one which has been indicated to be effective in modifying behavior through experimental group work by Asch (1951, 1956). Each group member verbalized a negative attitude toward the urination behavior and felt that whoever was doing it should stop it. In this example, the counselor would have increased the likelihood that the violator would have experienced dissonance concerning his behavior by eliciting from him a verbal statement which was contradictory to his previous behavior—that is, previous behavior: urinating on sleeping bags; verbal statement: "urinating on sleeping bags is wrong."

The counselor in the above example also provided the violator with a dissonance reducing alternative—stop urinating. The cessation of the behavior would be in agreement with the new attitude of "it is wrong to do." Thus, dissonance reduction would be achieved upon the cessation of the urinating behavior. The urination behavior ceased.

Role playing (Corsini, 1966; Moreno, 1946), a procedure often employed in group work with children, also provides opportunities for clients to "say" something contradictory to previous behavior or attitude. It follows, then, that role playing is another mode of creating dissonance (Janis & Mann, 1965), a state conducive to change.

Research findings also suggest that the probability of an attitudinal or behavioral change occurring is enhanced when the counselee "does" something that is contrary to his opinion or previous behavior (Allen, Hanke, Harris, Baer, & Reynolds, 1967; Aronson, 1959; Bandura & Walters, 1963; Margolius & Sheffield, 1961; Mills, 1958).

Counselors can foster dissonance-enhancing situations by providing opportunities for their clients to do something contrary to their previous behavior or opinion. Dissonance could be enhanced if a client joined in and participated with a small group concerning something he previously felt he could not or would not do. That is, if a client perceived that he was not able to perform a task and then discovered himself as a participating group member doing the task, he would experience dissonance (Festinger & Aronson, 1953). For example, suppose Tom is not completing his modern math homework. During an intake interview with the counselor Tom described his opinion as, "Modern math is for the birds." If Tom was provided the opportunity to join in and participate with a group who was using and enjoying some sort of "play object," which employed new math concepts, he would experience dissonance provided he recognized that his opinion and new behavior were not congruent with one another (Brehm & Cohen, 1962; Festinger, 1957). As indicated earlier, this dissonance would motivate Tom to promote consonance by changing his items of information to a congruent state. Because Tom is doing and enjoying the new math in a group it is suggested that his dissonance would be reduced by a modification of his opinion toward the new math. Similar analogies could be drawn with groups employing role playing (Corsini, 1966; Janis & Mann, 1965) or other kinds of play media (Ginott, 1961).

CONDITIONS CONDUCIVE TO DISSONANCE AND RESULTANT BEHAVIOR CHANGES

The effectiveness of such dissonance-creating events in producing counselee change, a change which is congruent with the event or newly obtained item of information, appears to be enhanced if the following conditions are met:

Condition 1. An environment is provided which is characterized by minimal (not a complete absence, but minimal) pressure and/or rewards while maintaining an accepting nonthreatening environment (Brehm & Cohen, 1962; Brock, 1962; Cohen, et al., 1959; Festinger, 1957; Festinger & Carlsmith, 1959; Janis & King, 1954; Mayer & Cody, 1968). Minimal reward or pressure seems necessary to evoke the desired behavior, or to motivate the student. Large reward or pressure can also evoke the desired behavior but tends to serve as a justification for the behavior (Festinger & Aronson, 1953). Thus, when experiencing large reward and/or pressure the client is likely to reduce his dissonance, not by changing previously held attitudes or beliefs, but perhaps by denying, distorting, or rationalizing away the dissonance-creating item(s) of information. An environment, then, characterized by minimal pressure and/or rewards while maintaining an accepting atmosphere, appears more effective in promoting attitudinal or behavioral change than one characterized by an absence or excess of pressure or rewards.

Condition 2. The counselor or group member who is emitting the dissonance-creating act is perceived by the counselee as similar to himself (Bandura, 1965a; Bandura & Walters, 1963; Burstein, Stolland, & Zander, 1961; Festinger, 1957; Landfield & Nawas, 1964; Mendelsohn, 1966; Mendelsohn & Geller, 1963; Stotland & Dunn, 1963; Stotland & Patchen, 1961). Individuals tend to be influenced by and interact more with those who are like themselves (Zander & Havelin, 1960). Moreover observers who believe themselves to be similar to models in some attributes are more likely to match other classes of responses of the models than are observers who believe themselves to be dissimilar (Bandura & Walters, 1963). Similarity, then, among clients and between counselor and client, appears positively related to interaction and behavioral change.

Too much similarity, however, appears to handicap the group's ability to function as a change agent. Dissonance apparently cannot be introduced in relation to an item of information if the group members are in complete agreement with one another concerning the item (Festinger, Riecken, & Schachter, 1956; Mitnick & McGinnies, 1958). For example, if the group members have the same prejudice or belief they will tend to reinforce one another's viewpoints (Festinger, et al.,

1956; Mitnick & McGinnies, 1958). Such behavior effectively maintains their consonance and prevents the introduction of desired dissonance. Thus, little, if any dissonance can be created about a topic or item unless there are differing viewpoints and/or behaviors represented within the group concerning the item. Group members, then, should probably be similar in some aspects, but should not have a similar or identical attitude if the goal is to change that attitude or resultant behavior.

Counselors can often increase group interaction, and thereby dissonance-enhancing situations by pointing out existing similarities among group members. Group size also appears to influence interaction Mayer and Baker (1967) have advocated that for maximal interaction group size should probably not exceed six for children from the upper elementary grades, and group sizes of less than six would be more appropriate for relatively immature or younger elementary school students.

Condition 3. Verbalizations or behaviors should not be too complex for the counselee to comprehend and imitate (Bandura 1965c, 1969). This condition is similar to Condition 2 in that verbalizations and behaviors emitted by a counselee are not likely to be too complex for fellow counselees to imitate if they are similar to one another. An attitude or behavior is more likely to be rapidly acquired by a counselee if the complexity of the stimulus is not too difficult, if the stimulus is not presented too rapidly for him to comprehend, and if it possesses some components which he has already learned previously (Bandura, 1956a, 1965b, 1965c). For example, a counselee may observe or hear a dissonance-creating behavior and not be able to imitate it due to its complexities In such a situation, the complex behavior must be broken down into its components before accurate imitation can occur. In addition, if a behavior or attitude exceeds the comprehension level of a counselee, it may not even arouse dissonance because it existence will not be meaningfully acknowledged. Consequently, the counselor needs to help his counselees become aware

58

of and understand the attitudes and behaviors of the other group members so that they will be able to incorporate such items into their attitudinal and behavioral repertoires. At times, this will mean that the counselor will need to simplify or verbalize in a clearer fashion various counselee behaviors or attempts at communicating with one another.

Condition 4. A model's behavior or statement (in this case the behavior or statement of the counselor or group member) receives positive consequences (Bandura & Kupers, 1964; Bandura, Ross, & Ross, 1963a, 1963b; Walters, Leat, Marion & Mezei, 1963). A model's statement or behavior which receives positive consequences is more likely to be imitated than a statement or behavior which does not (Bandura, 1969). Perhaps a statement or behavior which receives positive consequences appears to the observer to be more effective or better than his own attitude or behavior thus contributing to his dissonance or motivation to change.

Studies also suggest that an individual, or in this case, a counselee, is more likely to imitate another item of information if it is emitted by an individual who is perceived by the counselee as being attractive, important, or having high prestige. (Asch, 1948; Bandura, Ross, & Ross, 1963a; Lefkowitz, Blake, & Mouton, 1955; Toch & Schulte, 1961.) It would seem that in order for an individual to appear attractive, important, or prestigious he would have had to receive positive consequences for his previous and/or current behaviors. Perhaps, then, an individual would be more likely to imitate the behavior of a model referred to as attractive, important, or prestigious simply because he emits more effective behaviors (behaviors which receive positive consequences).

An example should help to illustrate: A client believed that he should not discuss his difficulties when at school. During the group session he heard another member discussing his school difficulties and he observed that this behavior was accepted and perhaps reinforced (positive consequences) by the counselor and the group. In the context of this condition, the client's dissonance would be enhanced because he heard a group member emit an effective act which was dissonant to his attitude. That is, the model's act of discussing his school difficulties, which the client felt should not be done, was probably perceived as effective by the client because it was accepted and reinforced by the counselor and the other group members. Furthermore, the positive consequences the group member received could have enhanced the prestige or importance of his behavior to the client. Such an event would enhance the likelihood that the group member's behavior would be imitated.

Condition 5. The counselee has a history of experiencing positive consequences for imitating or adopting the attitudes and/or behaviors of others (Lanzetta & Kanareff, 1959; Miller & Dollard, 1941; Toch & Schulte, 1961). That is, if a client has learned from his past experiences that he will receive positive consequences for imitating or adopting the behaviors and attitudes of others it is likely that he will continue to do so. However, if this has not occurred in the past he would be less likely to imitate a statement or behavior emitted from another regardless of the consequences it received. He is not likely even to attend to it (Bandura, 1965c, 1969). In such a situation dissonance would not have been created.

Condition 6. The counselee receives positive reinforcement for an emittance of his newly obtained item of information, statement, or behavior from the counselor and or group members (Bandura, 1965c, 1969; Bandura & Walters, 1963; Toch & Schulte, 1961). Once responses occur, the consequences to the behavior will largely determine whether these responses are strengthened, weakened, or inhibited (Millenson, 1967). Reinforcement appears to be particularly effective when applied to the responses of individuals experiencing dissonance (Corrozi & Rosnow, 1968; Kanareff & Lanzetta, 1960; Lesser & Abelson, 1959; Walters & Ray, 1960). In the group setting this condition could be employed by having the counselor or another group

59

member give positive reinforcement to a client for expressing an attitude or for exhibiting a behavior that was known to cause him dissonance. In an earlier example, a client did not think he should discuss his difficulties at school. Assuming that this attitude was known by the counselor, the client's eventual behavior change could be enhanced if the counselor reinforced the client when he did discuss his difficulties at school. As the client was reinforced this behavior would be strenthened, that is, the probability of it occurring again would be greater. As the reinforcement continued for each occurrence, the behavior would tend toward stability and gradually become a part of the client's repertoire.

DISCUSSION

The preceding suggests that dissonance theory can be combined with social learning theory in a manner which may prove to be highly effective in bringing about client behavioral and attitudinal changes through group counseling. Assuming that some or all the above conditions are met, a client seems likely to reduce his dissonance by changing his behavior and/or attitude so that it would become congruent with his newly obtained item of information. If the conditions are not met he is likely to reduce his dissonance, not by changing previously held attitudes, but perhaps through denial, distortion, or rationalization, thereby reducing or avoiding the dissonance-creating item(s) of information. However, such behavioral changes are usually not considered to be positive nor relatively permanent. Thus, if a behavior change is obtained without a corresponding change in attitude, the behavior may not persist. The conditions, then, might be important if persistent attitudinal and behavioral changes are desired.

Group counseling appears to offer an excellent environment for the creation of dissonance through the aid of segments of social learning theory. In such a setting more than one model is provided for each student to listen to, observe, and interact with. As a result of this interaction among members contradictory items of information are likely to be introduced in the group. Furthermore, group counseling provides several potential sources of reinforcement that could be used to aid clients in behavioral change. It would appear then, that group counseling, as viewed by the authors, could be a powerful instrument for assisting students in their developmental process. The reader should be cautioned, however, to view the conclusions reached as tentative and suggestive. The intent of this paper has not been to present absolutes but to present a point of departure for discussion and applied research. It is hoped that further research may delete, further substantiate, or add to some of the conditions and ideas which were briefly outlined.

ALLEN, K. E., HENKE, L. B., HARRIS, F. R., BAER, D. M., & REYNOLDS, N. J. Control of hyperactivity by social reinforcement of attending behavior. *Journal of Educational Psychology* 1967, 58, 231–237.

ARONSON, E. The effect of effort on the intrinsic attractiveness of a stimulus. Unpublished doctoral dissertation, Stanford University, 1959.

ASCH, S. E. The doctrine of suggestion, prestige and imitation in social psychology. *Psychological Review*, 1948, 55, 250–276.

ASCH, S. E. Effects of group pressure upon the modification and distortion of judgement. In H. Guetzkow (Ed.), *Groups, leadership and men*. Pittsburg: Carnegie Press, 1951.

ASCH, S. E. Studies of independence and conformity. A minority of one against a unanimous majority. *Psychological Monographs*, 1956, 70, (9 Whole No. 416).

BANDURA, A. Behavioral modifications through modeling procedures. In L. S. Krasner & L. P. Ullman (Eds)., *Research in behavior modification*. New York: Holt, Rinehart & Winston, 1965. (a)

BANDURA, A. Influence of model's reinforcement contingencies on the acquisition of imitative responses. *Journal of Personality and Social Psychology*, 1965, 1, 589–595. (b)

BANDURA, A. Vicarious processes: A case of no-trial learning. In L. Berkowitz (Ed.), *Advance in experimental social psychology*. Vol. 2. New York: Academic Press, 1–55, 1965. (c)

BANDURA, A. Social learning theory of identificatory processes. In D. A. Goslin & D. C. Glass (Eds.), *Handbook of socialization theory and research*, Chicago: Rand McNally 1969, in press.

BANDURA, A., & KUPERS, C. J. The transmission of patterns of self-reinforcement through modeling. *Journal of Abnormal and Social Psychology*, 1964, 69, 1–9.

BANDURA, A., ROSS, D., & ROSS, S. A. A comparative test of the status envy, social power, and the secondary-reinforcement theories of identificatory learning. *Journal of Abnormal and Social Psychology*, 1963, 67, 527-534. (a)

BANDURA, A., ROSS, D., & ROSS, S. A. Vicarious reinforcement and imitation. *Journal of Abnormal and Social Psychology*, 1963, 67, 601-607. (b)

BANDURA, A., & WALTERS, R. H. *Social learning and personality development*. New York: Holt, Rinehart & Winston, 1963.

BREHM, J. W. Increasing cognitive dissonance by a *fait accompli*. *Journal of Abnormal and Social Psychology*, 1959, 58, 379-382.

BREHM, J. W., & COHEN, A. R. *Explorations in cognitive dissonance*. New York: Wiley, 1962.

BROCK, T. C., & BLACKWOOD, J. E. Dissonance reduction, social comparison and modification of others' opinions. *Journal of Abnormal and Social Psychology*, 1962, 65, 319-324.

BRODBECK, M. The role of small groups in mediating the effects of propaganda. *Journal of Abnormal and Social Psychology*, 1956, 52, 166-170.

BURNSTEIN, E., STOTLAND, E., & ZANDER, A. Similarity to a model and self-evaluation. *Journal of Abnormal and Social Psychology*, 1961, 62, 257-264.

COHEN, A. R., TERRY, H. I., & JONES, C. B. Attitudinal effects of choice in exposure to counterpropaganda. *Journal of Abnormal and Social Psychology*, 1959, 58, 388-391.

CORROZI, J. F., & ROSNOW, R. L. Consonant and dissonant communications as positive and negative reinforcements in opinion change. *Journal of Personality and Social Psychology*, 1968, 8, 27-30.

CORSINI, R. J. *Roleplaying in psychotherapy: A manual*. Chicago: Aldine, 1966.

ELMS, A. C., & JANIS, I. L. Counternorm attitudes induced by consonant versus dissonant role playing. *Journal of Experimental Research in Personality*, 1965, 1, 50-60.

FESTINGER, L. A., *A theory of cognitive dissonance*. Evanston, Ill.: Row, Peterson, 1957.

FESTINGER, L. A., & ARONSON, E. The arousal and reduction of dissonance in social contexts. In, D. Cartwright & A. Zander. *Group dynamics research and theory*. New York: Harper & Row, 1953.

FESTINGER, L. A., & CARLSMITH, J. M. Cognitive consequences of forced compliance. *Journal of Abnormal and Social Psychology*, 1959, 58, 203-210.

FESTINGER, L., RIECKEN, H., & SCHACHTER, S. *When prophecy fails*. Minneapolis: University of Minnesota Press, 1956.

GINOTT, H. G. *Group psychotherapy with children*. New York: McGraw-Hill, 1961.

HOVLAND, C. Reconciling conflicting results derived from experimental and survey studies of attitude change. *American Psychologist*, 1959, 14, 8-17.

HOVLAND, C., & PRITZKER, H. Extent of opinion change as a function of the amount of change advocated. *Journal of Abnormal and Social Psychology*, 1957, 54, 257-261.

JANIS, I. L., & KING, B. T. The influence of roleplaying on opinion changes. *Journal of Abnormal and Social Psychology*, 1954, 49, 211-218.

JANIS, I. L., & MANN, L. Effectiveness of emotional role-playing in modifying smoking habits and attitudes. *Journal of Experimental Research in Personality*, 1965, 1, 84-90.

KANAREFF, V. T., & LANZETTA, J. T. Effects of success-failure experiences and probability of reinforcement upon the acquisition and extinction of an imitative response. *Psychological Reports*, 1960, 7, 151-166.

KEIRSEY, D. W. Transactional casework: A technology for inducing behavior change. Paper presented at the Annual Convention of the California Association of School Psychologists and Psychometrists, San Francisco, 1965. (Mimeo.)

KRUMBOLTZ, J. D. *Revolution in counseling: Implications of behavioral science*. Boston: Houghton-Mifflin, 1966.

KRUMBOLTZ, J. D., & HOSFORD, R. E. Behavioral counseling in the elementary school. *Elementary School Guidance and Counseling*, 1967, 1, 27-40.

KRUMBOLTZ, J. D., & SCHROEDER, W. W. Promoting career planning through reinforcement and models. *Personnel and Guidance Journal*, 1965, 44, 19-26.

LANDFIELD, A., & NAWAS, M. Psychotherapeutic improvement as a function of communication and adoption of therapist's values. *Journal of Counseling Psychology*, 1964, 11, 336-341.

LANZETTA, J. T., & KANAREFF, V. T. The effects of a monetary reward on the acquisition of an imitative response. *Journal of Abnormal and Social Phycology*, 1959, 59, 120-127.

LEFKOWITZ, M. M., BLAKE, R. R., & MOUTON, J. S. Status factors in pedestrian violation of traffic signals. *Journal of Abnormal and Social Psychology*, 1955, 51, 704-706.

LESSER, G. S., & ABELSON, R. P. Personality correlates of persuasibility in children. In I. L. Janis & C. I. Hovland (Eds.), *Personality and persuasibility*. New Haven: Yale University Press, 1959.

MARGOLIUS, G. J., & SHEFFIELD, F. D. Optimum methods of combining practice and filmed demonstration in teaching complex response sequences: Serial learning of a mechanical-assembly task. In A. A. Lumsdaine (Ed.), *Student response in programmed instruction: A symposium*. Washington, D. C.: National Academy of Science–National Research Council, 1961.

MAYER, G. R., & BAKER, P. Group counseling with elementary school children: A look at group size. *Elementary School Guidance and Counseling*, 1967, 1, 140-145.

61

MAYER, G. R., & CODY, J. J. Aspects of Festinger's theory of cognitive dissonance applied to school counseling. *The Personnel and Guidance Journal*, 1968, **47**, 233–239.

MENDELSOHN, G. Effects of client personality and client-counselor similarity on the duration of counseling: A replication and extension. *Journal of Counseling Psychology*, 1966, **13**, 228–234.

MENDELSOHN, G., & GELLER, M. Effect of counselor-client similarity on the outcome of counseling. *Journal of Counseling Psychology*, 1963, **10**, 71–77.

MILLENSON, J. R. *Principles of behavioral analysis.* New York: Macmillan, 1967.

MILLER, N. E., & DOLLARD, J. *Social learning and imitation. New Haven:* Yale University Press, 1941.

MILLS, J. Changes in moral attitudes following temptation. *Journal of Personality*, 1958, **26**, 517–531.

MITNICK, L. L., & McGINNIES, E. Influencing ethnocentrism in small discussion groups through a film communication. *Journal of Abnormal and Social Psychology*, 1958, **56**, 82–90.

MORENO, J. L. *Psychodrama.* New York: Beacon House, 1946.

OJEMANN, R. O. *A teaching program in human behavior and mental health: Book III. Handbook for third grade teachers.* (Rev. ed.) Cleveland: Educational Research Council of Greater Cleveland, 1967.

ROHEN, T. M., & MAYER, G. R. Public commit-ment and dissonance: Cognitive counseling. Southern Illinois University, 1968. (Mimeo)

SALZINGER, K., FELDMAN, R. S., COWAN, J. E., & SALZINGER, S. Operant conditioning of verbal behavior of two young speech-deficient boys. In L. Krasner & L. P. Ullman (Eds.), *Research in behavior modification.* New York: Holt, Rinehart & Winston, 1967.

SCHEIN, E. H. The effect of reward on adult imitative behavior. *Journal of Abnormal and Social Psychology*, 1954, **49**, 389–395.

STOTLAND, E., & DUNN, R. Empathy, self-esteem, and birth order. *Journal of Abnormal and Social Psychology*, 1963, **66**, 532–540.

STOTLAND, E., & PATCHEN, M. Identification and changes in prejudice and in authoritarianism. *Journal of Abnormal and Social Psychology*, 1961, **62**, 265–274.

TOCH, H. H., & SCHULTE, R. Readiness to perceive violence as a result of police training. *British Journal of Psychology*, 1961, **52**, 389–394.

WALTERS, R. H., LEAT, M., & MEZEI, L. Response inhibition and disinhibition through empathetic learning. *Canadian Journal of Psychology*, 1963, **17**, 235–243.

WALTERS, R. H., & RAY, E. Anxiety: Social isolation, and reinforcer effectiveness. *Journal of Personality*, 1960, **28**, 358–367.

ZANDER, A., & HAVELIN, A. Social comparison and intergroup attraction. *Human Relations*, 1960, **13**, 21–32.

BEHAVIORISTIC PSYCHODRAMA: A TECHNIQUE FOR MODIFYING AGGRESSIVE BEHAVIOR IN CHILDREN

William E. Ferinden, Jr., Ph.D.

This paper discusses *behavioristic psychodrama*, a term and approach devised by the author to modify aggressive "acting out" behavior through a combination of behavioristic psychodramatic and self-monitoring techniques.

The school psychologist is called upon to evaluate and counsel a great number of culturally deprived, socially maladjusted, and emotionally disturbed youngsters. We appear something like emergency repairmen for health workers, social workers, and educational personnel. The difficulty of such a position is not the interpreting of a child's emotional actions and behaviors, but the frustrations encountered in attempting to change or modify such behavior. In many instances parents are uninterested or uncooperative and, consequently, the psychologist in cooperation with the classroom teacher, must modify such behaviors within the learning situation.

The most difficult child to cope with within the classroom appears to be the aggressive youngster. The aggressive child, aside from physically attacking other children, may also express aggression in the form of childish behavior, profanity, open defiance and by facial or gestural cues.

Behavioristic psychodrama or behavior rehearsal includes many variations of the techniques as described by Moreno (1959), Wolpe (1958), and Gittelman (1965). The method utilized by the author is an approach in which the teacher involves the child in play acting a prescribed behavior which is considered inappropriate.

Self-monitoring behavior is the technique of counting behavior. Self-control techniques have been demonstrated to be effective in modifying behaviors ranging from poor study habits, Sulzer (1962), to stuttering, Goldiamond, (1965b) to the simplest application of self-monitoring, Kaufer (1967). Such a technique emphasizes self-control by which the child sets up conditions in his environment to bring about specific behaviors in himself. This technique of counting behavior provides immediate feedback and as such, the child becomes aware of the effect and consequences of his behavior.

METHOD

To illustrate a combination of the above techniques with children, an approach is described. Four fifth grade boys who manifested overall aggres-

GROUP PSYCHOTHERAPY AND PSYCHODRAMA, 1971, Vol. 24, pp. 101-106.

sive behaviors and who consistently disrupted the classroom were included in this study. Prior to implementing the above approaches, the author had worked with these children (ten, one hour counseling sessions) with a modification of behavior achieved within the counseling setting but with little or no carry over to the classroom. Prior to implementing the above techniques, each boy maintained an average base line of 15 disruptions per class day or a total of 60 class disruptions (average) a day for the entire group.

Most teachers attend to children much more quickly when they are naughty, acting childish, noisy, than when they are nice. Consequently, the teacher was requested to ignore the boys negative behaviors and reinforce only the positive behaviors.

The self-monitoring technique has its drawbacks as it requires the child to cooperate and participate in carrying out the procedures without direct supervision. The above procedure was presented in the public of the class and as such the four boys had to cooperate by making check marks for the occurrence of each negative behavior. All students in the class, as with the teacher, were requested not to react to the negative behaviors of the four boys and to maintain mental count of each time one of the four misbehaved. Each child included in the study was instructed to draw up a chart with each day of the week represented. Instead of attacking one particular behavior, the author attempted to modify all negative behaviors of each child by having the youngster place a check mark in the appropriate box for each negative behavior he displayed. The behavior chart was kept on the upper right corner of the youngsters desk.

Behavioristic psychodrama was implemented by requiring each of the four boys to act out the childish behaviors they had manifested that week (half hour sessions). At the completion of each of these half hour sessions the class was requested to discuss these behaviors and through role playing techniques etc. act out alternate more positive behaviors that each of the four children might practice during the week or in between sessions. At the end of each week, I returned to the class and through psychodramatic techniques had the four children again act out childish behaviors in general and those particular behaviors each boy himself manifested during the prior week.

Before the end of each session, the four boys were requested to act out positive alternatives to any negative behavior they may have manifested between sessions. By the third week, psychodramatic techniques were utilized involving play acting of only positive behaviors of each of the four children by themselves and by their classmates. In addition, self-monitoring behavior involved only the counting of positive ways of behaving during the class day. A total of 5½ hours sessions brought about a drastic change in each child's behavior.

Through the implementation of behavioristic psychodrama, these four children were able to play the role of themselves in the present; themselves at another time and in essence explore their own behavior while members of their class not only observed but participated as well. Each child in the study was afforded the opportunity to develop ego strength and to release tensions by practicing roles and interpersonal relationships with their classmates.

This combination of techniques proved quite effective and in fact, drastically reduced not one negative behavior in each child but reduced the occurrence of several childish behaviors and extinguished several others. The children realized that their classmates could be positive reinforces without having to resort to clowning, profanity, and facial or gestural cues. The class, in general, functioned much more effectively as the other children also benefited from the improved behaviors by vicariously imitating such behavior.

The teacher in turn was much more relaxed and as such facilitated a more congenial class atmosphere by not becoming emotionally upset as she ignored the negative behaviors and reinforced only the positive behavior.

CASE ILLUSTRATIONS

James, a 12 year old boy who was diagnosed as psychotic by the school psychologist presented the greatest problems, not so much in the expression of aggression but in his overall hallucinating actions, such as talking out loud, giggling, barking like a dog, making weird sounds and expressing many facial gestures. James came from a residential treatment center at mid-year and as such, had difficulty in making new friends. He was not well liked and to this author's knowledge, did not have one friend as a classmate. A sociometric evaluation placed James outside of the entire class group. He expressed several choices but no one chose him.

At the end of the first week, James had only 3 check marks for the entire 5 day period. His classmates attested to the fact that James was the best behaved and most honest of the four boys in monitoring his behavior. The class applauded James for his remarkable improvement. At the end of the second session, James had no checks for inappropriate behavior and at the class suggestion, he was not required to monitor his behavior the third week of the study. Similar results have been found with adult populations,

Rutner and Bugle (1969), but to this author's knowledge, very few studies have been conducted with children.

James had made several friends, became much more outgoing and for the first time in his life actually felt accepted and was accepted by his peers.

Craig, a very bright youngster, 10 years old, completed his first week with a total of 15 checks (45 less) than his base line. At the end of the second session, Craig's total for inappropriate behaviors numbered 5. However, his classmates felt he was not honest in recording his behavior and as such, felt his score should be doubled for cheating behavior. Craig had a total of 3 points for the final week of the study. Again, overall, this was a considerable depreciation in general aggressive behavior. In addition, the behavior of banging his head on the blackboard for attention was totally extinguished.

Roger, age 11, completed his first week and second week with 14 and 11 points respectively. Roger's third week of the study resulted in 0 points. His classmates felt he made the next to best overall improvement and many stated that they now enjoyed playing with Roger on the playground because he was no longer prone to pushing or shoving his classmates. This behavior which prevented Roger from being accepted by his classmates became totally extinguished.

Allen, age 11, the most mature member of the group, presented the most difficult problem with regards to overall improvement. Aggressive behavior did not increase from the base line of 15 points a day, however, Allen maintained a high level of aggressive behavior for the first week. In fact, Allen began to use profanity, a behavior which was not evident prior to conducting the study. When discussing Allen's behavior in front of the class, Allen became quite emotional and began to cry, stating that his classmates were all liars. Subject appeared to be more neurotic than the others, and the author, at this point had reservations about continuing Allen in the study. The class teacher's immediate response was to overact with a lot of tender loving care. However, Allen, being an extremely bright youngster, (able to pass all tests without paying attention or studying) had been successful in manipulating his teachers since the first day he entered school (case referred to special services at end of second grade). Allen developed a pattern of behavior in which he constantly disrupted the class for the entire school year. This behavior was reinforced as the teacher consistently drew attention to it. Only during the last 3 weeks of any term did this youngster settle down and conform to class norms as he always wanted to get promoted and knew enough not to push his teacher during such a critical time when she was making decision as to who should pass or fail. Since Allen was consciously aware of his negative behavior, I decided to continue him in the study.

Consequently, my initial approach with Allen continued with the class teacher's full cooperation. The only difference being that the class discussed Allen's behavior and ways in which members of the class could help Allen behave as a 5th grader. The other 3 boys also became involved in attempting to modify Allen's behavior. Consequently, the peer group began to emphasize only positive behavior. During the second week, Allen scored a total of 23 points and a total of 15 points for the third week of the study. After three group sessions in which behavioristic psychodrama and self-monitoring behavior was employed, Allen reported a considerable improvement in his behavior, however, he did not experience the growth that the other three boys had. Allen did report that while he often felt angry at his classmates and the teacher, he now felt much more able to inhibit aggressive responses. On follow-up, three months later, the classroom teacher reported a continued diminution of his aggressiveness, which had previously been a daily occurrence.

CONCLUSIONS

Behavioristic Reviewing, a term and approach devised by the author proved quite effective as a technique in modifying and extinguishing aggressive behaviors in children. By combining behavioristic psychodramatic and self-monitoring techniques, the children received immediate feedback in addition to witnessing the childishness of such behaviors. Such an approach appears quite effective when utilized in the presence of the peer group.

It is the job of the school psychologist to maintain each child within the mainstream of education and to make him ameniable to our educational program. The school setting does not lend itself to the long drawn out analytical approach and as such the school psychologist must work with surface behavior. Psychiatric clinics have long waiting lists and often produce little or no positive results. Such an approach described in this paper might be looked upon by others as harsh and cruel treatment. However, it is important to point out that the Linden school system as with any major city, encounters far more problems with children in one day than many school systems encounter in a year. Most important is that after an 18 month follow-up, all 4 children have adjusted satisfactorily to the educational setting and all have gone on to the junior high school apparently as well adjusted youngsters without secondary symptoms etc. This approach to modifying their behaviors was successful.

The results of this study reinforce my contention that the school psychologist, with a workable knowledge of behavior modification techniques can, as a consultant, aid in providing teachers with behavioral approaches to the elimination of inappropriate behaviors which interfere with the learning situation. Thus, a majority of children displaying any type of conduct disorder behaviors could be controlled in the regular classroom setting. The result would hopefully be a decrease in referrals for psychological services whereby the school psychologist could spend a greater amount of time in the capacity of consultant in preventing behavior problems and learning disabilities and in coping with the more seriously handicapped child.

REFERENCES

GOLDIAMOND, I. Self-control procedures in personal behavior problems. *Psychological Reports*, 1965, 17: 851-868. (a)

GOLDIAMOND, I. Stuttering and fluency as manipulatable operant response classes. In L. Krasner & L. Ullmann (Eds) *Research in behavior modification*. New York: Holt, Rinehart & Winston, 1965. (b)

GITTELMAN, M. Report on the Work of the Medical Committee for Human Rights in Mississippi. Paper read at Albert Einstein College of Medicine in New York, November 25, 1964.

KANFER, F. H. Self-regulation: Research, Issues and Speculations. Paper presented at the Ninth Annual Institute for Research in Clinical Psychology, University of Kansas, April 1967.

MORENO, J. L. Psychodrama. *American Handbook of Psychiatry*. Edited by Arieti, S. New York: Basic Books, 1959 (Ch. 68).

SULZER, E. S. Research frontier: Reinforcement and the therapeutic contract. *Journal of Counseling Psychology*, 1962, 9: 271-276.

WOLPE, J. Psychotherapy by reciprocal inhibition. Stanford, California: Stanford University Press, 1958.

NON-VERBAL TECHNIQUES: A MEANS OF FACILITATING
GROUP COUNSELING WITH CHILDREN

Richard J. Malnati, Ph.D.
Assistant Professor
Temple University

In recent years the use of non-verbal techniques as a means
of facilitating process in group therapy and encounter groups has
been described by Mintz (1971), Otto (1970) and Shutz (1967).
Few efforts, however, have been made to translate these tech-
inques into procedures which can be used by elementary school
counselors.

The purpose of this article is to illustrate four non-
verbal techniques suitable for group counseling with elementary
school children. The techniques can be employed by the counselor in groups and/or in consultation with the teacher in the
classroom.

Elementary school counselors working with children in group
counseling frequently are faced with practical problems such as:
(a) facilitating interaction and involvement, (b) eliciting
childrens' feelings about themselves and others, (c) facilitating the process of self-understanding, (d) maintaining the
child's interest in the group and (e) involving the silent
member(s).

Explanations for these occurrences are numerous. Typically,
counselor leadership style, composition and size of the group,
or age of group members are viewed as being major contributors to
the development of these problems in group counseling. An often
neglected explanation, however, is that counselors who work with
groups of children rely primarily on verbal techniques to generate interaction and involvement among group members. Counselors may overlook the fact that often children are not skilled
or comfortable in verbalizing their feelings about themselves and
the world. Moreover, children tend to have a relatively short
attention span and, therefore, an overabundance of verbal interaction challenges their ability to participate over an extended
period of time.

Introducing non-verbal exercises as an adjunct to verbal
techniques in group counseling offers children a means of interaction which is often more natural and easy for them. Children
learn about their world through physical participation as well
as through verbal interaction. They are willing to engage in
activities and games which can provide valuable learning experi-

ORIGINAL MANUSCRIPT, 1974.

ences about themselves and others. Participation, according to Komachack (1972): "provides the medium for communication between counselor and children and between each child and other children (p. 81)." Further, non-verbal exercises enhance the possibility of increasing the child's interest and span of attention during the group process.

Non-verbal exercises may be used for a wide range of purposes at different stages of group development. Some exercises may be employed to start the group or familiarize members to the group process. Others may serve the purpose of facilitating the occurrence of more accurate feedback or to break impasses between group members.

Described below are four examples of how non-verbal exercises may be utilized for different purposes at different times in group counseling:

"Trust Walk"

Objectives:

1. To initiate and facilitate interaction among group members.
2. To facilitate an awareness of trust among group members.
3. To stimulate discussion about trust and helping behaviors (i.e., relying on others, concern for others).

Materials

1. Blindfolds

Directions:

1. Blindfold half the members and assign them a partner.
2. Non-blindfolded members "guide" their partners to a pre-determined location.
3. Upon reaching pre-determined locations, roles are reversed.
4. No communication. permitted.

Discussion

1. How did members feel when they were blindfolded?
2. What were they thinking about as they were being guided (trust, concern, relying behaviors, etc., are usually generated)?

<u>Discussion</u>: (cont'd)

3. Did they trust the person helping them (why, why not)?

4. Allow children to give feedback on the degree of trust they felt in the person guiding them.

5. What kinds of "helping behaviors" facilitate the development of trust?

5. Discuss the importance of trust in group counseling.
   a. Why is it important for us to trust each other in this group?

"Positioning"

<u>Objectives</u>:

1. To highlight non-verbally the dynamics of why a group may not be performing effectively.
2. To help overcome subgroup development and facilitate group cohesiveness.
3. To make the group aware of members who do not feel they are part of the group and the reasons why.
4. To demonstrate how subgroup development or isolated membership may hinder the group process.

<u>Directions</u>:

1. No communication between members.
2. Group members asked to position themselves anywhere in the room according to how their feeling.
3. Allow members to "mill" until they have assumed their positions.
4. Members maintain their positions until group discussion of the exercise has been completed.

<u>Discussion</u>:

1. Examine distances of members from subgroups and other members.
2. Discuss why members positioned themselves as they did.
3. Discuss how positioning and/or subgrouping may effect the development of a good group.
4. Examine the feelings of isolated members.
5. Discuss if any members have ever felt alone and why.

"Non-verbal Gossip"

Objectives:

1. To acquaint members (to initiate the group).
2. To familiarize group members with the importance of non-verbal behavior.
3. To demonstrate how non-verbal messages may be misinterpreted.
4. To become aware of differences between verbal and non-verbal communication.

Directions:

1. Place members in a circle (seated or standing).
2. Leader asks members to close their eyes.
3. Leader whispers an emotion to a member who portrays it non-verbally to another member.
4. When a member has communicated the message, he may keep his eyes open.
5. Each receiver is alerted by a touch on the shoulder.

Discussion:

1. Upon completion of the exercise, the last member communicates what he believes was transmitted to him and the group discusses the experience.
2. Long pauses between members can be explored.
3. Differences between non-verbal and verbal communication can be described.
4. How non-verbal messages can be misinterpreted (go around individual members to see where the original emotion may have been lost).
5. Emphasize importance of listening as well as observing non-verbal behavior.

"Roleplaying Emotions"

Objectives:

1. To acquaint children with different feelings.
2. To facilitate interaction and involvement by group members.
3. To facilitate the development of self-awareness.

Materials:

    1. 3 x 5 cards
    2. Write names of different emotions on cards (i.e. bored, happy, angry, sad, joyful, scared, etc.).

Directions:

    1. Child picks a card and is asked to portray the feeling without speaking.
    2. Child may use facial expressions, gestures, or body movements to convey the feeling.

Discussion:

    1. Children guess what emotion was protrayed.
    2. Children asked if any have ever felt that way and why.

The non-verbal exercises described above are usually welcomed by children in counseling groups since they are game-like and pose minimal threat. Caution, however, should be exercised by the counselor when considering exercises which demand more confrontive behavior. Careful selection of exercises according to purpose, methods, and potential consequences (positive and negative) is warrented and essential.

The use of the non-verbal exercises with children in counseling groups, such as those presented here, should be viewed as an aid to the counseling process and not as a substitute for verbal interaction. However, this dimension lends an added degree of flexibility which enhances the group counseling process.

REFERENCES

Komachak, M. K. The activity-interaction group: A process for short-term counseling with elementary school children. Elementary School Guidance and Counseling, 1971, 6, 13-20.

Malnati, R. J. Non-verbal techniques for goup counseling in the elementary school. Paper presented at the American Personnel and Guidance Association, Regional Convention, Atlanta, Georgia, 1973.

Mintz, Elizabeth A. Marathon groups: Reality and symbol. New York: Appelton-Century-Crofts, 1971.

Otto, Herbert A. Group methods to actualize human potential: A handbook, Beverly Hills, California: Holistic Press, 1970.

Schutz, William. Joy. New York: Grove Press, 1967.

DANIEL W. FULLMER

Family group consultation

The purpose of this article is to help orient the practicing counselor to the method and applications of Family Group Consultation (FGC) and the Family Bond Inventory (FBI). The FBI is a recent development in FGC that has led to the possibility of identifying interpersonal conflicts within a family. This instrument would be used by professional practitioners to measure change in the relationships within the family during treatment. Adlerian family counseling, behavior therapy, group psychotherapy, or any method involving a family group could use the measuring techniques, as there is a cultural baseline for human behavior. This concept is similar to Skinner's idea (1971) of the culture as a set of reinforcement schedules.

London (1969) talks about behavior control by information, psychotherapy, hypnosis, conditioning, electronic tools, coercion, assault (punishment), drugs, and surgery. As counselors, we have an aversion to coercion as a controlling device. However, we embrace information and the means to influence by our preferred method of intervention. Family Group Consultation works because the forces operating in the consulting session are the same forces that operate in the family group outside the session. The primary force in family interpersonal relationships is the control exerted by one person's behavior over another person's behavior in the interaction process. If one person changes his behavior, other people need

Daniel W. Fullmer is a Professor, Department of Educational Psychology, University of Hawaii, Honolulu.

to change their response to him. However, if one person continues his usual behavior, every other person can continue to respond in the same fashion, and a redundant patterning of family group behavior continues (Fullmer & Bernard 1972).

Family Group Consultation (FGC)

The theory basic to the method of FGC states simply that behavior comes out of the relationship. The relationship is interpersonal, involving communication between two persons (dyad). The dyad is part of a group; the group is part of a community; the community is part of a larger social system, or culture. To change behavior in A, one must redefine A's relationship with B (Hall 1959). This is accomplished by exposing the control system used in a relationship to verbal interaction techniques and the Family Bond Inventory.

Son: What is this all about? Why are we here?
Mother: I don't think it is safe to talk about our troubles in front of him [son].
Father: [looked impotent in the social stress being pushed by the son and mother]
Counselor: Are you [family] always this stressed emotionally?
Mother and son: [together] What do you mean?
Counselor: You seem so upset that I pick up an emotionally tight climate, very distressed. Are you always like—

ELEMENTARY SCHOOL GUIDANCE AND COUNSELING JOURNAL, 1972, Vol. 7, pp. 130-136.

75

Son: Usually.
Mother: We didn't want to come. Doesn't the idea of telling it all to each other seem to be destructive?
Counselor: Oh, how so?
Mother: Giving up the secrets—I don't like it.
Son: What secrets? Now I'm curious. I want to be here.

Behaviorists expose the control system by focusing on the changed reinforcement schedules in the environment between B and A (Fullmer 1971). Adlerians say that person B followed the direction in the prescription given by the counselor, and logical or natural consequences followed (Fullmer 1971). Each of these is correct to a degree, no matter what method is used. The important variable is that information is selectively managed by the method of intervention. Family Group Consultation uses the familiar verbal model for managing the selection of information in counseling. Family members gather together for one to two hours and talk. The counselor (usually two counselors) tells the family or families that each person will speak for himself. This is the major guideline for exposing the information-behavior control system.

> *Mother:* This thing is not working. I think the whole business has just upset our family.
> *Son:* Things have really improved. I can see how to interrupt the fighting.
> *Father:* We have a long way to go.
> *Mother:* I don't care what you say, things are not good. You haven't helped.

Sessions are contracted by number. Initially there are four sessions; however, more sessions may be added if participants wish.[1] FGC, whether long-term or short-term, is only one of several intervention methods used. Frequently the range of clinical, educational, and social resources managed includes the full scope of mental health services (Blum 1972; Hart 1971).

The formula used to monitor and guide the verbal interaction in each session consists of the speak-only-for-yourself guideline, and in reference to time and place, an emphasis on the here-and-now rather than the then-and-there. However, references to past events are not uncommon, and future references are frequent in plans to try out new behavior and to change schedules of reinforcement. Family Group Consultation is not exclusive. Ideas from other approaches, such as child rearing ideas from Adlerian family counseling or behavior therapy strategies to change a specific habit or behavior, are frequently used. The counselor is responsible for the management of the type of behavior interventions used in FGC.

Conflict resolution and crisis management are major goals of FGC. If two people communicate, harmony and/or conflict may result. When their meanings match, we find more harmony than conflict. Conflict is usually present at some level in all interaction. The FGC method teaches techniques to resolve the conflicts, as it is unrealistic to attempt to avoid conflict in human relationships.

> *Son:* I don't see how our being here will help us. You [counselor] have not told us anything. We talk and you observe—is that all you do?
> *Counselor:* What would you like to have me do?
> *Mother:* I'm against being here. What do we need to do?

---

[1] Additional detailed discussions of the method may be found in Fullmer (1971) and Fullmer and Bernard (1968).

Counselor: Why not begin by describing an incident. Tell what happened before, during, and following the incident. Any incident will do.

Son: Like the one we had this afternoon before coming here?

Mother: I don't remember any incident.

Son: My school work.

Mother: [cut in] He is flunking two subjects in the last quarter of his senior year. He won't graduate. He was called in by the principal. [son did graduate]

Son: Only a little time was spent on the school work. Mostly, it was a school politics issue.

Mother: You are going to fail.

Son: I can re-do the twelfth grade.

The family members continued to expound and challenge each other and the counselor. The session ran over the one-and-one-half hours by thirty minutes because the family could not decide if they should return. They were told to go home and take with them the task of deciding. The counselor indicated that he was disinterested in working with people of such low motivation.

Counselor: After all, it is difficult work to meet with people like you. It is not difficult to see why you have problems with each other.

The family had a task. They left with directions to phone the center and leave the decision with the secretary. The following day a message was received. They would continue and complete the initial four sessions.

The family arrived on time for the second session. The first task was to complete the Family Bond Inventory, a projective inventory of family relationships. When each member completed the

task, the counselor asked for any reactions each person had during the exercise.

Mother: I thought it was silly.

Son: The emotional thing kept coming up.

Father: Yes, did you find it that way too?

Counselor: Anything else?

Mother: Emotional content? What do you mean?

Son: Well, you can't place yourself in relation to another person without thinking about whether you're angry or not.

Counselor: [to mother] What do you think everyone else will do when placing symbols? Do you think your son will place them like you did?

Mother: Yes.

Counselor: Tell us about it. How do you think he did it?

Mother: He [son] would place himself between his father and me.

The Family Bond Inventory seems to be an integral part of Family Group Consultation and the remainder of the article will be devoted to its use in FGC.

The Family Bond Inventory (FBI)

Purpose. The FBI will reveal each individual's perception of the key relationships in his family. The conflicts between family members can then be discovered. The findings can also be used to help learn how to resolve conflicts. The primary bonds or alliances between family members will be revealed through the placement of symbols representing each family member.

Directions. Given a blank sheet of paper, place symbols representing your family members:

F—father

M—mother

♂ —son

♀ —daughter

X—any significant other person who has regular contact with the family

Several life situations may be suggested. Be sure to include: (1) how you see your family members now; (2) how you wish they were, if different from how they are; and (3) any situation where an issue of disagreement may exist.

Number each sibling position, for example:

Boy ♂ oldest child

Girl ♀ second oldest child

Explain the X as a grandmother, aunt, etc.

Draw a circle around your symbol ⊙

Some suggested situations follow: (a) place the symbols in any manner you wish to show how you see your family; (b) show your family at a mealtime (indicate which meal); (c) show how your family is arranged for sleeping (sleeping pattern); (d) show how your family is arranged between 4 and 6 p.m., the re-integration period, and explain your choice. Add other situations as needed. When each person in the family group has finished, permit each other member to see each set of results. Exposure will not invalidate the results or future use of the inventory. The reason for sharing the placements is to discover each family member's reaction to each other's placement of himself. It is helpful to tape record this activity so that reruns can be made during further discussion.

Each person should look for differences and similarities between his placement of symbols and the placements of each other person. The reason is that differences in placement of symbols are concrete representations of possible conflicts. The counselor should verify this by asking each member to make his own statement about what he thinks the different placement means. The counselor may also interpret the results.

Interpretation of the FBI. In a cross-cultural study of personal space within the family group, Cade (1972) found that the basic organization principles within the family could be discovered through the placement of figures representing individual family members. The structure of organization in families in each culture studied (Japanese, Filipino, and American) show a hierarchy, with parents highest in status and power and children ranking from oldest to youngest. The relative placement of each person in the family reflects the structure, and defines the function each person can perform. Any violation of the cultural pattern signals a conflict between the persons in regard to their respective functions within the family structure. The relative status structure defines the relationships within the family. The relationship definition tells each person what to do and what not to do. Each person places himself as he sees and defines his relationship with others in the family. Other persons may disagree with one member's placement of himself, but two things remain significant: the pattern of placements and the personal distance between family members.

The normal family pattern and symbol placement for American families is from male to female and parent to child as shown in Figure 1. The examples shown are typical sample placements for families with normal or healthy interpersonal relationships. Deviations from these typical patterns usually signal a conflict-producing relationship. Deviations are

Figure 1

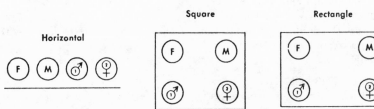

(Give each person a blank sheet of paper)
(Each example is placed on an 8½ by 11 page)

represented by placements which exceed the norm for the American family.

The normal circle symbols are ½-inch in diameter. Each symbol is normal when separated by 1½ to 3 inches, measured from center to center. Deviations of more than 3 inches represent potential conflicts. Four inches and more give results that may safely be representing major conflicts. Some examples of deviation patterns and personal distance produced by families in the initial sessions of consultation are illustrated in Figures 2, 3, and 4.

The subject of each conflict is then explored through verbal interaction in the family consultation session. The beginning of each discussion comes when placement patterns are first shared among family members. *Important:* When family members have arguments, the Family Bond Inventory will tell the counselor whether or not the interpersonal relationships within the family are normal. If the relationships are normal, conflicts can be resolved by the verbal interaction in family consultation. If the relationships are deviant, the definition of the relationships in question must be changed before conflicts will subside. The Family

Figure 2

Family A.   (Paper 8½ by 11 inches)

(Drawing made by male child, age eleven)

Figure 3

Family B.   (Paper 8½ by 11 inches)

(Drawing by girl child ♀, age nine)

Bond Inventory may also be used to redefine relationships and may be given over and over again without hazard.

How to use the results. The counselor may give oral reports to the family immediately.

> *Counselor:* Let's look. Here, take each one and pass them among yourselves. See if you all placed them alike.
> *Son:* Why did you put yours like this, Mom?
> *Mother:* [greatly surprised] What do you mean? I was just putting the symbols down the way it is.
> *Son:* Sleeping in a row?

The mother had tried to defeat the instrument by giving what she thought were bland responses. The directions given included the statement that anyone could rig the responses, but the person doing it would know it if he had lied. The pattern of placements would not look or feel correct. There was no attempt to confront the mother with what she had done. She was aware that the others knew what she had done.

The second session was a sharp contrast to the initial session. The son remarked about the difference. He wondered how two sessions could be so completely different. All interaction had been in relation to the instrument.

Near the close of the second session a task was assigned. The family was to begin by appointing one member each morning, on a rotation basis, to have the duty. The duty was to interrupt any escalating interaction by simply asking, "Hey, what's happening now?" The principle participants were to discuss what had just taken place. If the discussion began to escalate in a similar manner, then the process was to be repeated. Following detailed discussion of the directions, the family went home.

Figure 4

Family C. (Paper 8½ by 11 inches)

(Drawing by boy child ☿, age eleven)

The Family Bond Inventory revealed the existence of powerful normal relationships between family members (father-mother, father-son, mother-son). We learned from the instrument that the mother was not a reliable informant on family issues. However, she knew that everyone was aware of this shortcoming, and the potentially destructive interaction to confirm it was avoided. During the second and third sessions, the mother gave evidence of conscious effort to be more reliable.

The counselor must avoid "head trips" with the family about their behavior and stick with the description of one incident at a time: What happened? What happened just before, just after, and during the incident? What response did you make? What happened then?

The next stage involves helping each member of the family understand how to control his own behavior. Each family member learns to identify the sequence of cues which trigger emotional outbursts and loss of control. The individual can learn to manipulate his own input in interactions, which in turn controls responses from others. This is the only concrete source of control anyone has in an exchange of messages during an interaction with another individual.

Summary

In Family Group Consultation, like other group counseling approaches, everyone improves at his own rate. The gain is a more realistic evaluation of the functioning of each family member and the family as a whole. The family may then try to practice new behavior in the FGC sessions or at home.

The Family Bond Inventory helps to discover the emotional relationships that each person has with each other family member. The counselor may use results from the FBI to validate or invalidate his subjective perceptions of the family's interpersonal relationships. The results may also be useful as a measure of behavior change in an individual family member, or to help the family change behavior.

References

Blum, R. H. and Associates. *Horatio Alger's children: Role of the family in origin and prevention of drug risk.* San Francisco: Jossey-Bass, Inc., Publishers, 1972.

Cade, T. A cross-cultural study of personal space in the family. Unpublished doctoral dissertation. Honolulu: University of Hawaii, 1972.

Hall, E. T. *The silent language.* New York: Doubleday & Co., 1959.

Hart, P. Interpersonal distance in selected social and personal relationships as a measure of alienation among young middle class drug users. Unpublished doctoral dissertation. Honolulu: University of Hawaii, 1971.

Fullmer, D. W. *Counseling: Group theory and system.* Scranton, Pa.: Intext Educational Publishers, 1971.

Fullmer, D. W., & Bernard, H. W. *Family consultation.* Guidance Monograph Series II Counseling. Boston: Houghton Mifflin Co., 1968.

Fullmer, D. W., & Bernard, H. W. *The school counselor-consultant.* Boston: Houghton Mifflin Co., 1972.

London, P. *Behavior control.* New York: Harper & Row, 1969.

Skinner, B. F. *Beyond freedom and dignity.* New York: Alfred A. Knopf, 1971.

DONALD H. BLOCHER, RITA S. RAPOZA

A systematic eclectic model for counseling–consulting

One way to look at the emerging roles of psychological workers in educational settings is from an essentially ecological view (Blocher, Dustin & Dugan 1971; Danskin, Kennedy & Friesen 1965). From such a view the major professional goal of the student personnel worker (or consultant) is to help create and to maintain a network of learning environments in family, school, and community that will nurture the optimal development of every student. Most of the learning environments that presently exist within our families, schools, and communities are clearly not designed to provide the kind of psychosocial interaction that will optimize human development, so that the role of the personnel worker often becomes that of an agent of environmental change (McCully 1965). The counselor or personnel worker in effect becomes an applied social scientist and uses the tools afforded him by social and developmental psychology to facilitate positive change in those human systems that become his clients (Berdie 1972; Blocher 1969).

Within this framework the client may be seen as a single individual or as a social system, such as a family, classroom, or school organization. The kinds of treatments or interventions available to the counselor may include consultation techniques, small group work, or laboratory learning procedures, as well as the more traditional individual counseling approaches. Counselors may be engaged in process consultation within classrooms, teaching parent or teacher effectiveness courses, or running academic improvement or interpersonal skills groups. They could be involved with vocational decision making groups with students, or engaged in consultation and staff development activities with school administrators, as well as being occupied with individual counseling cases.

A major problem for counselors in developing this new ecologically based role has been the fact that traditional counseling theories and approaches were derived primarily from personality theories. These approaches have not been flexible enough to provide the conceptual underpinning necessary for the wide range of problems and settings in which the ecologically oriented counselor finds himself. Many such approaches are based primarily on clinical experiences with middle class adult neurotics engaged in insight-oriented psychotherapy. For several years leaders in the field have called for systematic eclectic approaches that will provide the flexibility needed to apply the kinds of specific interventions that have proved effective for specific problems of specific clients (Carkhuff 1966). The profession has almost abandoned its search for panaceas.

One attempt at developing a systematic eclectic approach for use by counselors

Donald H. Blocher is a Professor and Rita S. Rapoza is a counselor at Edgewood Junior High School, St. Paul, and a graduate student, Department of Educational Psychology, University of Minnesota, Minneapolis.

ELEMENTARY SCHOOL GUIDANCE AND COUNSELING JOURNAL, 1972, Vol. 7, pp. 106-112.

in educational settings is described very briefly here. The method is systematic in that it presents a specific sequence of activities in which the counselor engages. It is eclectic in that it utilizes several different sources of gain based upon relationship, cognitive, behavioral, and social psychological theories. The model is presented in flowchart form in Figure 1. It seems useful to comment briefly on its practical use. The rationale involved is described more fully elsewhere (Blocher & Shaffer 1971; Blocher, in press).

The systematic eclectic model assumes that the first step for the counselor in the process of intervening in a positive way with a client system (school, family, or individual) is to clearly understand his own professional identity and goals. These need to be clarified in relation to the needs and perceptions of the institutional framework and potential client population with which the counselor works. This may be expressed in a basic postulate:

1. The counselor understands himself and the systems within which he operates before he intervenes actively.

Now the counselor can actively scan the relevant learning environments with which he works to find opportunities to advance his professional goals. He operates from a proactive rather than a reactive stance. As he encounters groups and situations that may represent potential opportunities to facilitate growth in

Figure 1. Facilitating Change in Human Systems

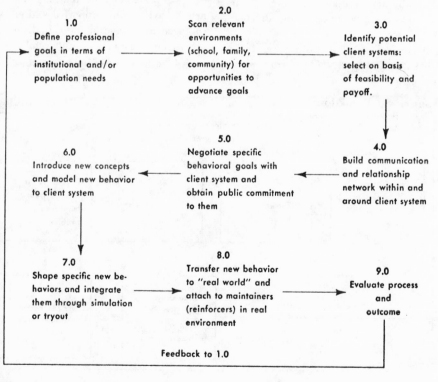

1.0
Define professional goals in terms of institutional and/or population needs

2.0
Scan relevant environments (school, family, community) for opportunities to advance goals

3.0
Identify potential client systems: select on basis of feasibility and payoff.

6.0
Introduce new concepts and model new behavior to client system

5.0
Negotiate specific behavioral goals with client system and obtain public commitment to them

4.0
Build communication and relationship network within and around client system

7.0
Shape specific new behaviors and integrate them through simulation or tryout

8.0
Transfer new behavior to "real world" and attach to maintainers (reinforcers) in real environment

9.0
Evaluate process and outcome

Feedback to 1.0

key human systems, he begins to build communication and relationship networks. These networks will allow open, honest, and important messages to be transmitted in many directions. This phase may be summarized in a second postulate:

2. The way to begin to help any human system is to listen to it and help it listen to itself.

After successfully establishing that relationship and communication network, the counselor becomes involved in open and direct negotiation. The counselor focuses on the specification of goals in behavioral terms, and the securing of open client commitment to these goals. A third postulate can be summarized:

3. Change in human systems occurs most readily when goals are clearly and mutually agreed upon and when public commitment is obtained in a contractual way.

Upon the completion of the negotiation phase, a whole-part-whole learning se-

quence is initiated. This sequence uses principles of information dissemination in order to obtain cognitive change coupled with social learning and operant shaping procedures, as well as simulation techniques drawn from laboratory learning wherever appropriate. This sequence can be summarized in the following way:

4. Human systems learn best when presented with clear general concepts and models, followed by error correction and discrimination training, followed by supervised practice with the newly acquired complex behaviors in safe settings.

The next sequence of activities is aimed at the transfer of learning and the maintenance of new learning in the actual environment of the client. The counselor follows up the client system as it attempts to respond to real problems in new ways. He attempts to arrange for the new behavior to be supported and encouraged by significant individuals or subsystems. The basic postulate follows:

5. The help-giving process is not com-

Figure 2. Breakdown of Evaluation Procedures

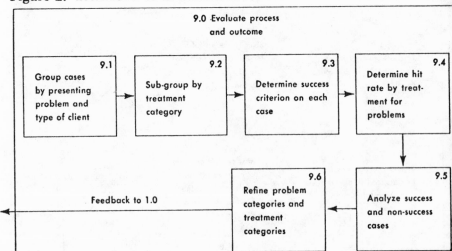

plete until the client system has successfully utilized its learning in the real situation and has experienced rewards for doing so.

The final sequence involves evaluation and is shown in Figure 2. Essentially, this phase involves the computation of success ratios for specific treatments with specific client problems and populations. This information is then used to improve performance and goal setting. The final postulate is simple:

6. Professional practice can only improve where accurate and immediate feedback is available about results.

The preceding discussion of this systematic eclectic model for counseling practice is necessarily very brief and abstract. It seems very complex and perhaps cumbersome. It has been employed successfully, however, in many practical counseling situations. The following is an example of its use in a junior high school.

The counselor's first function in the school was to write the following job description; this statement clearly defined her areas of expertise in relation to her personal needs and the needs of the educational institution she was about to enter. Administrators, supportive staff members, teachers, and parents used this outline as a stimulus for further negotiation and clarification of the school's and, counselor's goals.

I. Expertise in staff development and consulting with teacher-advisers in the following areas:
   A. Group dynamics
   B. Communications skills
   C. Decision making skills
   D. Study skills
   E. Student development
   F. Individual differences
   G. Vocational development
   H. Parental and/or family counseling

II. Training and expertise in consulting with staff and administration concerning problems of:
   A. Human relations
   B. Organizational development
   C. Curriculum development

III. Expertise and experience in organizing and conducting:
   A. Academic improvement groups
   B. Interpersonal skills groups
   C. Vocational-educational planning groups

IV. Skills in individual counseling with students who have special problems.

V. Ability to perform assessment and diagnostic activities in regard to the following types of problems:
   A. Learning difficulties
   B. Special referral problems (personality disorders and learning dysfunctions)
   C. Vocational aptitudes and interests

Example 1

An example of how this approach can be implemented is described in a consultation with a first year teacher, who had previously worked with the counselor. General dissatisfaction with what was happening in one of her classes brought the young teacher in contact with the counselor. Her request for help came in the form of asking the counselor to observe the class as she taught.

Before agreeing to enter the classroom, the counselor asked the teacher to define some specific behaviors that she wanted the counselor to observe during the process observation (Step 1, Figure 1). A set of group rating scales was used as a basis for negotiation in this particular case, because the teacher had some difficulty in defining these specific behaviors (Blocher, Dustin & Dugan 1971). After the behaviors were written down and explicitly agreed upon, the teacher and the counselor decided on the day and time of the classroom observation (Steps 2, 3, 4, 5, Figure 1). Throughout this preparation period the counselor was very much aware of the relationship she was trying to establish with the teacher. Her goal at this point was to insure the flow of expressive, instrumental, positive and negative communication (Step 4, Figure 1). This climate needed to be established before the results of the process observation could be given to the teacher.

Sensing that the teacher was nervous after her classroom presentation, the counselor tried to help her stay with some of the feelings she was experiencing (Step 4, Figure 1). With the communication open once more, the two studied the results of the observation and again negotiated until they agreed upon a plan of action (Step 5, Figure 1).

During the ensuing two sessions the counselor introduced her client to new ways of thinking about her students and herself, reinforced the teacher's attempts at new behaviors, and played the role of a student as the teacher tried out some personally difficult behaviors in the counselor's office (Steps 6, 7, Figure 1). The counselor was invited back into the classroom for a follow-up observation. Afterwards, in their evaluation session, the counselor asked the teacher if there were any one staff member that she liked and respected and could talk to about the skills she was trying to acquire. This person turned out to be a veteran teacher in another department. In a meeting where all three were present, the counselor served as a facilitator to insure that the goals were feasible and clearly defined and that the communication between the two teachers was direct and open (Step 8, Figure 1). Before terminating that session, the counselor and the new teacher once again reviewed the value of this particular approach and agreed upon another time to re-evaluate the situation (Step 9, Figure 1).

Example 2

Another example of the effectiveness of the systematic eclectic model is provided by six students who wished to increase their study skills in an academic improvement group. During the individual intake interviews, the counselor clearly defined her goals for the group and helped the students decide if their goals were appropriate for this particular group. Once this was determined, the counselor requested that the potential group member (a) declare his behavioral objectives to the group in either the first or second session; (b) commit himself to assisting other members in the group; and (c) let the group know of his decision to sever his relationship with them if he should find the group inappropriate for his needs after the first two meetings.

Even before the counselor met with the group, she showed evidence of following the first three postulates: She knew her own goals, tried to secure the right people for the right group, and obtained an oral commitment to individual and group goals. When the group convened, the objectives were redefined through the sharing of expectations. During the negotiation of group and individual goals, the counselor modeled the honest communication that she wanted the students to be using with each other. She also reinforced personal and relationship statements emitted throughout all of the group sessions. Students were paired up at the end of each meeting in order to jointly draw up a learning contract for the week. Each co-signed the other's written agreement (Steps 3, 4, 5, Figure 1).

Group members were soon able to congratulate each other on successes, no matter how small, and confrontations especially between partners over unfulfilled contracts were common (Steps 6, 7, 8, Figure 1). At the last session, the counselor had the students draw a picture of the group in terms of how they saw each member's participation and the group's movement toward its goals. This served as a departure point for a general evaluation and feedback session to the entire academic improvement group (Step 9, Figure 1).

Example 3

Knowing of her special interest in conducting inservice training for the staff, the principal called upon the counselor to design a workshop for 10 teachers to take place during the summer. The eight-day workshop ran for four hours daily and had several objectives: (a) to help the teachers meet community members with some degree of ease; (b) to compile a community resource directory for the school; and (c) to devise a plan that would assist these workshop teachers in encouraging other teachers in the school to make community contacts and to add to the community resource directory.

After hearing the principal's institutional goals defined, the counselor met with the teachers to obtain their professional and personal objectives for this project (Steps 1, 2, 3, Figure 1). In these discussions, the counselor functioned as a group facilitator and carefully listened to what was being said and helped the members to listen to each other (Step 4, Figure 1). Once the professional goals were clearly defined in terms of institutional needs, specific behavioral goals were agreed upon both in the large group and between those pairs who decided to work together (Step 5, Figure 1).

Group members, as well as the counselor, introduced new concepts and practical skills to each other (Steps 6, 7, Figure 1). This allowed the group to draw on the expertise of all of its members. Simulated task sessions coupled with a sharing of the previous day's field work experiences gave each member a chance to evaluate, critique, and reinforce others as well as himself (Steps 8, 9, Figure 1). The group began to pull together and collaborate on many decisions, such as the setting of goals for each meeting.

On days when some teachers were meeting with community members, the counselor remained in the school to keep the communication open and to get to know each staff member in the workshop better. This also proved to be an excellent opportunity for re-teaching small units involving concepts and skills on an individual basis. Another advantage of having some free informal time for the teachers came in the form of having the occasion to encourage and reinforce those relevant behaviors that had just been practiced in the community (Steps 7, 8, Figure 1). The counselor reinforced the teachers, and the teachers in a very short time were reinforcing each other.

At the closing session of the workshop the members reviewed their original goals to evaluate their progress. They then modified their project guidelines and appointed a committee to organize the information obtained from more than one hundred community contacts. They committed themselves to a jointly determined strategy for introducing and teaching their skills to the rest of the faculty. This strategy required that each project member identify one other member to serve as a support system to help share this project with his department. After filling out an evaluation questionnaire, members shared their evaluation of the entire workshop with each other. Personal feedback was given to every member of the group with communication open enough by this time for expressive, critical, and positive messages to be given and received (Step 9, Figure 1).

The counselor found all of the steps in the systematic eclectic model necessary in order to effectively work with various human systems. Although she had performed some of the steps intuitively before being introduced to the model, the conceptual framework provided her with an objective criterion against which to analyze her progress. This proved especially helpful when resistance and opposition appeared to be blocking further advancement of goals. She was then forced to study the sequenced steps and retrace some steps when necessary before proceeding.

In conclusion, the authors have discussed the systematic eclectic model and illustrated its use in the daily duties of a school counselor. The model described provides a systematic conceptual framework flexible enough to be used in a wide range of situations and interventions, including individual and group counseling as well as consultation and organizational development. The model also draws upon sources of gain in facilitating behavior change that include relationship conditions, public commitment, cognitive learning, social modeling, and operant shaping and reinforcement. The model attends to problems of transfer and maintenance of behavior usually ignored in therapeutically oriented systems.

References

Berdie, R. F. The 1980 counselor: Applied behavioral scientist. *Personnel and Guidance Journal*, 1972, *50*, 451–456.

Blocher, D. H. Counseling as a technology for facilitating and guiding change in human systems. *Educational Technology*, 1969, *9*, 15–18.

Blocher, D. H. Counseling process variables. In C. Pulvino (Ed.), *Proceedings of counseling workshop*. Madison: University of Wisconsin Press, in press.

Blocher, D. H.; Dustin, E. R.; & Dugan, W. E. *Guidance systems: An introduction to student personnel work*. New York: Ronald Press, 1971.

Blocher, D. H., & Shaffer, W. F. Guidance and human development. In D. R. Cook (Ed.), *Guidance for education in revolution*. Boston: Allyn & Bacon, 1971.

Carkhuff, R. Counseling research, theory and practice—1965. *Journal of Counseling Psychology*, 1966, *13*, 467–480.

Danskin, D.; Kennedy, C. E.; & Friesen, W. S. Guidance—the ecology of students. *Personnel and Guidance Journal*, 1965, *45*, 130–135.

McCully, H. The counselor: Instrument of change. *Teachers College Record*, 1965, *66*, 405–412.

WILLIAM HOWARD, JR., DAVID G. ZIMPFER

The findings of research on group approaches in elementary guidance and counseling

The use of group procedures at the elementary level has accompanied the recent growth of guidance in the early grades. Group activities have ranged from small group counseling with students to classroom guidance activities, have involved teachers and parents, and have spanned the developmental-remedial continuum.

Theoretical support for group counseling with elementary-age children has been established (Dinkmeyer, 1968; Dreikurs & Sonstegard, 1967). Likewise the importance of working with significant others to establish what Faust (1968) calls "effective learning climates" has been recognized and strongly supported in the American School Counselor Association's 1959 and 1964 Reports on Guidance in the Elementary Schools.

To date, enough group research has been done at the elementary level (K–6) so that we can begin to look for trends, guidelines for practice, and points of departure for future investigations. This review examines outcomes in terms of achievement and adjustment and focuses on the treatment population

William Howard, Jr., is an Elementary School Counselor in the Rochester (New York) City School District. David G. Zimpfer is an Associate Professor of Education at the University of Rochester.

(students, parents, teachers, and combinations thereof) and techniques employed.

Achievement-related studies

Both the existence and consequences of underachievement at the elementary level have been documented. For example, Barrett (1957) found a measurable pattern of underachievement at the fifth grade level, while Shaw and McCuen (1960) found evidence of underachievement by boys at grade one and distinctive patterns of underachievement in this group by grade three. For girls, traces of underachievement were first noticed at grade six, with distinguishable patterns emerging by grade nine. In a longitudinal study released by the Fels Research Institute (Kagan & Moss, 1962) it was found that the achievement of boys from 6 to 10 years of age highly correlates with adult male achievement.

Early attempts at remediation via group counseling with students focused primarily on the improvement of reading. Due to the efforts of Axline's (1947) work with second grade retarded readers and Bills' (1950) work with third graders, nondirective play therapy emerged as a potentially useful approach to the remediation of reading difficulties. Its most recent application by Moulin (1970), using 24 underachieving primary

ELEMENTARY SCHOOL GUIDANCE AND COUNSELING JOURNAL, 1971, Vol. 6, pp. 163-169.

level children, yielded significant improvement in the Non-Language Section of the California Test of Mental Maturity (CTMM) and in meaningful language usage as measured by the Illinois Test of Psycholinguistic Abilities.

Other techniques have also been found to be effective in improving reading performance, as indicated by Crider's (1966) use of selected group guidance activities with fourth graders, Strickler's (1965) combination of remedial reading instruction and group counseling, and Shatter's (1957) group counseling with fourth grade boys and their mothers.

In terms of overall grade point average, the multitreatment study of Winkler, Teigland, Munger, and Kranzler (1965) with fourth graders showed that boys receiving group counseling did significantly better than girls who were exposed to the same treatment.

Not all achievement-related studies have yielded such positive results. Ohlsen and Gazda (1965) found group counseling with bright underachieving 5th graders ineffective in improving the students' grade point average, as did Clements (1963) with 5th, 8th, and 10th grade male students. Crow's (1971) comparison of a variety of audiovisual guidance kits as stimulators to discussion and an unstructured group approach with sixth graders resulted in no improvement in their grades. Working only with parents, Samuels (1958) and Southworth (1966) likewise found group counseling ineffective in remediating reading difficulties and improving academic achievement.

Adjustment-related studies

Most educators agree on the importance of affective elements in the learning process. Support for their position comes from the studies of Coopersmith (1959), showing a correlation between a positive self-concept and achievement, and Glick (1969), revealing a correlation between achievement and high acceptance among peers. In addition, all of the achievement studies cited above, with the exception of Moulin (1970) and Samuels (1958), report significant changes in social-personal adjustment.

Many adjustment studies deal with the enhancement of sociometric status. Traditional group approaches have yielded conflicting results, with negative findings outweighing the positive. Variations in treatments have ranged from group counseling (Winkler, Teigland, Munger, & Kranzler, 1965) to different combinations of individual counseling, group counseling, and teacher-led group counseling (Biasco, 1966; Kranzler & Osmon in Kranzler, 1968; Mayer, Kranzler, & Matthes, 1967; Oldridge, 1964). While all these studies failed to lead to the desired results, Kranzler, Mayer, Doyer, and Munger (1966), using some of the same combinations, obtained positive outcomes. Schiffer (1967) also had positive peer rating change, using recreation leaders instead of teachers in placebo group sessions with children from 9 to 11 and their parents.

Consistently more positive results have been obtained through the use of behavior modification techniques, especially reinforcement, to enhance sociometric status of sixth graders (Hansen, Niland, & Zani, 1969), social acceptance among fifth graders (Barclay, 1967), and social approach behaviors of third grade boys (Clement & Milne, 1967). Aside from these interpersonally focused studies, reinforcement has been proven effective in situations involving the increasing of verbal output of sixth graders (Tosi, Swanson, & McLean, 1970) and promoting adaptive behavior (Hinds, 1968), but ineffective in promoting such behavior and changing attitudes of fifth and sixth graders when combined with insight methods (Kelly & Matthews, 1971). In addition to reinforcement, social modeling (Davis, 1958) is another behavioral modification technique that has shown potential for altering unacceptable behavior.

By the use of more traditional group counseling approaches, changes have been effected on numerous other adjustment variables, such as attitudes toward school, learning, peers, teachers, attendance, and self-concept (Crow, 1971; Lodato, Sokoloff, & Schwartz, 1964; Mann, 1968). In some cases teachers have successfully assumed the group leader role in order to bring about these social-personal changes (Bedrosian, Nathir, & Pearlman, 1970; Marx, Redding, & Smith, 1967; Mc-Nassor, Williams, & Rouman, 1958).

Despite the paucity of research and the newness of the concept, developmental group guidance, broadly interpreted as guidance for all children, has preventive implications for overall adjustment, as illustrated in the work of Anandam, Davis, and Poppen (1971) with feelings classes and Bedrosian, Nathir, and Pearlman (1970) with 30 discussion-provoking, need-focused stories. The effectiveness of orientation programs as one aspect of developmental guidance remains questionable (Kobliner, 1959).

The underlying assumption in working with significant others, such as teachers and parents, is that an effected change in their attitudes and manners of relating to children will lead to the improved performance and adjustment of the child. While teachers have responded favorably

to counseling (Berman, 1954; Otto, 1962; Patten, 1968) and consultation (Hume, 1970; Jones & Karraker, 1969) and parents favorably to counseling (Buchmueller, Porter, & Gildea, 1954; Carroll, 1960; Samuels, 1958; Schiffer, 1967; Shatter, 1957; Tamminen, 1957), the child's response has been mixed. Positive change regularly occurred in the children in adjustment-related areas (Buchmueller et al., 1954; Hume, 1970; Schiffer, 1967; Shatter, 1957) but inconsistently in reading and other achievement areas (Samuels, 1958; Shatter, 1957). Southworth's (1966) group counseling produced change neither in parents nor in their children.

At the present time relatively few studies have encompassed all three treatment populations simultaneously or separately. However, the ambitious work of Stormer (1967) and Lisle (1968) warrant the further exploration of the preventive-remedial potential of such comprehensive milieu approaches both on the academic and adjustment fronts.

Synthesis and discussion

A review of the research to date shows the overall direction to be more positive than negative. In the area of under-achievement in elementary school the results thus far have been overwhelmingly positive, as compared to what has been accomplished at the secondary school level. Reading is the subject most frequently chosen for experimentation; evidence to date shows nondirective play therapy to be the most effective approach at the primary grade level. Traditional group counseling is the most frequently applied procedure at the intermediate grade level, but it is questionable if it is the most effective approach here. Grade point average appears to be less affected by group procedures. Follow-up studies have not typically been done, however, and the accrued longer term results of group procedures on achievement in elementary grades, as Ofman (1964) found with college students, are not known.

In adjustment the results appear promising. Various affective factors have been positively influenced both by traditional insight methods of group counseling and by the recently employed behavioral modification techniques. Sociometric status appears to be the one affective criterion requiring further explanation. The majority of sociometric studies were concentrated within a six-year period, 1964 to 1969. During that time those studies which utilized traditional group counseling methods, whether led by a trained elementary counselor or not, proved somewhat disappointing. However, the few studies using behavioral techniques to improve peer status are encouraging, judging from their consistently positive outcomes. Developmental group guidance has also shown itself capable of producing positive outcomes on various affective variables.

The success of group approaches with teachers and parents is most encouraging when one speaks of developing effective learning climates. In the majority of studies involving the counseling of parents, the consequent positive changes in their attitudes toward their children facilitated the overall adjustment of their children and in some cases enhanced the children's achievement. The fact that teachers in particular have responded quite well as recipients of counseling and consultation and as leaders of group activities is equally encouraging for the promotion of developmental guidance

as defined above, for it is through the teacher that the elementary school counselor will most easily be able to reach all children.

There are some limitations in the reviewed research. Group procedures research to date in elementary guidance and counseling has focused mainly on the older student population, relatively little having been done with the kindergarten or primary grade student to grade two. If, as previously reported, underachieving patterns and their accompanying adjustment correlates are established by grade three, then it behooves us to focus more of our guidance efforts on the early primary grades. Prevention, and likewise remediation, will require early identification and involvement. They may also require greater investments of time, in terms of both longer treatment duration and later follow-up evaluations to show their effects. They may also require different measuring instruments that are sensitive to the rapidly changing and developing elementary school student.

The apparent concentration of research at the remedial (corrective) end of the continuum as opposed to the developmental (preventive) end is yet another limitation, as is also the present preoccupation with the outcomes rather than the processes of group procedures experimentation.

Finally, there is a need for more guidance and counseling research at the elementary school level so that it will equal the amount performed at other levels of education.

References

Anandam, K., Davis, M., & Poppen, W. A. Feelings . . . to fear or to free? *Elementary*

School Guidance and Counseling, 1971, *5,* 181–189.

Axline, V. M. Non-directive therapy for poor readers. *Journal of Consulting Psychology,* 1947, *11,* 61–69.

Barclay, J. Effecting behavior changes in the elementary classroom. *Journal of Counseling Psychology,* 1967, *14,* 240–247.

Barrett, H. O. An intensive study of 32 gifted children. *Personnel and Guidance Journal,* 1957, *36,* 192–194.

Bedrosian, O., Nathir, S., & Pearlman, J. A pilot study to determine the effectiveness of guidance classes in developing self-understanding in elementary school children. *Elementary School Guidance and Counseling,* 1970, *5,* 124–134.

Berman, L. The mental health of the educator. *Mental Hygiene,* 1954, *38,* 422–429.

Biasco, F. The effects of individual counseling, multiple counseling, and teacher guidance upon the sociometric status of children enrolled in grades four, five, and six. *Dissertation Abstracts,* 1966, *27,* 223.

Bills, R. E. Non-directive play therapy with retarded readers. *Journal of Consulting Psychology,* 1950, *14,* 140–149.

Buchmueller, A. D., Porter, F., & Gildea, M. C. L. A group therapy project with parents of behavior problem children in public schools. *Nervous Child,* 1954, *10,* 415–424.

Carroll, W. T. The use of group counseling in the modification of parental attitudes concerning the guidance of children. *Dissertation Abstracts,* 1960, *20,* 4388.

Clement, P. W., & Milne, D. C. Group therapy and tangible reinforcers used to modify the behavior of 8-year-old boys. *Behavior Research and Therapy,* 1967, *5,* 301–312.

Clements, T. A study to compare the effectiveness of individual and group counseling approaches with able underachievers when counselor time is held constant. *Dissertation Abstracts,* 1963, *24,* 1919–1920.

Coopersmith, S. A method for determining types of self-esteem. *Journal of Abnormal and Social Psychology,* 1959, *59,* 87–94.

Crider, M. M. A study of the effectiveness of group guidance upon personality conflict and reading retardation. *Dissertation Abstracts,* 1966, *26,* 4438.

Crow, M. L. A comparison of three group counseling techniques with sixth graders. *Elementary School Guidance and Counseling,* 1971, *6,* 37–42.

Davis, D. C. A group technique for the modification of certain behavior reactions (kindergarten level). *Dissertation Abstracts,* 1958, *18,* 2075–2076.

Dinkmeyer, D. C. *Guidance and counseling in the elementary school: Readings in theory and practice.* New York: Holt, Rinehart & Winston, 1968.

Dreikurs, R., & Sonstegard, M. Rationale of group counseling. In D. Dinkmeyer, *Guidance and counseling in the elementary school: Readings in theory and practice.* New York: Holt, Rinehart & Winston, 1968. Pp. 278–287.

Faust, V. *The counselor-consultant in the elementary school.* Boston: Houghton Mifflin, 1968.

Glick, O. Person-group relationships and the effect of group properties on academic achievement in the elementary school classroom. *Psychology in the Schools,* 1969, *6,* 197–203.

Hansen, J. C., Niland, T. M., & Zani, L. P. Model reinforcement in group counseling with elementary school children. *Personnel and Guidance Journal,* 1969, *47,* 741–744.

Hinds, W. C. A learning theory approach to group counseling with elementary school children. *Dissertation Abstracts,* 1968, *29,* 2524-A.

Hume, K. E. Counseling and consulting: Complementary functions. *Elementary School Guidance and Counseling,* 1970, *5,* 3–11.

Jones, B. A., & Karraker, R. J. The elementary counselor and behavior modification. *Elementary School Guidance and Counseling,* 1969, *4,* 28–34.

Kagan, J., & Moss, H. *Birth to maturity.* New York: Wiley, 1962.

Kelly, E. W., Jr., & Matthews, D. B. Group counseling with discipline-problem children at the elementary school level. *School Counselor,* 1971, *18,* 273–278.

Kobliner, H. The effects of a pre-entrance orientation course on the adjustment of sixth grade pupils to junior high school. *Dissertation Abstracts,* 1959, *20,* 588–589.

Kranzler, G. D. Elementary school counseling: An evaluation. *Elementary School Guidance and Counseling,* 1968, *2,* 286–294.

Kranzler, G. D., Mayer, G. R., Doyer, C. O., & Munger, P. F. Counseling with elementary school children: An experimental study. *Personnel and Guidance Journal,* 1966, *44,* 944–949.

Lisle, J. D. The comparative effectiveness of various group procedures used with elementary pupils with personal-social adjustment problems. *Dissertation Abstracts,* 1968, *28,* 4485-A.

Lodato, F., Sokoloff, M., & Schwartz, L. Group counseling as a method of modifying attitudes of slow learners. *School Counselor,* 1964, *12,* 27–29.

Mann, P. H. The effect of group counseling on educable mentally retarded boys' concepts of themselves in school. *Dissertation Abstracts,* 1968, *28,* 3467-A.

Marx, S., Redding, J., & Smith, L. A program of group counseling in the elementary school. *Elementary School Guidance and Counseling,* 1967, *2,* 33–42.

Mayer, R. G., Kranzler, G. D., & Matthes, W. A. Elementary school counseling and peer relations. *Personnel and Guidance Journal,* 1967, *46,* 360–365.

McNassor, D., Williams, L., & Rouman, J. A small activity group project. *Group Psychotherapy,* 1958, *11,* 137–143.

Moulin, E. K. The effects of client-centered group counseling using play media on the intelligence, achievement, and psycholinguistic abilities of underachieving primary school children. *Elementary School Guidance and Counseling,* 1970, *5,* 85–98.

Ofman, W. Evaluation of a group counseling procedure. *Journal of Counseling Psychology,* 1964, *11,* 152–159.

Ohlsen, M. M., & Gazda, G. M. Counseling underachieving bright pupils. *Education,* 1965, *86,* 78–81.

Oldridge, B. *Assessing outcomes of group counseling for underachieving bright fifth graders and their parents.* Quarterly Progress Report to Cooperative Research Branch of U.S. Office of Education, 1964.

Otto, H. Spontaneity training with teachers. *Group Psychotherapy,* 1962, *15,* 74–79.

Patten, B. B. Group counseling with teachers and teacher-student perceptions of behavior. *Dissertation Abstracts,* 1968, *29,* 1454-A.

Samuels, A. F. The effect of intensive group discussion on certain attitudes of mothers toward children with reading disabilities and the relationship of changed attitudes on the reading growth of their sons. *Dissertation Abstracts,* 1958, *18,* 2216.

Schiffer, A. L. The effectiveness of group play therapy as assessed by specific changes in a child's peer relation. *American Journal of Orthopsychiatry,* 1967, *37,* 219–220.

Shatter, F. An investigation of the effectiveness of a group therapy program, including the child and his mother for the remediation of reading disabilities. *Dissertation Abstracts,* 1957, *17,* 1032.

Shaw, M. C., & McCuen, J. T. The onset of academic underachievement in bright children. *Journal of Educational Psychology,* 1960, *51,* 103–108.

Southworth, R. S. A study of the effects of short-term group counseling on underachieving sixth grade students. *Dissertation Abstracts,* 1966, *27,* 1272–1273-A.

Stormer, G. Milieu group counseling in elementary school guidance. *Elementary School Guidance and Counseling,* 1967, *1,* 240–254.

Strickler, E. Educational group counseling within a remedial reading program. *Dissertation Abstracts,* 1965, *25,* 5129–5130.

Tamminen, A. W. An evaluation of changes in parents' attitudes toward parent-child relationships occurring during a televised program of parent panel discussions. *Dissertation Abstracts*, 1957, *17*, 1268–1269.

Tosi, D. J., Swanson, C., & McLean, P. Group counseling with nonverbalizing ele-mentary school children. *Elementary School Guidance and Counseling*, 1970, *4*, 260–266.

Winkler, R. C., Teigland, J. J., Munger, P. F., & Kranzler, G. D. The effects of selected counseling and remedial techniques on underachieving elementary school students. *Journal of Counseling Psychology*, 1965, *12*, 384–387.

Group Counseling:

By Charles F. Combs, Benjamin Cohn,

Edward J. Gibian and A. Mead Sniffen

APPLYING THE TECHNIQUE

THE AUTHORS have recently conducted a series of experimental projects designed to demonstrate the values of group counseling as a technique in the public school. They worked in practical situations in regular school buildings and within the limits of the usual school curriculum. From· these experiences certain common patterns of procedure relating to the use of group counseling have become apparent.

Group counseling is often the most feasible tool available to the counselor in reaching the difficult or troubled student. It seems to be especially effective when applied to adolescents. Many studies have emphasized the importance of a peer group to the adolescent; the concept of group counseling capitalizes on this peer group identification.

Group counseling is a social process. The persons involved approach problems at their own speed within the safety of a social setting. Here they may explore problems that are important to them within the security of a group of peers who share their problems and with whom they identify. Moreover, they may do this without fear of external direction or the pressure of adult coercion. The adult whom they experience within the group is an adult in a new role—the helpful, non-judgmental, non-threatening adult.

In addition to these advantages, group counseling offers to the school the attractiveness of an efficient use of the counselor's time, energy and influence for dealing with personal problems. Thus the counselor may work with greater numbers of those students who need help most or present the greatest threat to smooth school operation.

The counseling pattern to be used in any particular school must be tailored to the school system in which it is to be applied. A counseling program must always meet the needs of the framework within which it exists. If it does not meet these needs, it will soon cease to exist.

Counseling must be experienced, then, as helpful not only to the students but also to the administrators and, particularly, to the teachers of the students who are being counseled. Involvement of administration and faculty will avoid the hazards of a counseling program that may otherwise be viewed by these people as capricious or threatening. They should be drawn into the formation of the group counseling program, and there should be continual feed-back in order to maintain a high level of involvement.

Selection of Students

The classroom teachers must be made to feel that they are active participants in the selection of candidates for the group. The opinions and reactions of the faculty and administrators are extremely valuable to the counselor in identifying the dis-

THE SCHOOL COUNSELOR, 1963, Vol. 11, pp. 12-13.

ruptive student, the gross underachiever and others who are of deep concern to the school.

Likely candidates for group counseling may also be identified by studying school records. For instance, if the purpose of the proposed group is to deal with the disruptive or disorderly, school records will often have valuable indications of such previous difficulties. If the basic presenting problem is underachievement, candidates may be identified in terms of differences between measured capacity and achievement, or teachers' recorded comments of classroom difficulty.

Forming a Group

It is important in a new or formative program that the groups be carefully balanced. The members of a group should have a common presenting problem, but they should also have different levels or degrees of the problem. The counselor who tries to establish a group composed only of the most severe and recalcitrant persons who present a particular problem is almost assuredly foredoomed to disappointment. Members of the projected group should present mild as well as severe evidence of a particular problem.

The composition of a group will also be determined by the maturity of its members. It must be borne in mind, in this respect, that groups having both boys and girls will present certain special types of problems. For instance, on the junior-high-school level, in the same age range, there may be wide variations in maturity of the two sexes and in their psychosocial readiness to discuss certain issues.

In the final analysis, of course, the composition of the group will, to a larger extent, be predetermined by the period of the day that prospective members will be available.

Since group counseling is, insofar as possible, non-coercive, the composition of the group will depend upon the identification of the members with each other and with the counselor. As groups are instituted and as members experience success and satisfaction, other students will hear of them and will volunteer for these and for future groups.

Size of Group

The size of the group will depend on several major factors: the maturity of the students who are being considered for the projected group, the level of adjustment that they present and the topic to be discussed.

Elementary school children seem less capable of deferring their actions and reactions than are older children. The elementary-age child seems to be neither as verbal nor as group-oriented as the junior-high or secondary-school student. Therefore, a small group of four to six seems to afford these younger children a better opportunity to interact with their peers and to gain social experience than they would find in a larger group. The counselor must also be a more active group member with this age child than with older students.

At the junior-high and secondary-school levels, the optimal size seems to be six to eight students, depending upon the students and the topic or purpose for which they will be meeting. The more antisocial or antischool the attitudes of the group members, the lower the number that can be easily handled within the group. In a group of eight, each member seems to have an opportunity to talk and yet also to listen or to be less active when he wishes.

As the group size increases, the number of its interactions seems to increase geometrically. Beyond ten members the number of interactions definitely hampers the progress of the group. In counseling with aggressive students, even a group of eight is often too large. Six seems to be a more practical size.

Physical Setting

Group counseling in regular school buildings must, of necessity, use existing facilities. One of the appeals of this technique is that it does not require a glorified setting and can be easily adapted to what is available. The authors have successfully conducted group counseling sessions in regular classrooms, locker rooms, store rooms, cafeterias, stages of auditoriums, conference rooms and small offices.

Ideally, the room where the students meet should be as plain as possible. The optimum room size for a group of six to eight students seems to be about 15' x 15', with a round or square table having a seating capacity of approximately ten people.

There should be enough room between members of the group so that, while they can readily communicate with all of their neighbors, they are not so close to others that they are tempted into diversionary activity. It is also highly desirable to have a soundproof or isolated room, so that any noise of the group will not disturb the rest of the school.

With students having academic difficulties it is also important that there be as little distraction as possible. The room should be small enough that the individual cannot readily back away from the group or walk about the room in a manner that would be distracting. While groups are meeting, the central office should be requested to cut off the public address system and telephone calls to the room.

Length of Session

At the junior-high and secondary-school level, the length of group counseling sessions will usually be determined by the length of the class period. In the elementary school, the class periods will not comprise so great a complication. Group counseling sessions seem most effective when they are of 35 to 45 minutes' duration. Sessions lasting less than 30 to 35 minutes do not seem to allow a group to approach and develop topics. On the other hand, sessions that last longer than 45 minutes may result in boredom.

Initiating Counseling

There are certain techniques that may be of help to the beginning group counselor who is concerned about the important step of initiating the counseling sessions. A sample of an initial structuring might go somewhat as follows:

"I think we all know each other. We are going to meet during this period, in this room, every week for the next ___ weeks. We're going to be getting together to try to solve problems that we all share. Everyone in this group, for instance, seems to have a lot more ability than is actually being used. Somehow, something is getting in the way and keeping each one of us from being all that we can. We are going to be meeting together to try to find out what some of these reasons are and what we can do to solve them.

"While we are here in this group we are going to talk about anything that is of concern to us. We can say anything we want in any way that we want. Obviously there are going to be some limits. We don't want to disrupt the rest of the school, and of course we can't destroy any of the equipment in this room—or each other, for that matter. But other than these limits, I want you to feel free to express yourselves in any way you like.

"What we say in this group is our business. Nothing we say here is to

98

be told to anyone outside of the group by you or by me. No one else is going to know what goes on here—that's our business. I am here to work with you and perhaps help you to work through the problems, but together we may be able to work something out which will help us all. We must all work together; we must all try to understand each other.

"Okay, who would like to begin?"

Very definite "Rules of the Game" can assist group members in adjusting to the new situation. Certain of the authors, for instance, have found it useful to distribute mimeographed material to the members of the group, somewhat as follows:

Rules of the Game

1. Group counseling is a cooperative job. We must all work together to help each other solve problems.

2. We can't solve problems if we refuse to look at them honestly. Let's try not to let our previous ideas get in our way.

3. Try to really listen to what the person next to you is saying. Don't just try to convince him that you're right. Listen to what he says, just as you expect him to listen to you when you have something to say.

4. Stick with a topic; don't get side-tracked. Wait until the rest of the people seem to be willing to let a topic rest for a while before you try to change it.

5. Speak whenever you have something to say. Don't be afraid to speak up even if what you have to say isn't particularly clear in your own mind. But on the other hand, be careful not to cover up what you mean to say by saying too much.

6. One of the best ways you can help the others is to let them know that they are not alone in what they feel. If you have experienced the same feeling, tell them. You may be surprised to find that you will be able to understand more about the way you feel as you find yourself talking to others about how they feel.

7. Don't feel that you have to come to a group solution or agreement. The purpose of the group is to explore problems together. The decision that you as a person come to must be your own. The only solutions that are good for you must be those that have a personal meaning for you. Someone else's answer may not apply to the way you feel.

8. A group discussion goes along best when everybody trusts each other. Be careful that the others don't feel that you are making fun of them. If you are going to work together and solve problems, you're going to have to trust each other. The more quickly you get to know the others and they get to know you, the more quickly this group is going to "pay off" for you.

Atmosphere

The group counseling situation must be a permissive one. There must be an openness to all of those experiences that can and should be explored within the framework of the educational setting. The counselor must be experienced by the students as an accepting and facilitating adult. However, he must also remember that he is operating within a school framework and that there are certain limits and restrictions by which the group must abide. Permissiveness does not mean anarchy.

The limits observed must be those which are really necessary to the functioning of the group. Children and adolescents find that the security of limits is very important. They are in formative social periods and find security in the periodic restructuring of the group and of its aims. This often enables them to abandon courses of action which they may have already begun to experience as largely unrewarding.

The control of the topics to be explored should be in the hands of the students. It should be their decision to change the subject of discussion and, if necessary, to reorganize the group. The problems presented by the group should be explored where possible in terms of generalized, rather than specific, situations. The boy who presents the group with a specific problem about one certain teacher should find the group discussing behavior of teachers and pupils in general. The counselor must be careful, when clarifying a specifically presented problem, to re-present it in its more general framework.

The counselor must continually attempt to draw out the members of the group, to be aware of the feelings of the counselees and to reflect these feelings to the group. The counselor serves as a catalyst. He clarifies the statements that the group makes and the feelings expressed. He reflects these sentiments in a way that allows each member to examine his own feelings and the group to explore their feelings together. Thus he crystallizes feelings and meanings.

The authors have found that members of the group seem to have built-in controls for the depth of problem they are willing to explore. A topic will be handled only if the group feels it can actually deal with and solve the problem. When the group or particular members feel beyond their depth or not yet prepared to deal with a subject, progress may be effectively blocked by their lack of participation or their changing the subject. Restlessness, resistiveness, aggression or hostility often appear at this point.

If the counselor pushes the group too fast toward a particular solution or even toward a particular problem, the group will usually try to stop him and will give indications that he is losing them. If he responds to these signs and slows down or stops and allows the group once again to assume control and catch their breath, psychologically, the group will usually move ahead rapidly.

The counselor must always seek to respond to the true feelings underlying the statements that the counselees make. He must not fall into the trap of responding to the content of what the students say or, worse yet, to his own needs and attitudes toward these problems.

The members of the group will often test the sincerity of the counselor (who is, after all, a representative of the adult society) and the other members of the group. Before they will reveal themselves or explore problems of deep meaning to them, they must have faith in the integrity of the other members of the group.

As they become able to express

their pent-up feelings and needs within the safety of the group, they test and reorganize their perceptions of themselves and of the world around them. Essentially, they are groping toward greater self-adequacy and greater self-acceptability. As they work through group problems, they will be able to see new relationships and will thus become more effective individuals.

Duration

It is very important to establish at the beginning of a series of counseling sessions a definite duration for the group counseling experience. This seems to give structure to all members of the group so that they can more readily judge the available time remaining. That is, each group member can assess the gains already achieved at any point in the series and the time needed to reach a goal.

Group counseling seems to be most effective on a one-period-per-week basis, running approximately 15 to 20 weeks. Of course, the needs of the particular school will largely dictate the initiation and duration of counseling.

The timing of the start of a series of group counseling sessions is important. Members of the group seem to be more able to tolerate interruptions in counseling after the group has been well established rather than in the formative period, when consistency seems to be very essential. Members often feel rejected if they experience a break in the group pattern in the early periods. It is important that group sessions not be started shortly before Christmas or Easter vacations or semester breaks, for if the formation of a group is thus broken the members may return rather coldly to the group.

The greatest gains from group counseling will take time. The counselor should not be too concerned if there is a lack of observable difference in behavior or attitude early in the counseling process. Counseling often seems more effective if the groups terminate after the designated period and reopen at a future date.

It may be that the group will decide to close prior to the originally decided length of time. The counselor should beware of becoming so personally involved with the group that he feels that an expressed desire for closure is a rejection of himself. If the counselor is unthreatened by the request for closure, the problem of closure will be a rather simple one.

If the counselor is informed by the group that they feel they have discussed all they want to at this time, he should begin structuring for closure. However, he should also leave the door open for them to return. He might say, for instance:

"Okay, some of you seem to feel like stopping. Let's take a vote on it and decide. If as a group we decide to quit at this time, let's begin to taper off over the next few sessions. We'll review what we've discussed and what conclusions we've come to. If in the future we as a group or as individuals want to come back, we can resume this group or start a new one."

It is often in the discussion of closing that many problems not previously discussed will come up. This gives additional material for the tapering-off sessions. Two to five sessions should be used for closing. However, the control should be entirely in the students' hands. If the group decides on four sessions for tapering off, and then later decides to stop after two sessions instead, this is their prerogative.

During the tapering-off sessions, the counselor should assist members of the group to summarize, clarify and restate the problems that have been covered. He should help them discuss the various solutions they have previously explored. It is very important that all members of the group have the opportunity to express themselves on the various problems and their own unique solutions.

The tapering-off sessions are exceedingly important since some students may be deeply threatened by the idea of the closure of the group. They may find it quite difficult to give up the relations formed in the group.

Conclusions

Group counseling is an exceedingly valuable tool, far too seldom used within the regular school framework. Its advantages are manifold:

1. In dealing with several students simultaneously, it spreads the effect of the counselor and at the same time preserves his effectiveness.

2. It seems to be more readily accepted by students in that, since it occurs within a peer group, it is not as "different" or as threatening to them as individual counseling.

3. It makes effective use of the social setting and peer identification.

4. The adult experienced by students in group counseling is unique in that he is accepting of them and facilitating their experiences, rather than imposing an external judgment. He is a resource, a catalyst and, perhaps, a new kind of adult.

5. Often the establishment of counseling groups within the school may facilitate individual counseling and other new opportunities to meet the needs of the students.

The authors would like to emphasize that group counseling is not an art known only to a few practitioners who possess unique skills and talents. Group counseling is a technique that is effective and highly efficient of the counselor's time and energy. Most important, it is a technique which lies well within the capabilities of the perceptive school counselor.

Innovative Tool for Group Counseling: The Life Career Game

Barbara B. Varenhorst

TWENTY ninth grade students in a low ability social studies class in a junior high school in Southern California were sitting around in a circle discussing Laura, a hypothetical student introduced to them through the Life Career Game. The counselor leading the discussion had asked the group whether they thought Laura would get much satisfaction from getting an education; would Laura want to go on to some type of college or school after high school? The unspoken answer to that question was immediate shaking of heads by several students, indicating "No."

"Why don't you think Laura is interested in an education?" asked the counselor.

For a moment there was silence, then one girl blurted out, " 'Cause she takes the easy way out."

Another girl quickly spoke up and said, "Laura faces problems from home and pressures from school. If she wouldn't give in to these pressures and would work them out, she would really have something, but she won't."

"Why do you say that? What do you see in the Profile of Laura that makes you think this?" asked the counselor.

"Because she always takes the blame for what her brothers and sisters do. She doesn't stick up for herself."

"Yeah, she can't think much of herself if she would do that," volunteered another student.

"Oh, and you think that if a person takes the blame for something that she didn't do, she doesn't think very much of herself and that she is taking the easy way out?" asked the counselor.

"Sure, and getting an education isn't easy. You got to like yourself in order to work to get grades and an education," commented a boy.

From here the counselor led the group into thinking about what may cause a person to lose faith in himself. Was Laura born that way? At what point did Laura finally give up in liking herself or wanting to fight for her own rights? Reactions came quickly from others in the group, and

Barbara B. Varenhorst is Consulting Psychologist, Palo Alto Unified School District, Palo Alto, California.

THE SCHOOL COUNSELOR, 1968, Vol. 15, pp. 357-362.

soon students were talking about their own home lives and their relationships to parents, brothers, and sisters. They also dwelt on what happens to them at school and how they felt about grades and ability and success in life. Students were examining experiences and events in their personal lives affecting what they were presently doing and how they felt about themselves and one another. They were sharing different ways of feeling and dealing with what happens to a person and were pointing out from personal examples that many problems *can* be overcome. Laura was soon forgotten and they were involved with one another. Laura was always there to fall back on if the discussion became too personal or uncomfortable or if they wanted to make a point without being directly personal. Within one hour, meaningful, relevant topics were uncovered and explored. The students did most of the talking, and the teacher commented that one or two students who had never said anything in class before were talking. No restlessness or fooling around took place within that period in a class that usually exhibited such behavior.

The innovative tool that facilitated this discussion was the Life Career Game, developed by Dr. Sarane Boocock of Johns Hopkins University and adapted for guidance purposes for both the junior and senior high school by the author of this article. It is a simulation technique whereby teams of students playing the Game attempt to plan the most satisfying life for a hypothetical student over a period of eight to ten years, beginning in junior high for junior high school students and in the eleventh grade for senior high students. Students do their planning by deciding how this hypothetical student, described in a capsule profile, would spend his time during a typical week of each of these years. Outcomes or consequences of these decisions are fed back to teams in the form of game points or scores which are determined by probability data based on U.S. Census statistics and national surveys. Each year represents a round of the Game and for each round a team will get an education score, a job score, a family life score and a leisure time score.

Part of the purpose of the Game is to demonstrate that if one wants something in life, one must exercise initiative. For example, if a team desires a job for their Profile student, they must go to the Job Table where they fill out a job application and are told whether or not he got the job. Likewise, if they desire some post-high school education, the team would go to the education table and apply for admission to the school of his choice. If at sometime they desire to have their student marry, or have children, they would go to the Family Table where they fill out appropriate applications. Each of the outcomes for these various applications is decided by use of spinners and dice, introducing the probability data. After each round of the Game teams must draw from a series of unplanned events cards which simulate the luck or chance factors in life, such as getting a promotion, losing a job, or being drafted.

Inherent in these cards is the concept that with certain planning one can control these "chance" factors to a degree that one can begin to see and experience that life planning can fall into patterned ways under one's control.

A critical part of the Game is the critiquing that takes place at various times throughout the planning. Although students can learn a great deal from participating in the Game, it is during discussion periods where decision-making is shared that the great potential of the Game is revealed. Not only are students acting as model decision-makers for their peers, but in defending their planning, students are forced to examine critically and declare personal goals and values. The immediate feedback in terms of scores seems to be sufficiently realistic to involve students in a vicarious experiencing of the implications of their decisions and consequently to force them to confront the meaning of these decisions. These reactions are shared in a variety of ways with others in the group who are playing the Game.

For those counselors who have used traditional group counseling or group guidance as a tool in counseling, the potential of this technique may be obvious. Counseling in groups has some unique advantages for affecting behavior change that is not possible in a one-to-one relationship. Perhaps this is true because many of a student's problems may arise out of inability to function in groups or from improper learning from group experiences. Therefore, through creation of a group, led by a skilled leader, individuals may be taught new or more adequate behavior skills for living in society and conducting their lives toward desired goals.

Group dynamics can be utilized to teach communication skills. Many students do not know how to talk to one another, to convey ideas, to elicit information from others, to indicate emotion or feeling or to present themselves whereby they receive the reinforcement or rewards that they desire. Some students are able to both learn a new role of behaving by observing the behavior of others within a group and by rehearsing and practicing a new role in relation to others within the group. Still others may get a clearer understanding of the patterning of society, the division of authority and sources of reinforcement and the positions that one can occupy within this structure. For many, a group may help to clarify ideals and goals by testing out and reacting to values and goals expressed by its members.

Advantages of Group Counseling

The advantages of a well constituted and skillfully led group for accomplishing such purposes are several:

1. Group counseling is for the most part a verbal technique. Although some students may learn something from sitting and listening to others, most of that which takes place in a group is done verbally. There not only is pressure to speak in such groups, but to declare, defend and interpret for the benefit of all what a person is thinking and feeling. There is also assistance from group members and the leader in expressing these things.

2. By creating a new group environment students are provided a legitimate practice ground for trying out new ways of behaving. This new environment is secure enough, in a sense, because students know they can leave behind the group and the consequences of their actions, if they so desire. Their survival as a person does not depend on their being successful with these people. Therefore, they do not have as much to lose in trying out new roles and saying less than the "safe" thing.

3. Students are exposed to a variety of models who demonstrate alternative ways of behaving or solving problems. Since these models are their peers who face similar problems, they are potentially powerful models for effecting behavior change.

4. The conditions of reinforcement are or can be under the systematic control of the counselor and therefore can be used efficiently to affect social learning. Sources of reinforcement are also more available from members of the group who frequently take the role of co-counselors in the process and functioning of the group. If the climate of the environment is sufficiently different and safe, members will receive honest reactions to their ideas and values. These honest reactions work to affect decision-making for future actions and behaviors.

Relationship of the Game to Group Counseling

If all of this can be accomplished through group dynamics, then why should a counselor utilize a fairly complicated tool such as the Life Career Game? Or what is the relationship between group work and the Game? Do they not serve different purposes? In answering such questions one may be led to a better understanding of the process of groups and the unique potential of the Life Career Game, for the simulation serves to overcome some of the difficulties inherent in group work.

1. **The counselor:** In order for a group to realize its potential for accomplishing unique behavior changes, certain conditions must be met and controlled. The counselor himself is the critical factor in mobilizing the group to move and progress towards its intended goal. Although the group members do the actual work, the counselor must be so skilled that he initiates the process, utilizing the materials provided by the members, for a focused purpose. This is a very difficult task to accomplish and one that may falter at various times before the potential is realized. This also

means that sufficient time must be available for the group to become integrated, begin work and achieve some results. Meeting once a week even over a period of a year may not be a sufficient amount of time to do this.

2. **Composition of group:** Another factor affecting group counseling success is the composition of the group itself. Even with careful screening of members for the group, certain behaviors may be demonstrated on the part of individuals that had never been observed previously by the counselor. Such behaviors may hinder the process of the group or seriously handicap it.

3. **Resistance to involvement:** The movement of groups may be slow and aimless due to the natural resistance that exists in problem-oriented experiences. A person not only dislikes admitting to a problem, but may find it hard to be associated with additional reminders of his problem through exposure to others with similar problems. Likewise, people have a natural tendency to cover up and avoid those areas where one is most inadequate rather than to unveil and display them, particularly if one doesn't feel a relationship to people with whom one will be associating in other school activities. Young people cannot "turn on" their problems easily at one particular stated time each week when, in essence, they are told to do so. Consequently, much time may be spent in avoiding topics by fooling around, talking about inconsequentials or distracting the thread of verbal interaction that may be directed at problem subjects. There are times, too, when a person does not feel like talking about problems and "getting all depressed." Students may ask if they can join a "happy" group,

lamenting that the bright sunny day must be turned into gloomy discussions. Or members of the group may not feel an involvement with the others or their problems, feeling detached and aloof.

The strengths of the Life Career Game uniquely provide for these critical conditions, working to overcome the problem areas present in traditional group work. This is particularly true with respect to resistance to involvement and the avoidance of problem areas.

Counseling another person creates immediate involvement. The fact that teams are planning a life of a person like themselves is strongly motivating. As several students have said, "We feel a responsibility for this person and how he or she will turn out. It is almost like being a parent to the student." Frequently students will assign last names to the Profile student and name the children that this student may have when married. At one point a team playing the Game came up to apply for children and found that they could have a child. When this was announced to the class there was unanimous applause. The angry reactions and arguing that sometimes occur over the results of decisions indicate further the degree of involvement created by the Game. Teams can't seem to walk away from "their" student.

Although it is obvious that students are revealing their own problems, feelings, biases, values, etc., in the plans they enact for the Profile student, in discussions they can always hide behind this hypothetical person. They can "pretend" that they are discussing a person apart from themselves and therefore can look at problem areas more directly. After a few sessions with the Game, they quite naturally slip into direct personal reference and begin sharing with one another their own admitted feelings and ideas, the initial awkwardness having been broken by the attention that could be focused outside themselves. For example, when one student came seeking a job for George and was interviewed for the job, the boy said, "Well, I work in the cafeteria and I would kind of like to follow in my dad's footsteps . . . oh, I'm supposed to be talking about George, not me!" Not only had he immediately answered from his own experience, but he even had chosen a job that he would like to have himself. Another student, on getting George's grades for the junior year in high school, looked at the scores and said with a confused look on his face, "But *I* get *good* grades!"

The group is naturally integrated over the busy work of the Game. As students talk about what they have done with George, or Mary, or Mike, they are actually becoming acquainted with one another. They have heard opinions, seen reactions, and discussed attitudes and values. Since teams have a specific task to perform which, if not done, means the Game cannot continue, they must talk to one another and they must come to compromises over differing opinions of what to do with their student. By the time they have played a few rounds of the Game they are perhaps more acquainted with students in the group than they have ever been with any other peer group. When they know one another, they can talk more openly and more honestly to one another about personal matters.

Although the counselor must be skilled in leading discussions regarding the decisions that have been made or the many topics that are possible resulting from the Game, she too can utilize the Profile student as the anchor for personal discussions. The emotional tension and anxiety that may be present in traditional group work for both the group and the counselor can be relieved by using the simulated student. This frees the counselor to think more clearly and be more relaxed in his role. Also, the counselor who administers the Game is merely the dispener of the system, not the evaluator, judge or interpreter. On value issues, the Game rather than the counselor or group member can be criticized. This is an important consideration for effective group work.

The Game by its very purpose is preventive rather than crisis-oriented. Students are experiencing that by getting information, looking at consequences, and following certain paths, they can avoid problems, not just in the Game, but in their own lives. They feel that it is constructive rather than depressing and that one can even have fun and laugh while playing.

The composition of the group is not nearly as important here as it is in group counseling. The experience with the Game has shown that the more heterogeneous the group is, the more interesting the playing can be. Everyone has to plan a life and everyone has ideas regarding that life. These ideas can be shared even with someone quite different from oneself. In this way, extreme focus is taken away from certain individuals within a more homogeneous group.

Finally, more can be accomplished in a much shorter length of time than in traditional groups. Students are talking about meaningful topics sooner and even in a more systematic way than in other types of counseling groups. The issues seem to be clearer in the Game and the purpose for sharing and planning more meaningful. They know from the start what their goal is—to plan a satisfying life for a hypothetical student—and they know the steps to accomplish this. This brings them to direct confrontation with personal values and goals, which they do not necessarily have to expose to others or even admit, but which are revealed throughout all the decisions they have made for "their" student.

Although traditional group work was exciting to the author, there was always a feeling of frustration and helplessness in attempting to accomplish stated purposes for such groups. Since using the Life Career Game during the last three years, some of these desired goals have been realized and in a much shorter period of time. Although the effort and work to use the Game is greater, the benefits outweigh these efforts. Specific information has been taught, which was seldom done or possible in regular groups; students have examined values, a process that was difficult to achieve in other ways; students have related in meaningful ways to a small group of peers and in so doing have learned from them and shared with them. And, perhaps the most significant factor of all, students have demonstrated what they have learned by specific behavior changes, such as staying in school when dropping out was being considered, talking to counselors, teachers and parents for information, and beginning to study more. They have become critical of use of leisure time and have exercised initiative in personal decision-making. These outcomes suggest some evidence for further use and exploration with the Life Career Game.

Gestalt therapy interventions for group counseling

WILLIAM R. PASSONS

The growth of group counseling has been influenced by several theoretical frameworks. Rogers (1970) emphasized the value of human interaction in facilitating the actualization of resources available for changing one's perceptual and assumptive world. Behavioral group approaches have been demonstrated as being effective for learning behaviors in problem solving and competency (Krumboltz & Thoresen 1969).

Gestalt therapy, as developed by the late Frederick Perls (Fagan & Shepherd 1970; Perls 1969; Perls, Hefferline & Goodman 1965) also has many contributions to make to group counseling. Many practicing counselors, however, are unaware of the implications of Gestalt therapy for their work.

The purposes of this paper are threefold. First, a few of the basic tenets of Gestalt therapy will be described and related to counseling. Second, several Gestalt interventions applicable to group counseling will be presented. Finally, the interventions will be discussed vis-à-vis their nature and application.

A BRIEF OVERVIEW

What commonalities does Gestalt therapy have with counseling theories? Probably the most salient parallel is their common goals.

We have a specific aim in Gestalt therapy, and this is the same aim that exists at least verbally in other forms of therapy, in other forms of discovering life. The aim is to mature, to grow up [Perls 1969, p. 26].

Maturing can be considered as being comprised of two interrelated dimensions. First, maturing is "the transcendence from environmental to self-support [Perls 1969, p. 28]." Given the limits of his level of development, the individual is encouraged to assume responsibility for his own behavior. The second major dimension of maturity is the extent of integration within the individual. A person who is integrated functions as a systematic whole, comprised of feelings, perceptions, thoughts, and a body. There is little energy lost within his organism, and he is capable of responding appropriately (for him) to meet his needs.

In Gestalt therapy the principal means

PERSONNEL AND GUIDANCE JOURNAL, 1972, Vol. 51, pp. 183-189.

for facilitating responsibility and integration is the enhancement of self-awareness. These changes, however, are not forced or programmed. Rather they are allowed. As Perls (1969, p. 17) stated it: "This is the great thing to understand: that awareness per se—by and of itself—can be curative."

Necessarily, then, Gestalt interventions are designed to enhance awareness of the person's "now" experience—emotionally, cognitively, and bodily. As such, many of the interventions lend themselves to group counseling.

SELECTED INTERVENTIONS

The use of these interventions does not license the counselor as a Gestalt therapist. Rather they are offered as alternatives through which the counselor can increase his behavioral repertoire and hopefully his effectiveness.

Enhancing Awareness. There are two periods when the group member's awareness of his "here and now" are especially significant. One is at the start of the session. The other is after a critical event during a meeting. "Now I am aware of . . ." can be useful in both circumstances and can be employed by having members volunteer responses or by going around the group. (In the following examples, L is the group leader and Co is the counselee.)

L: To start today, I'd like each person to finish the sentence "Now I am aware of . . ."
Co_1: Now I'm aware I am ready to start.
Co_2: Now I'm aware of my test this afternoon.
L: What are you aware of here in this room?

L: Having heard about Jim's situation, I'm wondering what the rest of you are aware of now.
Co: I'm aware that I sometimes feel the same way.

Responding to this intervention teaches the group members to attend to their immediate experience. It can thus be a natural opener and a means to enhance the group's productivity tone at the outset. It can also be useful for diverting attention away from one person and back to the group by having each person reflect on his own experience.

Personalizing Pronouns. Idiomatic English dilutes personal awareness. For example, "How's it going?" is often answered by the impersonal "Things are fine." To circumvent these speech patterns and their deleterious effects on group interaction, counselees can be asked to personalize their pronouns.

Co: We can never please our parents!
L: Can you change the "we" to "I"?
Co: I can never please my parents!

Co: It is comfortable in here today.
L: What is the "it"?
Co: Me. I am comfortable in here today.

What can be expected from this intervention? Experience is owned rather than depersonalized through projecting. The awareness of one's own situation and responsibility is differentiated from that of "everyone's." Other group members are more likely to be responsive to a person who is speaking of his own experience.

Making Contact. In the initial phases of the group, members are often reticent about speaking for fear they will not be heard or understood. To facilitate contact, the group leader can invite the counselees to speak directly to a member of the group.

Co: I don't know what to do about . . .
L: Try saying this to someone here.
Co: Okay. Bill, I don't know what to do about . . .

Co: Nobody here understands me.

L: Can you ask someone whether or not that is so?

Co: Judy, do you understand what I'm saying?

Several desirable effects can result from this intervention. Speaking *to* someone enhances the speaker's awareness of his feelings by making his message a disclosure that is shared. The person spoken to is engaged directly and is more likely to respond, often leading to an exchange that precipitates responses from other group members. Making contact can be very effective in facilitating interaction that is pivotal to trust and cohesiveness within the group.

Changing Questions to Statements. Many group members use questions to mask messages or keep the focus off themselves. Many questions are not really questions at all but camouflages for statements. The group leader can deal with this situation by helping counselees to change some questions into statements.

Co: Bob, do you *really* think you'll be able to do that?

L: What are you *really* saying to Bob?

Co: I don't think he'll be able to do that.

L: Say that to him.

———

Co: Why are we wasting so much time?

L: Tell us what you are trying to say with that question.

Co: I don't like it that we're wasting time!

Encouraging changes of this type facilitates growth and communication. The questioner learns to accept the responsibility for expressing himself explicitly, and the person questioned is less likely to be confused by the mixed message and can respond more directly to the statement. Making the implicit more explicit can enhance the level of communication within a group.

Assuming Responsibility. There are many ways people attempt to shirk responsibility for their behavior. One of the most prevalent of these is through use of the word *can't*. In many instances "can't" means something other than "unable to:" Often it means "won't." Asking counselees to experiment with "won't" as a substitute for "can't" will often result in uncovering the dynamics involved in the impasse. Also, students can be asked to report on an experience of theirs and conclude it with "and I am responsible for it."

Co: I just can't study.

L: Would you try saying "won't" instead of "can't"?

Co: Okay. I just won't study.

L: Can you feel that it is you not doing it? What do you imagine would happen if you did?

———

L: I would like each group member to state something he is doing, thinking, or feeling and complete it with "and I am responsible for it."

Co$_1$: I am not sure what to say, and I am responsible for that.

Co$_2$: I am worrying about my boyfriend, and I am responsible for that.

Many counselees experience some relief when "won't" feels more genuine than "can't." They feel more in control and are more ready to examine their fears. Also, a "won't" is often a manifestation of defiance. It is important to help counselees realize and integrate the strength that is evidenced in defiance. Owning and accepting this strength is necessary in order to rechannel it for constructive use. Learning to assume responsibility helps the group members experience themselves as doers rather than persons whose locus of control is external.

Asking "How" and "What." One of

the surest ways to elicit pat answers, intellectualizations, and fruitless rationalizations is to ask counselees why they do or feel something. This is not to imply that understanding the purposes of behavior is not meaningful to counseling; it is. Asking why, however, causes three main problems. First, it often precipitates a search for the prime cause, the supreme insight that will unlock the mysteries of behavior and result in instant and effective behavior change. Second, "why" is too easily answered by "because . . . ," which places responsibility on an external or unknown locus of control. Third, "why" leads the person into "figuring things out" in a cognitive, problem solving fashion that rarely enhances the experiencing and understanding of emotions.

One way to break the "why" chain that many counselees put on themselves is to ask instead "how" and "what."

Co: I don't know why I keep getting into all this trouble.
L: Maybe you could tell us how you do it.

___

L: Why do you say that to your father?
Co: Because he is mean.
L: What are you trying to do?
Co: Show him he can't push me around.

Asking "how" and "what" permits the individual to get into the experience of his behavior. These words presuppose that he is doing something and facilitate his awareness of the processes he employs as means of doing it. They demonstrate respect for the person's ability to become aware of his motivations through examining his experience. They help the individual realize and accept the responsibility for his behavior.

Sharing Hunches. There are occasions when one member is tempted to react to or interpret the behavior of another.

The manner in which he does is significant for the subsequent interchange. Flat interpretations, even when somewhat valid, will often elicit defensiveness and flight from the subject. To avert this, counselees can be encouraged to preface statements with, "My hunch is . . ." A good preliminary for introducing this intervention is the "I see/I imagine" exercise, in which group members pair up and take turns looking at each other, stating what they see in each other and what they imagine it means. Each pair is observed by the remaining group members. The group leader helps make differentiations between seeing and imagining.

Co: I see you are fidgeting all around, and I imagine you are nervous. I see you are turning red and laughing, and I imagine I was right. I see you looking at me, and I imagine you are wondering what I am going to say next.

___

Co: Jill, from what you are saying you must be very afraid of your mother.
L: George, Jill didn't mention this fear. Maybe you could tell her that that is your hunch.

The speaker becomes aware that he imagines more than he sees or knows about another person, and he learns to assume responsibility for the projective elements of his perceptions. To say "you are . . ." is stating a quasi-fact that leaves room for acceptance or nonacceptance of a binary nature, thus making denial that much easier. Furthermore, exploration is not facilitated, as a prerogative has been usurped. A statement such as "My hunch is that you are afraid of her" allows the person greater freedom to own and explore his feelings without being coerced or manipulated.

Bringing the Past into the Now. Much of counseling is concerned with past events. Too often, however, such concerns are dealt with in the past tense and not worked on in the present. A rehashing of history rarely yields changes in thoughts, feelings, or behavior. To prevent being stuck in the past—the safest way to discuss a problem—group members can be asked to bring their feelings into the now.

Co: I felt awful when I hit her.
L: That was then. How do you feel about it now?
Co: Now I don't feel so bad.

———

Co: Boy, was I ever confused. I was running around and didn't know what to do.
L: Larry, could you try to tell us about it as though it were happening now?

Dealing with the current state of the feeling facilitates experiencing it so that it can be clarified, understood, and accepted. A person's becoming aware of how he maintains a feeling from the past can clarify his responsibility for the feeling. He can become aware of how he—and perhaps he alone—is now berating himself or suffering unnecessarily over some past event. Working in the present brings life and excitement into the situation. It also permits exploring for alternative behaviors that are present only in the now.

Expressing Resentments and Appreciations. Gestalt therapy suggests that where there are resentments there are also appreciations. If the latter were not present, there would be no reason for a person to hold onto that which he resents, be it another person or a situation. The reasons for holding on are appreciations. The counselor can facilitate growth in individuals and the group by helping counselees express both their resentments and appreciations. In addition, this intervention can be used to deal with unfinished business during the postmortem of the meeting.

L: Eric, you and George have mentioned a lot of things you dislike about each other.
Co (Eric): Yeah, and they're all true.
Co (George): Oh, baloney! A lot you know.
L: Now can you try to tell each other some things you appreciate about each other?

———

L: I would like to close today's session by asking those members to speak who want to express what they appreciate or resent about today's meeting.
Co_1: I resent that it has to end.
Co_2: Lou, I appreciated hearing about your . . .

This intervention yields advantages to individuals and the group. The expresser becomes aware of and learns to handle ambivalences. For example, he can sometimes like and dislike the same person, including himself. Owning both experiences helps integrate splits that lead to either-or anxiety. Similarly, the expression of both resentments and appreciations is helpful in confrontations within the group. The confronter experiences the range of his feelings for the other. The person confronted, on hearing what is appreciated about him, is more open to considering the validity of resentments expressed about him.

This procedure can be quite helpful to counselors who are afraid of what might happen when one group member is "attacked" by another. It can be used to temper viciousness and reduce the fear of confrontation. Using this intervention at the end of the meeting can permit individuals to express unfinished business that might otherwise continue to nag and finally develop into a resentment of another person, the group, or oneself.

Using Body Expression. A person operates as a system. All behavior is meaningful and important, including non-

113

verbal and involuntary expression of the body. The counselor can try to see body expressions as cues of a person's experience—not to interpret certain postures and voice intonations as being associated with certain feelings but rather to enhance awareness and to note how verbal and body expressions match. Inconsistent matches suggest areas for further exploration.

Co: I am really upset over flunking my math test.

L: Are you aware that when you said that you had a slight smile? What is there to smile about in the failure?

———

Co: It's all over. I'm not mad at Bob anymore.

L: I notice that your hand is clenched as though to make a fist.

Recognizing the lack of a match facilitates confrontation with oneself. A person can more readily deal with his feelings when he becomes aware that he is trying to evade himself. In the case of the boy who flunked his math test, examination of the sly smile could lead to the boy's exclamations of how gleeful he feels in getting back at a pushy mother. Group members can quickly learn to detect discrepancies in verbal and nonverbal communication among themselves and can broaden their scope for understanding one another.

APPLICATIONS IN COUNSELING

These interventions may be used within many counseling orientations. Brammer (1969) indicated that many systems of counseling and therapy hold similar values but "have different styles of carrying them out [p. 194]." Thus, as the counselor develops style, he is well advised to stay informed about the many sources of theoretical and procedural in-put. Gestalt therapy, with its emphasis on increasing responsibility and integration, shares underlying values with most counseling theories. The interventions presented in this article are "different styles of carrying them out."

Prior to using them in a group, the counselor might practice the interventions on his own behavior to acquaint himself with the internal dynamics involved in their use and to gain a sense of their validity. Learning the interventions experientially will also facilitate modeling them in the group. It is expected that counselors will differ considerably as to which of the interventions they may wish to adopt.

It is important that the interventions, especially one such as substituting "won't" for "can't," be introduced by a statement such as "Let's give this a try and see how it goes." In this way, if the intervention does not match the person's experience, he will not feel as though he failed, since the task was presented in a tentative way to begin with.

Timing is an important element in introducing the interventions. Generally, it is preferable to work them into the group early and at noncritical moments. It is desirable to introduce the interventions one at a time rather than presenting them as a list of "things to do." And perhaps the most crucial element of timing is the readiness of the group member. The counselor should always be sure that he or another group member does not attempt to coerce an individual into doing something he does not want or does not appear ready to do.

Often one of the most valuable outcomes of the interventions is a followup discussion about the experience of using them. For example, in discussing the "making contact" intervention, counselees would share feelings about how they relate to others. This sharing also facilitates trust and thus adds to the counseling potency of the group.

These interventions are generally used by Gestalt therapists with an individual in a workshop setting, while the other persons participate vicariously. Thus, while the interventions have been discussed in this article in terms of their use in group counseling, the counselor may apply them to his work in individual counseling as well.

Gestalt therapy is rich in theory and practice that can be of significant value when judiciously assimilated into counseling. Hopefully, the introduction of these interventions to group counselors can be a beginning to the realization of these resources for our field.

REFERENCES

Brammer, L. M. Eclecticism revisited. *Personnel and Guidance Journal*, 1969, *48*, 192–197.

Fagan, J., & Shepherd, I. L. (Eds.) *Gestalt therapy now: Theory, techniques, applications.* Palo Alto, Calif.: Science and Behavior Books, 1970.

Krumboltz, J. D., & Thoresen, C. E. (Eds.) *Behavioral counseling: Cases and techniques.* New York: Holt, Rinehart & Winston, 1969.

Perls, F. S.; Hefferline, R. F.; & Goodman, P. *Gestalt therapy.* New York: Dell, 1965. (Originally published: New York: Julian Press, 1951.)

Perls, F. *Gestalt therapy verbatim.* Lafayette, Calif.: Real People Press, 1969.

Rogers, C. R. *Carl Rogers on encounter groups.* New York: Harper & Row, 1970.

Values clarification—
a tool for counselors

SIDNEY B. SIMON

Even guidance counselors get headaches and retreat to bed when indecision surrounds them. Oh, to be able to choose, to know what we want, and to act on the decisions we make; these are life's chores for all of us.

There are the giant decisions, like whether or not to take off the two years and get that degree. Or to go into hock for a summer and make the pilgrimage to Bethel and the National Training Laboratory. Or maybe to go into psychic debt and attend a nude touchy-feely group.

It is a matter of values, and guidance counselors would do well to learn something about the processes of values clarification, not only for helping others but also for getting their own heads together.

For several years my colleagues and I have been training people in values clarification, and we have worked out a fairly comprehensive theory and rationale for the work (Raths, Harmin & Simon 1966). As the theory of values clarification began to receive wide acceptance, we turned our energies toward devising numerous strategies, techniques, and exercises for helping people of all ages to clarify their values. This article describes six different experiences based on values clarification theory. The strategies are taken from Simon, Howe, and Kirschenbaum (1972).

I hope you will first experience these exercises by doing them yourself. I think you will find out some interesting and exciting things about the values you hold —or don't hold. Then, as you work with others, you can adapt the strategies and make them fit your specific job situations. These strategies are also very useful in the teacher training role I enjoy seeing counselors take in some schools. Classroom teachers are very grateful for receiving additions to their repertoire of relevant things to do with students.

STRATEGY #1:
EITHER-OR FORCED CHOICE

Purpose
This exercise asks students to make a choice between two interesting alternatives. In making their choices, students have to examine their feelings, their self-concepts, and, of course, their values.

Procedure
The teacher asks students to move the desks so that there is a wide path from one side of the room to the other. Then the teacher asks an either-or question, such as "Which do you identify with more, New York City or Colorado?" Posting one of the words on each side of the room, the teacher asks those who favor New York City to go to one side and the Colorado choosers to go to the other. Each student then finds a partner on the side he or she has chosen, and the two of them discuss the reasons for their choice: what there is in their lives that made them pick what they did. About two minutes is just about the right time for exploring, and then everyone returns to the center of the room for another either-or choice. This time the choice might be: "Are you more of a loner or a grouper?"

Persons interested in Values Clarification are urged to write to Values Associates, Box 43, Amherst, Mass. 01002 for a brochure and other information.

PERSONNEL AND GUIDANCE JOURNAL, 1973, Vol. 51, pp. 614-618.

Five or six pairs of either-or choices work out about right, and the students are encouraged to pick a new partner each time. Here are some other useful either-or's: "Are you more political or apolitical?" "Are you more like a motorcycle or a tandem bicycle?" "Are you more like a gourmet meal or a McDonald's hamburger?"

This seemingly silly little exercise tends to involve groups of people rather quickly in beginning to look at their values, their choices, and some of the reasons they came to believe what they do.

STRATEGY #2:
SPREAD OF OPINION

Purpose
The either-or forced choice opens up the idea that rarely can we easily be squeezed into tight right or left positions. We are all more complex than that. Particularly where highly charged emotional values choices are in the offering, we would do well to teach students how to look at an issue on a spread-of-opinion basis.

Procedure
Groups of five or six people are formed. Each group chooses or is assigned a controversial issue. Some possibilities are: population control, premarital sex, legalization of marijuana, what to do about welfare, legalization of abortion, and open marriage. Each group then identifies five or six legitimate positions on their issue. Each student takes one of these positions (running to delightful extremes at either end) and writes a paragraph defending it. The paragraphs are dittoed up and given to the other members of the class, who, in turn, supply the other students with ditto sheets on the spreads of opinion from the topics they have been working on.

They all circle the position on each topic to which they can give their allegiance, and they are then asked to rewrite it so that it states as clearly as possible exactly what they believe on that

topic. In the process they will have considered the other alternatives, and the choice they make will be closer to a real value.

An interesting variation is to have each group write their spreads of opinion on a large sheet of newsprint and then have the class members wander around the room and read the various opinions. Then all members of the class may be given a chance to state orally their own positions on any of the issues.

Guidance counselors often run into a student who they sense is thinking very narrowly and unimaginatively about an issue that has come up. The spread of opinion opens horizons *and* people.

STRATEGY #3:
ALTERNATIVES SEARCH

Purpose
Choosing from among alternatives is a recurring theme in values clarification. In fact, we go so far as to say that nothing can be a value unless it has been consciously chosen from a fairly extensive number of alternatives. This activity is designed to provide students with practice in searching for alternatives. It also teaches the process of brainstorming, which is such a useful tool for all people, especially values clarifiers.

Procedure
Students are asked to form groups of four or five people. They are instructed to act as a team in developing a list of alternative solutions to a problem given by the teacher, working by combining their creative energies and piggybacking on each other's ideas. There is a tight time limit, which adds to the excitement of the game. Three to five minutes is about right, although a lively topic could run longer.

One group is asked to read their list, and then other groups add ones that they have thought up but that the first group did not, and so on, until the longest possible and most incredibly creative list has been generated. Students are then asked to pick three alternatives that really suit them the most and, finally, to rank order those three. Here are some topics that are quite delightful to work with: (a) ways to send love long distance, (b) ways to save time in everyday living, (c) where to go on a cheap date, (d) things to do to improve race relations in the school, (e) how to celebrate the new season of the year.

Students really need to see the power of a group searching for imaginative alternatives. A careful following of brainstorming rules often generates some marvelous ideas. I wish more faculties would try this strategy; the place to begin might be with the guidance staff.

STRATEGY #4:
TWENTY THINGS YOU LOVE TO DO

Purpose
In a world where the put-down, or the killer statement, is as prevalent as is a commercial on TV, we need to find ways for more of our students to seek and find self-validation. It may well be one of the best antidotes we have to the often hostile and aggressive world our students live in.

One of the most self-validating things we have ever discovered is this strategy, which gets students to look at the things they *love* to do in life.

Procedure
Ask students to get out a sheet of paper and number from 1 to 20 down the center of the page. Then, as fast as they can, in no particular order, and without the usual caution (this is not to be handed in, and no one else will see it), they are to list any 20 things in this beautiful life that they *love* to do.

Remind them of that brilliant line from *Auntie Mame,* "Life is a banquet, and most sons of bitches are starving to death." As they start making their lists, they may giggle and yuk up a bit, but ride with it. They know that this list is serious business. In fact, it is really their life, since what they love to do may describe better than most things just where they are in their efforts to make some sense out of the buzzing confusion and chaos of this thing called existence.

As the students are listing their 20 loves, it sometimes helps to suggest that they think about the four seasons and what they like to do as each one rolls around (unless you don't live in New England and don't get four seasons). It's also useful for them to think of special people in their lives and get down on the list what they love to do with those special people.

After the students have listed 20—and give them plenty of time—show them the following way of coding their list of 20 loves.

1. Place a $ sign next to any item that costs more than $3 each time it is done.

2. Place a P by each item that, for you, is more fun to do with people and an A next to the ones you prefer doing alone. (Stress that there is nothing inherently good in doing things with people or doing them alone. The point is that we each need to know what we truly love and in what way we love it.) You can use the code letter S to stand for some special person with whom you prefer to do that item.

3. Place the letters PL by any item that requires planning before you can do it; that is, it requires a phone call, a letter, an appointment, the obtaining of tickets, and so on.

4. Place the coding N5 next to those items that would not have been listed five years ago.

5. Place the letter R next to all the items that have an element of risk to them, either a physical risk or an emotional risk. (Again, stress that what might not be risky for some might be risky for others. There is no right or wrong answer to what you as an individual consider risky in your life.)

6. Place asterisks in front of the five items you love to do the very most. (Think of someone you love. Would that

118

person have placed those five so high on her or his list?)

7. Finally, record by each item the date you did it last.

Something very profound happens to people who make a list of 20 things they love to do and then repeat it three or four months later. Merely inventorying those things in their lives in this way seems to bring about very productive changes in people. Perhaps it is what happens with any experience in which we take time to take stock of our lives. In any case, I urge you who are reading this article to take the time to make your own list of 20 things you love to do and code it in some ways so that you will learn more about your own life.

STRATEGY #5:
"I LEARNED" STATEMENTS

Purpose

This strategy brings important closure to a values clarification experience. It ties it up, crystallizes new learnings, and generally gives some thrust to the new learnings ahead.

Procedure

The teacher prepares a chart consisting of certain sentence stems. The chart may be posted permanently in the room, or a ditto may be made of it for students to keep in their values journals. The sentence stems are:

I learned that I . . . .
I relearned that I . . . .
I became aware that I . . . .
I was surprised that I . . . .
I was pleased that I . . . .
I was disappointed that I . . . .
I see that I need to . . . .

The students are asked to think silently for a few minutes and piece together some completions of these sentence stems. It is pointed out that each "I learned" statement has the pronoun "I" in it twice. These statements are not about other people or about factual information from books; they are about our own lives and what we have learned

about our own reactions to life. I am convinced that there is no better way to process a great deal of our own living than to make "I learned" statements. It would be extremely useful after a counseling session for both the counselor and the client to make them. And we might learn multitudes if we did them after faculty meetings, after cocktail parties, or after some conflict with our own children.

STRATEGY #6:
OPPOSITE QUADRANGLES

This is a relatively new strategy that could be very useful to a counselor in a one-to-one counseling session and is equally helpful in a group situation. Again, I urge the counselor to try it out on himself first.

Purpose

As part of the ongoing work of values clarification to help students find out what they deeply prize and cherish, this exercise combines two areas and uses the contrasting elements of each to lead to some discoveries.

Procedure

Ask students to divide a sheet of paper into four sections. Ask them to list in the first section 10 people they really, really like to spend time with (give enough time for this). Ask them to list in the block to the right of that data 10 places they truly enjoy going to. The places can be big, such as cities, or little, such as special rooms in their homes. This list becomes their favorite places inventory.

Ask them to list in the lower left-hand section five or more people with whom they don't like to spend time. Students may be a bit uncomfortable about this listing, but encourage them to do it as honestly as they can and get as many names on it as they can. Stress that these are people they actually do spend time with but with whom they would prefer not to. In the lower right-hand section they should list five or more places they avoid going to, places that are not the most pleasant places in the world for them.

When they are all done, they have before them some interesting data on opposites: people they like to be with and people they don't like to be with; places that are fun to go to and places that are not so great.

Below are some clarifying questions that help examine the data, questions to which there are no "right" answers. One of the powerful ideas behind values clarification is that it tries very hard (not always successfully) to avoid moralizing or backing a student into a corner and expecting him to come up with an "acceptable" answer. It is truly a process of inquiry, of search, and its beauty is in the art form of questions that help people make sense out of the bewildering array of alternatives confronting them.

Perhaps it would be wise to state the three basic elements behind any values clarification strategy. First, we elicit some value-laden data for examination. We frequently use the phrase "We are going to inventory some things from the warehouse of your lives and experiences." Second, we accept the students' values statements in as nonjudgmental a way as possible. Third, we push the clarification a notch by looking at the data with some of the tools of values clarification. The following values clarification questions, which make use of the data elicited from the four opposite quadrangles, are in the repertoire of tools.

1. What would it be like if you took the 10 people you like best to the place you like least?

2. Would it make those places any better? Would those places ruin the people you like? Just what would happen?

3. What changes would you have to make in the places you don't like in order to make them enjoyable for you?

4. When was the last time you took the people you like (any of them) to the

places you like? Are there any plans you would like to make to do just that?

5. What could be done for the people in the lower left-hand quadrangle to raise them into the "good guys" list? Or are they truly hopeless? Comment on this.

6. Can you make some "I learned" statements from doing this opposite quadrangles exercise?

SUMMARY

These six strategies grew out of our work in values clarification. I think they are very useful to counselors and teachers, and you may be wondering why I believe so strongly in their use.

It is easy to be shocked by the statistic that 50,000 people die each year in automobile accidents in the United States, and death is not to be treated casually, but I am more shocked by the statistic that most people live at about a mere 15 percent of their potential.

On the other hand, I get a rush of genuine pleasure when I think of how people who know who they are live their lives. There is real joy in watching people who know how to cry and how to laugh and who see in the wonder of existence room for themselves to grow. At the center of such growing is a deep commitment to working on a set of values by which to live. Such people in search send out a radiance that is full of spirit stretching, alternative increasing, and zest making. The processes of values clarification help to enhance the delight that comes from being truly alive. Guidance counselors who learn more about values clarification would have a valuable tool to add to their repertoire of helping, healing, and caring.

REFERENCES

Raths, L.; Harmin, M.; & Simon, S. *Values and teaching.* Columbus, Ohio: Charles E. Merrill, 1966.

Simon, S.; Howe, L.; & Kirschenbaum, H. *Values clarification: A practical handbook of strategies for teachers and students.* New York: Hart, 1972.

Exploring Sex-Role Stereotyping and Social Change in Groups

OR

"Look! Look!
Look at Jane Watching Dick Run!"

BY

Ms. Audrey Maslin
Temple University

Quite recently a new responsibility has been placed on counselors--that of helping young people become aware of changing sex roles and of preparing young women to assume a more instrumental, proactive role in society. This article will present one means of meeting this responsibility. It advocates the use of group counseling to raise awareness in students--male and female, elementary and secondary--and in their teachers and counselors of ways in which they may be both the targets and the perpetuators of societal stereotyping of the sexes.

Because sex-bias stems not only from rules and laws but also from the more subtle concepts of what is "traditional" or "appropriate," most people need an opportunity to explore their feelings and attitudes, as well as the facts. Group counseling can provide a personally meaningful encounter with the effects of sexism in society.

Counselor responsibilities have always included the espoused aim of helping each individual toward optimum development of full human potential. Whatever this phrase is intended to mean, it surely must imply that the capacities to think and to work, to cry and to fight, to achieve and to decide, to be autonomous and caring, are not limited to one sex or the other.

ORIGINAL MANUSCRIPT, 1974.

121

The point is that both sexes are capable of more varied and less stereotypic aspirations, behaviors, and feelings than our society has encouraged or allowed. Both sexes will benefit from the freedom to develop along a broader spectrum without artificial limitations, and counselors can actively work toward this end.

Counselors are beginning to understand in new ways that our charge to help others develop fully has not always been fulfilled. The case has been made both within and outside the counseling profession that we have been negligent, especially toward women and girls (see Appendix A). The call has gone out from feminist and humanist groups, as well as from state and federal governments, for counselors and teachers to end their own sexist attitudes and practices, and to initiate actions that will allow students to understand, resist, and overcome sex-stereotypic pressures. As in the case of overt and covert racial discrimination, what is called for is counselor self-examination and active, compensatory measures. The question is no longer "if?" or "why?", but "how?"

Consciousness-raising (or C-R) groups, which have been the method of choice of feminist organizations, have proven among adult women and men to be a successful means of raising awareness of sexist attitudes and practices in oneself and others, of clarifying feelings about sex-roles and societal expectations, and of strengthening individuals to effect changes in the habits and goals.

It is the author's contention, gained from participation and from the testimony of other participants, that C-R groups are not essentially different from counseling groups, and that they, therefore, provide a model for counselors to use in schools. Some elaboration of this position appears later, as well as suggestions for using and modifying the model to meet the needs of particular client groups.

Counselors who want to better understand the issues at hand before beginning groups will find in Appendix A a list of source materials on sexism and counseling.

Appendix B provides a list of available materials and references which can be used by counselors in planning and running group sessions on sex-roles. It includes sources of information on employment trends, discussion topics, attitude questionnaires, films, and models for group organization and process. Also included are articles of special interest to teachers and males.

Who Needs Consciousness-Raising?

Nearly everybody does. Societal attitudes, laws, domestic arrangements, employment practices, and personal relations between the sexes are changing. Many people are confused, resistant, fearful, or unaware. Some are sympathetic, yet unsure of their own positions and the personal implications of societal change.

The need for consciousness-raising is especially apparent for students, teachers, and counselors--both male and female, at the elementary as well as the secondary level.

High school girls. If one client group can be designated as most crucially in need of sex-role counseling, it is probably high school girls. It is well established that high school and college females experience conflicting motives to achieve and to be considered sexually attractive and marriageable. Many girls have already compromised their ambitions and identities by high school age. High ability girls are often still in conflict in college.

These motives--to achieve and to be desirable in sex and marriage--are not, of course, intrinsically conflicting. However, most girls get the double-bind message society sends--"It's okay to be smart and capable, but not too smart and capable. Remember, your status and your identity depend on the man you marry."

These young women need to know that nearly half the women in the United States are now working outside the home, and that they themselves will probably hold jobs for 25 or 30 years during their lives. They need to know that women can now head for high paying and prestigious jobs, and that this is true in the factory as well as the office. They need to know that women can be forest rangers, crane operators, and stock brokers. And they need to know that one out of twenty women do not marry, and that even more do not stay married.

Young women need a chance to explore their expectations and feelings concerning marriage and sex in the context of changing sex-roles in society. How do they feel about passively waiting to be "chosen?" How do they feel about being chosen on the basis of beauty, or sexual "virtue," or willingness to take a back seat? To what extent do they repress or conceal their own abilities and ambitions in order to be popular with boys? These are questions a group counselor might introduce.

A counselor might test their awareness of the traditional expectation that girls will not accomplish much in the world, and of the likelihood that in the eyes of many their success will be measured by the husband they "catch?" How do girls feel about this? Can they anticipate the effect on themselves of being expected to enjoy satisfactions primarily through the achievements of husband and children, rather than experiencing achievement firsthand?

A group counselor might encourage high school girls to consider who are the women whom they most admire, and why. But what criteria do they value themselves? How do they evaluate other girls and women? Do their own behaviors help perpetuate female stereotypes and self-denigrations? Or a counselor can suggest they note and discuss the behavior of women they know. Do these women seem to get what they want by indirect means and by manipulating the emotions of others, rather than by openly and directly stating and obtaining their desired goals? Perhaps the group members have noticed their mothers belittle themselves in certain respects in order to allow fathers to feel important or superior. Do the girls think their fathers need this?

The big question under which all of the above can be categorized is "What does it mean to be a woman in today's society? What is essential to being a woman and what is merely traditional?" These are the kinds of questions explored by women in C-R groups, each examining her own experiences and feelings. In the high school group each individual will realize she can decide the elements which will make up her life (education, work, marriage, children, service to others) and each can consider alternate plans, priorities, and timing of these elements.

High school boys. The need for high school boys to explore similar questions may be not so obvious, but is nearly as great as for girls. One reason is the effect upon young women of their perceived attitudes and expectations among significant men in their lives. It has been shown repeatedly that women's perceptions of desirable or ideal feminine behavior in the eyes of men, although usually more stereotypically feminine than the actual ideals men hold, are highly influential upon the aspirations and behavior of young women. Another reason is that young men will find themselves living and working with women in a society that is no longer so apt to assume male supremacy.

But perhaps the best reason is that boys, too, can be negatively influenced in their own development by sex-stereotypes. They need to question why, for instance, it should be unmanly to weep or to need and accept help, or to work as a ballet dancer or nurse or preschool teacher. They can explore their feelings about the expectations placed on them by society to "succeed." By what criteria do they evaluate their own masculinity and human worth?

Counselors can encourage group members to consider why their wives and sisters should not earn more than they, if the women are able and in a more lucrative field? Do they believe that having a wife who is economically and emotionally dependent makes a man more manly? Would they expect a wife to value her husband's achievements more than her own?

Group members might discuss such questions as: Why should a man prefer basketball or fishing to art or cooking? Do they feel that a job or a task is somehow devalued if women can do it as well as men? Do they feel uncomfortable in the company of, or in competition with, capable, assertive girls? What are the qualities they value in girls and which attract them to girls? Do they think in terms of sexually "good" girls and "bad" girls?

Again, the basic question is "What does it mean to be a man in today's society? What is essential, and what is merely traditional?"

Elementary school students. It is well recognized that sex stereotypes start early. Even before kindergarten the effect of societal expec-
tations--what is appropriate and desirable for boys
and for girls--can be seen in the verbal and physical behavior, the mode of interpersonal relationships, and the value system of young children.
Schools reinforce these stereotypes in many ways.

Girls are typically rewarded for being pretty,
compliant and sweet, neat and clean, dependent and
charming (even flirtatious). Boys are complimented
for being real boys ("He's all boy!" or "That's my
little man!") if they are rough and tough, messy,
assertive, brave (meaning "don't cry"), and dom-
inating. Woe to the boy who likes clothes or colors, doesn't want to fistfight, and cries when he
is sad or hurt! We've got a sissy on our hands!

Although the "tomboy" and the capable, assertive girl do not fare quite as badly in our
eyes as the "sissy" boy, nevertheless, such girls
receive their greatest rewards when they show
signs of being beautiful, pleasing, and compliant
--not for their physical or intellectual achievements.

By age seven girls already know that boys
can be doctors or astronauts or store owners
when they grow up, but that they will be mommies
(or possibly teachers or nurses). Readers, texts
and picture books overwhelmingly employ males as
their central characters (the doers, the ones
the story hinges on). Typically, book illus-
trations show men in the jobs and occupations and
boys building the raft or improvising a play
train. Women, on the other hand, are usually
shown looking pretty in the kitchen with apron
and broom (although they occasionally appear
assisting the doctor or helping children). Girls
are typically depicted as watching the boys'
activity, cleaning up, helping Mommy, or playing

house, and are hardly ever in a creative or instrumental role activity. In books girls are almost always younger and more in need of help than
their brothers.

School books are not the only source of sex
stereotyping. Teacher behavior, as well as school
procedures, which reinforce these limitations by
sex have come under scrutiny recently and are
discussed further in this paper. We are concerned
in this section with the _effect_ on elementary
school girls and boys, and with _what_ _can_ _be_ _done_
_by_ _counselors_ to counteract it.

Group counseling can provide a means for
children to become aware that women hold many
kinds of interesting and meaningful jobs. They can
learn that motherhood and fatherhood are family
roles, not occupations. They can discuss their
feelings about the differential ways they are
treated by parents and teachers because they are
girls, or boys. They can examine the expectations they believe are held for them because of
sex.

In groups, children can talk about men and
women whom they admire, and why. They can compare notes about real life people whose life
styles they know are different from that of
picture book characters and families. Most
children are aware that there are one-parent
families and working mothers, that families are
made up of combinations of siblings whose personalities and roles vary not by sex and that
families establish different ways of distri-
buting household tasks and responsibilities.

Elementary students might express and overcome any feelings of inadequacy or resentment
about meeting the sex-role expectations of others
--"they want me to be more boyish (or girlish)."

Perhaps the most valuable learning through groups would be the recognition that girls and boys are alike in more ways than they are different--that they are more human than they are male or female.

Teachers. Most teachers and administrators would object and plead innocent to charges of discrimination by sex. The author believes they are largely unaware that their attitudes and behaviors have an insidious, if subtle, effect. Many teachers are not yet aware that in several states schools have been directed by governors and top education officials to eliminate overt and covert sexism, to provide counseling to students and sensitization to teachers, and to include the topic of nontraditional roles for women in the curriculum and in library and classroom materials. Group sessions led by a sensitive, informed counselor should prove an effective means for arousing self-awareness in a school staff.

Just what is it that teachers and school policies do to foster sex stereotyping and its consequent limitations of choice? Sources listed in Appendix B document such blatant practices as restricting certain classes or extra-curricular activities to one sex; teachers paying more attention to and interacting more with boys, while tending to ignore compliant girls or to treat girls' comments lightly; and teachers assigning classroom helper tasks or leadership jobs by sex.

Although conscientious or high-achieving girls are rewarded for their good student behavior, it is somehow made known that achievement and success are more crucial for boys. Boys are more often informed of future paths where their schoolwork might lead. Even top-student girls often receive more praise for their charm and looks than for their achievements.

It is common practice for girls' sports teams to receive a fraction of the budget allowed boys' sports, and for awards to girl athletes to be of less value than those for boys. One elementary school went so far as to privately explain to the real winner (a girl) that the award for highest-ranking student would be presented to a boy to avoid "hurting the feelings" of the boys in the graduating class. They knew she would understand!

Group counseling with school faculty and staff should aim at 1) self-discovery of sex-biased attitudes, 2) discovery of sex-discriminatory teacher behaviors, classroom practices, and school policies, and 3) development by members of positive actions that each can take in curriculum and classroom activities.

Materials such as films, attitude questionnaires, and research findings can be used to introduce topics for exploration in the group. As trust within the group develops, members can share personal experiences of sex discrimination and effects upon their own lives of sex-role stereotyping.

Once an awareness is created of the issues involved, teacher group members can examine together the attitudes of individual members and can trace possible effects of these attitudes upon students. Members will want to share observations of sex-biased incidents in the school and new realizations of their own behavior. Ideally, teacher groups should have members of both sexes and of different ages for maximum input.

Other client groups. Some other clients who can especially benefit from group counseling on changing sex-roles are:

1) College students -- Additional emphasis can be placed on career and marriage planning, consideration of alternate life styles, and sexual behavior.

2) Premarital couples -- An opportunity can be provided for couples to share expectations and ambitions for self and the other, to examine the bases of their relationship, and to formulate plans which allow full development for both partners.

3) Married couples -- Especially effective where marriages are troubled because of dissatisfaction with sex-role expectations, or in healthy marriages where more personal growth is desired.

4) Professionals and students in training -- Doctors, lawyers, nurses, social workers, psychologists, and clergymen have all been accused of perpetuating sex-role stereotypes and thereby failing to help clients. Most frequent accusations are of paternalistic or condescending treatment of females and of restricting individual growth by emphasizing traditional norms.

5) Women in transition -- Divorcees or mothers embarking on careers are often confused over self-concept, responsibilities, and interpersonal relations.

6) Middle-aged "empty nest" mothers and patients with depression symptoms -- Emphasis should be placed on redefining self in terms beyond family roles.

7) Employers, husbands, lovers, and fathers
-- Many men want to avoid perpetuating
the "male mystique" at the expense of
women and children, while others feel
irritated or threatened by current shifts
from tradition.

Why Group Counseling?

As stated earlier, adult women have found
consciousness-raising in groups to be a highly
successful means of helping women to find an individual identity not imposed by sex-role definition. By almost all criteria, the feminists'
C-R model is essentially the same as typical
group counseling.

Because sexism, like racism, is a pervasive
societal phenomenon which finds expression in
both blatant and subtle practices, it can be
assumed that no one has been untouched by its
effects and that no one is completely blameless
of perpetuating it, albeit without conscious
intent.

The group provides a permissive, confidential
atmosphere where members can examine their own
experience in terms of sexism and societal change.
Although material sources (readings, games, films,
quizzes) can be used to introduce topics, members
will benefit most if discussion focuses on each
one's direct experience, rather than on general-
ities. Most fruitful are feelings (resentments,
doubts, threats, hopes) and firsthand observations
or recollections of incidents involving self and
others. Members can help each other to formulate
and strengthen new concepts, goals, and attitudes
toward others which are free of sex-stereotypic
bias.

Perhaps the greatest gain from group experience can be the knowledge that one is not alone--that others are also resentful, guilty, fearful, or confused. Feminists have found that men and women have often been made to feel that they were somehow weak, deficient, or maladjusted individuals if they did not wholeheartedly accept all aspects of traditional bipolar sex-roles.

The group can provide the discovery that "it is not I, after all, who is maladjusted; it is others who do not recognize and allow my individuality." A corollary learning is "how do I, in turn, unconsciously impose damaging sex stereotypes on others?" And for some, the most significant learning might be "I am too well adjusted to traditional stereotypes, at the expense of my own development."

The goal here is a new ability to recognize sexism in oneself and others in behaviors which were formerly taken for granted. For most people this new ability results in a stream of sudden realizations, each one leading to further insights. The phenomenon is so common after consciousness-raising that feminists refer to these realizations as "clicks." Their experience shows that once the "clicks" start coming, change is on the way.

Background for counselors. The following are
references to writings which establish the need for
and the issues entailed in sex-role counseling and
special counseling for women and girls.

Challenges to counselors:

Birk, J. M. and Tanney, M. F. Career exploration for high school women: A model.
Available from American Personnel and Guidance Association, 1607 New Hampshire Avenue,
N.W., Washington, D.C.

Brady, R. P. and Brown, D. B. Women's lib and
the elementary school counselor. Elementary
School Guidance and Counseling, 1973, 7 (4),
305-308.

Cook, B. Roles, labels, stereotypes; A
counselor's challenge. Journal of the
National Association of Women Deans and
Counselors, 1971, 34 (3), 99-105.

Counseling women. Special issue of The
Counseling Psychologist, 1973, 4 (1), 131.

The counselor and the feminist protest. CAPS
Capsule, Spring, 1971. Available from ERIC
Counseling and Personnel Services Informa-
tion Center, 611 Church Street, Ann Arbor,
Michigan, 48104. ERIC Document CG 400 037.

*Gardner, J. Sexist counseling must stop.
Personnel and Guidance Journal, 1971, 49
(9), 705-714.

Looft, W. R. Sex differences in the expression of vocational aspirations by elementary school children. Developmental Psychology, 1971, 5 (2), 366.

Mathews, E. E. (Ed.) Counseling girls and
women over the life span. Monograph available from National Vocational Guidance Association, 1607 New Hampshire Avenue, N.W.,
Washington, D.C.

Minnesota Department of Education. Women and
the world of work: A career education
resource guide. Available from Pupil
Personnel Services Section, Minnesota
Department of Education, St. Paul,
Minnesota. 1972.

Owens, L. H. Toward more meaningful counseling with women. Paper presented at the
American Personnel and Guidance Association
Convention, March, 1970. ERIC Document ED
040 407, CG 005 311.

Pietrofesa, J. J. and Schlossberg, N. K.
Counselor bias and the female occupational
role. Wayne State University, 1970. ERIC
Document ED 044 749, CG 006 056.

Women and counselors. Special issue, Personnel and Guidance Journal, October, 1972
issue, 51 (2).

        Available from Pennsylvania Department
of Education, Box 911, Harrisburg, Pennsylvania, 17126:

*Bem, S. L. and Bem, D. J. Training the woman
to know her place. Social Antecedents of
Women in the World of Work. 1973.

School administrators' memorandum 544. A
directive from the Secretary of Education
of the Commonwealth on sexism in education.
September, 1972.

<u>Sexism</u> <u>in</u> <u>education</u>: <u>Joint</u> <u>task</u> <u>force</u> <u>report</u>.
1972.

Available from United States Department
of Labor, Women's Bureau, 3535 Market Street,
Philadelphia, Pennsylvania:

<u>Automation</u> <u>and</u> <u>women</u> <u>workers</u>. 1970.

<u>Counseling</u> <u>girls</u> <u>toward</u> <u>new</u> <u>perspectives</u>.
1966, 35¢.

<u>Expanding</u> <u>opportunities</u> <u>for</u> <u>girls</u>: <u>Their</u>
<u>special</u> <u>counseling</u> <u>needs</u>. 1971.

<u>Help</u> <u>improve</u> <u>vocational</u> <u>education</u> <u>for</u> <u>women</u>
<u>and</u> <u>girls</u> <u>in</u> <u>your</u> <u>community</u>. 1971, 10¢.

<u>New</u> <u>approaches</u> <u>to</u> <u>counseling</u> <u>girls</u> <u>in</u> <u>the</u>
<u>1960's</u>. 1965, 30¢.

<u>Underutilization</u> <u>of</u> <u>women</u> <u>workers</u>. 1971, 35¢.

*Federbush, M. <u>Let</u> <u>them</u> <u>aspire</u>: <u>A</u> <u>plea</u> <u>and</u>
<u>proposal</u> <u>for</u> <u>equality</u> <u>of</u> <u>opportunity</u> <u>for</u>
<u>males</u> <u>and</u> <u>females</u> <u>in</u> <u>the</u> <u>Ann</u> <u>Arbor</u> <u>public</u>
<u>schools</u>. Available from author, 1000
Cedar Bend Drive, Ann Arbor, Michigan,
48105. 1971, $2.25.

Grant (West), A. <u>Report</u> <u>on</u> <u>sex</u> <u>bias</u> <u>in</u> <u>the</u>
<u>public</u> <u>schools</u>. Available from NOW, 28
East 56 Street, New York, New York, 10022.
$2.25.

*Reprints available from KNOW, Inc., P.O. Box 86031
Pittsburgh, Pennsylvania, 15221.

Materials and models. The following are
materials which counselors can use either as models
of sex-role counseling in groups or as learning
materials for direct use by group members.

Delworth, U. Raising consciousness about
sexism. Personnel and Guidance Journal,
1973, 51 (9), 672-674.

Specific suggestions for brief warm-up
exercises as openers for beginning groups.

Jett, M. Blue-collar occupations attract more
women, mainly for the money. Wall Street
Journal, April 16, 1973, 1.

Sexism in education. Emma Willard Task Force
on Education, University Station Box 14229,
Minneapolis, Minnesota, 55414. $3.50.

A comprehensive booklet containing position
articles, mini-courses, games, quizzes,
lesson plans, and discussion openers;
excellent bibliography of books, articles,
and audio-visuals.

United States Department of Labor,
Women's Bureau, 3535 Market Street, Philadelphia, Pennsylvania:

Background facts of women workers in the
United States. 1970.

Careers for women. A series of individual
pamphlets on nontraditional female occupations. 10¢ each.

Changing patterns of women's lives. 1971.

The myth and the reality. 1972.

Twenty facts on women workers. 1973.

Why women work. 1970.

Vetter, L. and Sethney, B. J. Women in the work force: Development and field testing of curriculum materials. 1970. Available from The Center for Vocational and Technical Education, The Ohio State University, 1960 Kenny Road, Columbus, Ohio, 43210.

This project report describes objectives, methods, materials used, and evaluations of a systematic effort to increase knowledge and influence vocational planning in 7th, 9th, and 11th grade girls.

Women and the world of work. A packet developed for counselors and available from Department of Education, State of Minnesota, Capitol Square, 550 Cedar Street, St. Paul, Minnesota, 55101.

Feminist Consciousness-Raising Groups:

Gornick, V. Consciousness ♀. The New York Times Magazine, January 10, 1971, 22, 77-82.

Pogrebin, L. C. Rap groups: The feminist connection. Ms. Magazine, March, 1973, 1 (9), 80-83, 98-104.

Women's Collective of Stratford, Connecticut. Consciousness raising. 15¢.

Films:

Growing up female. Available from New Day Films, 267 West 25th Street, New York, New York, 10001.

Jobs and Gender. An 18-minute sound film strip available from Guidance Associates, Pleasantville, New York, rental $30-$39.

Masculinity and Femininity. A 21-minute sound
film strip available from Guidance Associates, Pleasantville, New York, rental $40-
$44.

Modern women: The uneasy life. One-hour film,
#5S1047, rental $4.75. Available from
Department of Audio-Visual Extension, University of Minnesota, 2037 University Avenue, S.E., Minneapolis, Minnesota, 55455.

Attitude Questionnaires:

Englehart, P. Women in flux; A self-survey of
sex role attitudes. Impact, Winter, 1972,
1 (2), 31-34.

Sexism in education. Emma Willard Task Force
on Education, University Station Box 14229,
Minneapolis, Minnesota, 55414. $3.50.

Spence, J. T. and Helmreich, R. The attitudes
toward women scale. An objective instrument to measure attitudes toward the rights
and roles of women in contemporary society.
JSAS Selected Documents in Psychology,
American Psychological Association, 1200
Seventeenth Street, N.W., Washington, D.C.,
20036.

For Teachers:

Horner, M. Why bright women fail. Psychology
Today, 1969, 3 (6), 36-38, 62. A report on
conflict in college women between motive to
achieve and fear of "unfeminine" success.

Howe, F. Sexual stereotypes start early.
Saturday Review, October 16, 1971. A re-
counting of the school's role in perpetuating stereotypic behavior through textbooks,
teacher attitudes, classroom experience, and
administrative policies.

Howe, F. Sexism, racism, and the education
of women. Today's Education, May, 1973,
62 (5), 47-48.

Miles, B. Women's liberation comes to class.
Scholastic Teacher, (Elementary Teacher's
Edition), November, 1971, 9-10. A discussion of sexism in the elementary school
classroom, with practical suggestions for
change.

Sadker, M. and Sadker, D. Sexual discrimination in the elementary school. The
National Elementary Principal, October,
1972, 52, 41-45.

Stern, M. (Ed.) Women in education: Changing
sexist practices in the classroom. American
Federation of Teachers, AFL-CIO, 1012 14th
Street, N.W., Washington, D.C. A collection
of articles and resource materials for use
by teachers and students.

Vroegh, K. Masculinity and femininity in the
elementary and junior high school years.
Developmental Psychology, 1971, 4 (2), 254-
261.

GROUP THERAPY WITH AFFLUENT, ALIENATED, ADOLESCENT DRUG ABUSERS: A REALITY THERAPY AND CONFRONTATION APPROACH

THOMAS EDWARD BRATTER

Description of Group Setting

Sponsored by the Village of Scarsdale, a group therapy program has been designed to provide affluent, alienated, adolescent drug abusers an opportunity to convene with an academically trained group therapist in a casual atmosphere. Groups meet at different times in different locales four times a week. More than 325 youngsters have attended at least five sessions during the projects two-and-a-half years. There currently is a nucleus of 20 youngsters who attend the majority of sessions. Group membership, where participation is voluntary, changes with each session. The average attendance has been 16 with the range being 71 to six. Participants ages have varied from a great-grandmother to preadolescent with the preponderance being 14 to 18.

Any community resident can attend. Adult presence does not seem to inhibit the character of the sessions and it appears as if adolescents enjoy their company. Significantly, when parents attend at the invitation of either a participant or the group therapist, their youngster becomes more active than he is at other times. These adolescents apparently want communication with their parents but also want their independence.

Each session format remains flexible. Youngsters arrive and depart at various times. Usually there is no predetermined agenda since group membership changes. The group is committed to convene while working with an individual. The longest session has been seven hours; the shortest one hour, with the average being three hours. The length of the session pressures the individual to make a commitment to change his behavior.

The Target Population and Families: Their Social-Psychological Characteristics

The target population serviced currently attends the same high school, lives in a middle to upper middle class suburban community within convenient commuting distance to a large urban center. Collectively, the adolescents have described a disillusionment—indeed, an absolute rejection—of their parents' values. Having been labelled as failures and viewing themselves in this fashion, these adolescents have decided to withdraw from a system which appears inimical and dehumanized. While failure is painful, it represents an abdication from commitment, involvement, and responsibility. Failure is tolerated because youngsters frequently rationalize that had they made the effort, they probably would have succeeded. By using this self-destructive adaptive mechanism, the drug abuser avoids learning that he might not be as intelligent or powerful as he previously believed. Their drug involvement spans the spectrum: occasional marihuana use to heroin addiction.

The families of these adolescents are cultured and well-educated, successful in their professions, affluent, and some are socially prominent. Many of the families became so involved either in pursuing affluence or social prominence that their youngsters earlier in their lives felt neglected and rejected. Many are exposed to extreme permissiveness, inconsistent or inadequate limit setting. While the family constellation remains intact, there seems to be little genuine love and concern. There is a rage when the parents feel embarrassed by the behavior of their children, and conversely, the children feel rejected because no one cares about them.

Reprinted with permission from the editor and the author from PSYCHOTHERAPY: THEORY, RESEARCH AND PRACTICE, 1972, Vol. 9, No. 4, pp. 308-313.

Group Dynamics: Coping with Reality and Accepting Responsibility

A primary short-term goal is to diminish current drug abuse by encouraging abstinence without enforcing it. Anyone who attends a group while under the influence of drugs incurs the wrath and disapproval of the members. Consequently, few attend in an intoxicated state.

Utilizing a confrontation-teaching-interpretative-reasoning approach, the group demonstrates to the drug abuser the irresponsible and self-defeating aspects of his behavior. The individual becomes aware of the impact of his behavior, begins to understand the consequences of his acts, and attempts to become more responsible to himself, others, and society. Emphasis is placed on the "eigenwelt" (the relation to one's self)—i.e., the immediate experience. The individual must acknowledge his perceptions of the conflict, the problem, his irresponsibility, etc. He must focus on the "here and now" in the group setting and cannot delay, evade, and/or hide. One person generally becomes the focal point. He begins to relate to his conflicts amidst much hostility from his peers. Self appointed advocates, protectors of the weak, are discouraged. This becomes an odyssey which the person must take alone (Yablonsky, 1965). The ritual requires that the individual risk being ostracized by self exposure which involves putting aside his defenses. Any sort of protective support denies the individual the adult experience of both defending and relying on his own resources as he must do in everyday activities. While there is a dialogue between the adolescent on the hot seat and the therapist; peer involvement is preferred. The individual, gaining the candid opinions and admonishments of his peers regarding the more destructive elements of his behavior, considers a new orientation and behavior.

After each appraisal, the individual is confronted about whether or not he wishes to change—i.e., to act more responsibly—or does he wish to continue his "madness?" During this therapeutic inquisition, which forces the person to recognize the "stupidity," "immaturity," "irresponsibility," self-defeating" aspects of his behavior; he begins to experience discomfort, humiliation, and rejection. For perhaps the first time in his life, the adolescent is forced to accept total responsibility for his behavior and cannot rationalize the causes. Behavior is stressed. The goal of treatment is directed toward the termination of irresponsible and self-destructive behavior.

Once the individual has accepted responsibility for his actions, he is encouraged to make a commitment to change his behavior. Of tantamount importance is the knowledge that the group will not accept any excuse for a violation of the commitment. In extreme cases, a formal, written contract has been drafted which has been signed by the person on the hot seat. Refusing to accept any excuse reinforces the notion that people can control their behavior. If, however, the participant cannot determine positive behavioral alternatives, the group will make specific suggestions regarding improved functioning. This might involve teaching the individual how to behave so as to ensure a maximum probability of success. In addition, two or three members either will volunteer or be asked to serve as quasi-consultants who will advise the individual and report any contractual infractions. When the person begins to discard his failure identity and actively experiences some success, he begins to feel much better about himself. He experiences a sense of gratification because he can assert himself as autonomous without being self-destructive. The adolescent learns that he possesses the elements of freedom of choice as well as the capacity to grow and develop. While he cannot control external conditions, any person can control his responses to these conditions. (This is an affluent, powerful, and atypical group who has access to many opportunities the general population does not.)

The Group Therapist: His Role

Adolescents have a distrust of their parents, their teachers, and their government. With drug abusers, furthermore, the twin fears of detection and subsequent incarceration combine to produce much suspicion and hostility which must be neutralized before any meaningful relationship can be established. It is imperative for the group leader to prove himself worthy of their confidence.

Since there exists an age differential and

great social distance between the therapist and the adolescent, the professional is thrust into various father roles for the group constituency—i.e., the good, the bad, the accepting, the rejecting, the strong, the weak, the understanding, the punitive (Samorajczyk, 1971). In this situation, the group therapist becomes the parent whose tolerance must be tested—i.e., to determine behavioral and therapeutic limits, to absorb personal insults, etc. The therapist should attempt to avoid becoming the inconsistent father. In this group situation, the leader often assumes a charismatic role. Some seek parental approbation, encouragement, understanding, acceptance, and/or reinforcement. Many project their hostility, anger, mistrust, and/or rejection. There are those who remain ambivalent. The most important question which must be answered before the therapist can gain entry is: DOES HE REALLY CARE ABOUT ME AS A HUMAN BEING?

By answering questions about himself with candor when it seems appropriate, the therapist both allays distrust and simultaneously becomes a responsible role model (Glasser, 1965).

Questions will be asked about the group therapist's personal views regarding drugs. Has he used any? Which ones? What does he believe? Assuming the therapist believes that any chemical depending on the quantity and quality consumed may become compulsive when utilized either to avoid or to deny the uncertainties and anxieties of life, he should affirm his commitment to a drug-free life style. The professional, by adopting a chemically-free life style, proves it is possible to function productively and be happy without any dependency on drugs.

The Therapeutic Relationship: The Therapist's Commitment

While reviewing 20 years of research concerning the therapeutic working alliance, Swensen (1971) concludes that "the successful psychotherapist is the one who genuinely cares about, and is committed to his client . . . The really crucial element in the therapist's contribution to therapeutic success is the therapist's commitment to the client." There are two ways which the therapist can demonstrate this commitment:

First: To maintain high expectations of improvement and performance. By demanding the best of any person emphatically states that someone cares enough about him not to accept a mediocre record. It is important to note that the drug abusing adolescent feels worthless because few people, if any, continue to believe he has any potential. Clinically, the high expectation of the therapist differs from parental pressures because there is neither a possessive demand nor any reflection on the group leader personally if goals are not attained. The therapist must be willing to risk by becoming involved with the youngster. To some degree, the group leader should be affected by progress and/or failure. As soon as a goal is attained, a more ambitious one should be set. While momentarily frustrating, the explicit message communicated to the adolescent is that he has more ability than he currently dared to believe. Conversely, if the adolescent fails to attain or maintain high standards, therapist can share candidly his disappointment. The quality of disappointment is not pejorative but connotes concern with high expectations. These adolescents equate caring commensurately with the amount of energy expended. The louder the yell, therefore, the more the adolescent feels reassured. According to Glasser (1969, p. 24) these adolescents need adults "who will work with them again and again as they commit and recommit until they finally learn to fulfill a commitment. When they learn to do so, they are no longer lonely; they gain maturity, respect, love, and a successful identity."

Second: To function in the role of advocate. An attendant integral part of the helping relationship would be the therapist's commitment to action on behalf of his client. The group therapist becomes an advocate where he may be required to pressure aggressively—i.e., to confront agencies—for special consideration on behalf of a youngster. In his effort to secure direct services, the therapist becomes his client's advocate, his supporter, his champion, his representative. In many respects this role is similiar to the attorney who protects his client's interests and attempts to negotiate the most favorable deal—even at the expense of an adversary. The professional must be willing to jeopardize his reputation and challenge directly the public agency, the bureaucracy (Bratter, 1972). This pressure might enable the client to secure what he needs to continue his growth and development—i.e., a college placement, an adjournment in court, etc.

Before agreeing to assume the advocate role for any participant, the group leader traditionally shares the decision-making responsibility with the group. Mobilizing the collective resources of the group enables the therapist to appraise accurately any growth and development. In order to ensure candor, the group is notified that the leader's reputation is their asset, because if he were to lose his credibility, he would no longer be in a position to elicit favors and preferred services. The group, as an entity, has a vested interest in the performance of the individual for whom the therapist endorses. The group reinforces any growth and development and exerts pressure for continued commitment and responsibility. If, however, an individual is informed by the group that he does not deserve the leader's support, he is informed specifically what he must do to receive the endorsement. Becoming joint partners in the adolescent's battle enables both the group and the therapist to make more ambitious demands on the youngster to continue to actualize his potential.

Case Study: A Behavioral Analysis

As a successful business executive, Craig Kantor's father, 47, was rarely home during his son's childhood and adolescence because his work day started at 7:00 and ended twelve hours later. Mr. Kantor has been described by each of his three sons as being emotionally remote, overly demanding, judgmental, and punitive. As a child, Craig feared his father's authority. He was a compliant child who would repress his anger until he became exhausted. Consequently, his father has remained omnipotent. Socially sophisticated, Mr. Kantor appears extroverted and pleasant. His intelligence facilitates pleasant and scintillating conversation. He seems self-assured.

Mrs. Kantor, 46, never wanted boys. She has devoted much of her life to pampering herself, and thereby, has neglected her family. She cannot relate to her sons and feels threatened by them. When they disappoint her, she becomes vindictive. Their frequent disappointments and failures tend to confirm to her that she is a failure. Mrs. Kantor constantly berates herself.

The three sons feel abandoned by their parents who frequently dine at restaurants or spend time at their country club. The family rarely eats together and has no common interests. Each of the sons, at different times, have described their parents as being "emotionally dead." There seems to be a marital conflict which has been seething for several years. This is compounded because Mrs. Kantor has bestowed her affection on Craig who becomes the target of his brothers and father's rage.

Since his mother perpetually diets and has numerous prescriptions for amphetamines and tranquilizers to enable her to sleep; there has been a well-stocked medicine cabinet. Mr. Kantor nightly has several cocktails before and after dinner. At fourteen, the adolescent started using marihuana. Shortly thereafter, he began experimentation with his mother's barbiturates and amphetamines. Craig nurtured the image of a drug abuser to the point where his knowledge of medication—the generic names, the pharmacology, the appropriate dosage, etc.—was extensive even if judged by medical standards.

Craig's earliest recollection of failure was in the fourth grade when he was not promoted. Eight years later he was suspended from the high school because of truancy. (He was suspected of being a major illict seller of drugs by both the high school and police.) A few days after his suspension, Craig returned to the school not only to challenge authority but also to test limits imposed by the authorities. When he refused to leave the premises and became belligerent, the police were summoned. With less than two months remaining in his junior year, Craig was expelled indefinitely. He had jeopardized his turbulent and unproductive school career. Since they could neither understand nor help their 18 year old son, Mr. and Mrs. Kantor insisted that Craig begin analysis. The use and abuse of amphetamines, barbiturates, and the hallucinogens reached their zenith during the period when Craig was being seen by a psychiatrist. In order to help Craig control his impulsive behavior, librium

was prescribed. When his patient did not re-
pond to thorazine (which Craig admitted he
old), the physician suggested placement in a
psychiatric residence. Mr. and Mrs. Kantor
elt relieved because this placement would remove Craig from the household. In addition, a
psychiatric diagnosis confirmed mental illness
which would exonerate Mr. and Mrs. Kantor
rom any responsibility. Their guilt would be
ameliorated because they were purchasing ex-
ensive medical treatment.

Two months after he started his analysis,
raig attended group therapy because several
f his friends did. He was hostile and abusive
o the group leader. Through a process of
mbolic association, Craig fantasized that the
oup leader was an extension of his father.
isplacement permitted the adolescent to ver-
alize frightening emotional feelings without
e fear of retaliation or even recognizing the
rson for whom such feelings were intended
iginally. The adolescent group, Craig felt,
ould protect him against the adult-father-
erapist. Simultaneously he could impress ev-
yone with his ability to be the bad boy.
aig was put on the hot seat in the second
ssion he attended. During this session, Craig
hibited much defensive grandiosity while he
ed to convince the group of his emotional
ness. One of his favorite activities was to
ive his sports car at excessive speeds while
der the influence of LSD. Whenever asked a
estion, Craig would offer an elaborate auto-
graphical explanation to justify his self-de-
ting behavior. He seemed to enjoy the fact
at he was manipulating the group to believe
was unable to control his impulses. In an
ort to discourage this dynamic, the group
der either interrupted or attacked the ado-
cent's answers. Behavior became the pri-
ry consideration. Craig was unable to de-
d his irresponsible and self-destructive acts
en questioned: "What kind of a person
ves his car at high speeds when tripping?"
at kind of a person deliberately gets him-
f expelled and then provokes the police?"
thin an hour-and-a-half, Craig had been
ced to evaluate his behavior. He had re-
ved some candid feedback from his peers
arding his self-destructive behavior. The
lescent concluded that he had been moti-
ed by stupidity rather than illness and was,

in fact, able to control his behavior. He exhibited insight because after the group he verbalized a feeling of relief that he no longer felt
compelled to play the game of deception—i.e.,
of being sick.

During the next session, his disasterous academic performance was examined. Craig admitted deliberately failing examinations because he feared any success would establish a
precedent. He did not wish to be subjected to
any pressures to achieve or attain success.
Most adults, at this juncture, had decided he
was "too disturbed to be helped" and avoided
him. He acknowledged having fundamental
doubts as to whether he was capable of sus-
taining any type of success. Despite this fear
of success, Craig decided he wanted another
chance to learn even if he would risk failing.
(Several months later, Craig admitted he had
felt pressured by the group. He had been con-
fident that neither his parents would finance
private school nor the local high school would
re-admit him.) The group leader convinced
the high school to consider granting the adolescent credit for his attendance at a graduate
psychology course which the therapist was
scheduled to teach at a university. Before
Kantor would be permitted to take the graduate course, a contract was negotiated which
included no drugs for the duration of the
course, perfect attendance, and completing all
assignments on time. Craig agreed to regulate
his behavior and to conform to the provisions.
Toward the end of the course, Craig violated
his contract and smoked marihuana. An entire
graduate class focused on his need to test authority which jeopardized his position, his
self-destructive and irresponsible behavior. The
repetition pattern was discussed. The class decided that since Craig had violated his contractual agreement with the group leader, he
must petition the school on his own and explain why the therapist no longer would support him. As a condition for continuing the
graduate course, another contract was negotiated which had more stringent stipulations
such as lengthening the drug-free period to
three months, more responsible behavior at
home, and an additional assignment. By continually raising his behavioral expectations of
Craig, the group therapist communicated a
faith and optimism few still maintained. Craig

was awarded two points of academic credit and was readmitted to high school. He was two years behind his graduating class. As an additional incentive, the group leader mentioned he would attempt to secure a college placement at the end of his first semester of his junior year. The college placement was contingent on a "B—" average. The adolescent returned to school feeling much better about himself. He entered into a mutually gratifying relationship with a girl who was considered to be one of the brightest and most talented in the junior class. This relationship further reinforced his recently improved concept of self. Craig questioned his ability to sustain an intimate interpersonal relationship, and consequently, sabotaged it. Consumed with depression and despair, his academic average fell to a "C" for the term. Because he had contained his self-destructive behavior, the high school and college agreed to permit Craig to enroll and receive credit.

Prior to leaving for college, Craig gave assurance he would achieve a "B" average and remain drug-free. Toward the end of the semester, the adolescent duplicated his pattern of self-destructive behavior and was notified by the college not to return after finishing the term. Significantly, however, after receiving his suspension, Craig completed the semester with a "B—" average. His drug involvement had been confined to four episodes.

Craig, who is in the unique position of having completed one semester at college, still needs a year of high school for his diploma. In one year, however, much of his self-destructive behavior has been eliminated. In an effort to continue to whet Craig's desire to actualize his potential, the group therapist located another incentive. Recognizing Craig's fantasy wish to become a psychologist, a program was contacted where the youngster could be trained as a paraprofessional and receive a group leader's certificate. The program required 500 hours of classroom participation. An agreement was reached whereby Craig would abstain from drugs for one year, to pursue his education until he completes his college degree, and eliminate all self-destructive behavior. Nine months ago, Craig received his group leader's certificate. One month ago, he passed the high school equivalency examination. Currently, he moved out of his house and secured full-time employment. He has been accepted to a prestigious and competitive New York State college and plans to matriculate on a full-time basis starting January 1973.

When placed on a behavioral continuum there is considerable evidence to suggest that he has begun to limit his self-destructive behavior while actualizing some of his potential. His prognosis currently is guardedly optimistic. Perhaps, one day, Craig Kantor will become a psychologist.

RESULTS

The behavioral results of this reality therapy-confrontation approach where the therapist becomes an advocate have been dramatic. In almost three years, twenty adolescents who had terminated or been expelled from school have returned. Ten are attending college without having a high school diploma. Six have received their high school equivalency. Twenty who were addicted to the opiates, are drug free. Nine are employed in meaningful work.

REFERENCES

BRATTER, T. E. Treating adolescent drug abusers in community-based interaction group program: Some philosophical considerations. *Journal of Drug Issues*, 1(3), 237-252, 1971.

BRATTER, T. E. The therapist as advocate: treating alienated, unmotivated, drug abusing adolescent, paper presented at the Society for Adolescent Psychiatry, Inc. (New York Medical College) April 1 1972.

GLASSER, W. *Reality therapy: a new approach to psychiatry.* New York: Harper & Row, Publisher 1965.

GLASSER, W. *Schools without failure.* New York Harper & Row Publishers, 1969.

SAMORAJCZYK, J. The psychotherapist as a meaningful parental figure with alienated adolescents. *American Journal of Psychotherapy*, XXV: 1, 115, 1971.

SWENSEN, C. H. Commitment and the personality the successful therapist. *Psychotherapy: Theory Research, and Practice*, 8(1), 34, 1971.

CHAPTER IV

GROUP PROCEDURES WITH THE CULTURALLY DIFFERENT

THE THERAPEUTIC RELATIONSHIP UNDER VARYING CONDITIONS OF RACE

LaMAURICE H. GARDNER

The theoretical and research literature on such topics as the so-called "Negro personality," and the dynamics of the intra- and inter-racial relationship patterns of blacks contain little established scientific data. There is too much evidence of distortion and misunderstanding, based upon failure to control for more or less subtle ethnocentric "racial experimenter effects" (Sattler, 1970). As blacks have become increasingly familiar with the contents of this literature on race, they have recoiled from its misrepresentations and its potential for reinforcing the negative racial stereotypes which continue to divide our nation.

For this reason many blacks have called for a moratorium on all further efforts by white investigators to study and explain the psychological and social characteristics of blacks. Investigators have, by and large, failed to appreciate the methodological complexities involved in psychosocial research under inter-racial conditions. And although early research in the physical sciences demonstrated the need to control for "the human equation" in the collection of scientific data, it has been only in recent years that behavior scientists have begun to concentrate research efforts upon the effects of experimenter and subject bias and expectancy on results obtained in otherwise well designed studies (Rosenthal, 1966). The results of these investigations demonstrate that experimenter variables may, and often do, influence such dimensions of research as data collection, hypothesis testing, and the interpretation of results.

In a recent paper on *Racial "Experimenter Effects" in Experimentation, Testing, Interviewing and Psychotherapy*, Sattler (1970) made the following observations:

The studies show that subjects are influenced by the experimenter's race. However, the extent and direction of the influence depends on many factors including (a) the task content, (b) instructional set, (c) reinforcement conditions, (d) geographical location of study, (e) subject variables such as age, race, family background, socio-economic level, and attitudes, (f) experimenter variables such as race of experimenter team, attitudes, residence, and socioeconomic level, and (g) dependent measures (p. 155).

Sattler's paper presents an excellent overview of issues and findings in inter- and intra-racial behavioral research. But as he points out, the literature on the effects of race on therapist-client interaction in psychotherapy is weak and fairly one-sided. Few controlled investigations have been attempted in this area of study. And although several articles have attempted to detail the parameters of white therapist-black client interaction, few exist on the subjects of black therapist-white client or black therapist-black client relationships. This paper attempts a more detailed examination of therapist-client relationships in psychotherapy under varying conditions of race, with an emphasis on ways both therapist and client expectancy and bias contribute to the clinical phenomena on which writers have based their contributions to the psychology of race.

WHITE THERAPIST—BLACK CLIENT
Therapist Variables

Because of the nature and orientation of our society, its members are characterized by an almost universal tendency to unconscious racial bigotry (Rosen and Frank, 1962). Recognizing this, a number of writers have noted the need for white and black psychotherapists to come to terms with their feelings about race before attempting to treat members of minority groups (Adams, 1950; Curry, 1964a; Grier & Cobbs, 1968; Heine, 1950; Rosen & Frank, 1962). A large portion of the literature on the personality and interaction patterns of blacks

PSYCHOTHERAPY: THEORY, RESEARCH AND PRACTICE, 1971, Vol. 8, pp. 78-87.

has issued from observations made by therapists during psychoanalytically oriented therapeutic relationships. It is to this literature that therapists, black and white, frequently turn when preparing to work with their black clients. Too often this literature is digested uncritically and with little realization that paper never refused ink. Thus, when the therapist approaches his black client he may harbor assumptions, mental sets, and beliefs of questionable validity, gathered from the professional literature, from the attitudes and pronouncements of his training supervisors, and from his own conscious and unconscious attitudes about blacks.

Psychoanalytic training attempts to examine conscious and unconscious attitudes and dispositions that may impair objective understanding and rapport with clients. Nowhere in psychoanalytic literature, however, is there an indication that training analysts give adequate attention to the analysis of unconscious anti-Negro prejudice in white candidates, such as the patronizing and paternalistic attitudes which so frequently characterize psychoanalytic papers on the "Negro personality."

Although psychoanalytic writers have made important contributions to our understanding of the interaction between native endowment and psychosocial experience in the shaping of individual personality, their contributions to the understanding of personality development and adaptation in blacks contain a curious admixture of objective reporting, ethnocentric distortion, up-dated racial mythology, paternalistic exhortation, and poppycock. Thomas (1962) has noted that cultural stereotypes regarding the inferiority of the American Negro appear frequently in psychiatric and psychoanalytic literature. But instead of offering genetic-constitutional explanations for this supposed inferiority as was true of the earlier literature (cf. Klineberg, 1944), the current trend is to account for it in dynamic experiential terms, based upon the well documented oppression and discrimination blacks experience.

A frequently cited study by Kardiner & Ovesey (1951) provides a good example of this trend. Based upon the psychoanalytic and psychodiagnostic investigation of twenty-five black clients, they described the following

characteristics as being fairly prominent in the personality organization of blacks.

1. Superficiality
2. Apathy and Resignation
3. Repressed hostility
4. The wish to be white
5. Identification with feces
6. Intragroup aggression
7. White ego-ideal
8. Inclined to gamble
9. Magical thinking
10. Inclined to alcoholism
11. Unconsciously resentful and anti-social
12. Weak superego development
13. Disorderly, unsystematic
14. Sexual freedom
15. Reject education
16. Poor discipline in childhood
17. Maternal neglect and rejection
18. Little respect for parents
19. Psychologically crippled
20. Distrustful
21. Live for the moment
22. Hedonistic

These formulations are intended to describe a modal personality pattern in terms of which the entire black group is to be understood. Such an approach to the psychosocial study of groups is nothing less than methodological recklessness (Doob, 1965). Far less subtle examples of stereotypic thinking in white therapists are also found in the literature. In an early article, Lauretta Bender (1939) wrote that characteristic traits in black children such as laziness and the ability to dance are reflection of specific brain impulse tendencies. More recently there has been a tendency by some writers to suggest that the greatest psychological tragedy to befall the black man in the United States was his premature emancipation. Hunter and Babcock (1967) have proposed that with the emancipation proclamation "the psychologically immature Negro was given the choice of remaining within the symbiotic plantation-slave common membrane or delivering himself into the world external to it. In view of his unprepared ego, the permission to individuate, given by law to the Negro slave in 1863, was essentially a useless privilege" (pp. 160-161). Wilson and Lantz (1957) also expressed the belief that the conditions of slavery were more favorable to the psychological security of blacks. They argued that the increasing incidence of mental illness and psychological uncertainty among blacks directly associated with the movement of the group towards equality with whites.

These assertions are undocumented and hardly qualify as scientific. They are paternalistic, ethnocentric, and no more rational than the following statements of a European psychiatrist studying the Tembu of Africa. He wrote:

Although the scarcity of meat in the diet is no doubt conducive to stock theft, the native's general attitude towards food and his stomach is indicative of powerful oral needs, which reflect the infantile nature of his culture (Doob, 1965, p. 394).

Here the obvious association between poor diet and concern with the digestive apparatus is overlooked due to pre-formed attitudes about African culture and the mentality of its people. It is this specific tendency to impose unconscious racial stereotypes on the material produced by blacks, which constitutes the greatest source of threat to real understanding and effective psychotherapeutic interaction in the white therapist-black client combination. The ways in which these attitudes influence diagnostic and treatment relationships with blacks are many. Hollingshead and Redlich (1958) have already demonstrated the tendency of white, middle-class therapists to discriminate against the poor and members of minority groups.

Yamamoto et al. (1967) showed that in a clinic staffed by white professionals, blacks are less likely to receive dynamic individual or group psychotherapy, are seen for fewer sessions, and have higher attrition rates than white clients. These investigators found a significant positive relationship to exist between therapist ethnocentricity and black attrition rates.

Recognizing the frequency with which conscious and unconscious racial bias influence the white therapist's perception of his black client, it is not surprising that they often report that black clients tend to be resentful and suspicious (Rosen & Frank, 1962), difficult to establish rapport with (St. Clair, 1951), untreatable or unreachable (Calnek, 1970), incapable of insight, etc.

A disclaimer must be entered at this point. What is being said here should not be taken to imply that it is more desirable that black clients have black therapists. Not at all. My purpose here is only to highlight the extent to which unconscious racial attitudes *may* cause white therapists to misunderstand and misinterpret the behavior of blacks. Black therapists have their own problems keeping unconscious racial attitudes from influencing their work with black and white clients. We will deal with these later. Basically I hold with Heine (1950) that the only barrier to the effective treatment of black clients by white therapists is the therapist's own unresolved racial prejudice. White therapists who are more or less free of racial prejudice, and who have achieved the skill and psychological integrity necessary for the conduct of psychotherapy, may be as effective with black clients as with any client.

Let us turn now to some of the specific challenges and pitfalls common to the white therapist-black client situation.

The history of race relations in the United States has so sensitized us all that the initial phase of any interracial relationship between strangers is likely to be characterized by cautious attempts by each party to discern gross or subtle indications of the racial attitudes of the other. And on the basis of what is perceived or fantasied, each party adjusts his behavior in such a way as to minimize vulnerability and maximize the ability to cope. When the therapist is white and the client black, due consideration must be given the complicating aspects of culturally conditioned interaction tendencies, which will influence transference and counter-transference phenomena, but are actually independent of them (Curry, 1964a).

If the white therapist deals with his personal conflicts through defensive flight and avoidance, the black client who stirs unconscious racial attitudes in him, is likely to be rejected either through referral to another therapist or through the use of more impersonal treatment procedures such as drug therapy. On the other hand, the therapist may resort to defensive denial and fail to recognize and deal not only with his own racial feelings, but also those of his black client.

Frequently observed in white therapists working with black clients is the tendency to ward off their own racial hostility and conflict by resorting to strong reaction formations. Where this is the case the therapist may mani-

149

fest an inclination to be oversympathetic and overindulgent in an effort to conceal feelings of guilt over his racial attitudes (Adams, 1950). Or he may overlook severe psychopathology in his black clients (Grier & Cobbs, 1968) and attribute the source of all their problems to cultural and racial conflict (Adams, 1950).

Client Variables

The black client entering psychotherapy with a white therapist is likely to experience considerable anxiety about racial differences (Kennedy, 1952). These anxieties may take such forms as fear, suspicion, verbal constriction, strained, unnatural reactions, feigning stupidity (Sattler, 1970), "acting white" (Calnek, 1970), integration, or open resentment (Rosen & Frank, 1962) and hostility (St. Clair, 1951). Regardless of the form his anxieties assume, the black client in the initial stages of psychotherapy with the white therapist will consciously and unconsciously subject him to a series of tests to determine the extent to which he is accepted as an individual and is free to express feelings which might make him particularly vulnerable to rejection, insult, and humiliation. Because this is most often the case in the white therapist-black client relationship, the development of a working alliance (Greenson, 1967) may be delayed longer than would be the case in an intraracial situation. This delay has caused some therapists to believe that with black clients it is difficult to establish rapport and a workable therapeutic relationship (St. Clair, 1951).

The black client who fears alienating his white therapist by expressing resentment of the discrimination to which he as a black is subjected, may actually repress and deny ever having suffered its malignant effects (Sattler, 1970). He may also demonstrate what Waite (1968) has called the "nigger complex," systematically avoiding any behavior that might be taken to exemplify the fabled attributes summarized in the stereotype of "the nigger." Such a client will have special difficulty expressing feelings and fantasies associated with the hostile transference (St. Clair, 1951) and may strongly repress oedipal material because of the taboo against sexual competition with the white male (Adams, 1950).

On the other hand, some black clients will react to the interracial therapeutic situation by overemphasizing their blackness and the patterns of discrimination to which they have been exposed. In this manner they may use their minority status (a) to conceal basic personality difficulties (Sommers, 1953), (b) to put the therapist on the defensive, (c) to avoid personal involvement in the therapeutic task by substituting social problems for personal ones (Heine, 1950) or (d) to express, through displacement and acting-out a deeply entrenched hostility toward authority (St. Clair 1951). Adams (1950) has noted that blacks characterized by oral demanding tendencies may spend considerable time in psychotherapy discussing racial problems, being happy to find discrimination where there is none and rather unhappy to find evidence that they are being treated fairly.

Each black client will deal with his interracial motives and anxieties in his own unique manner. And his ego will resort to the same coping and defensive patterns which characterize his efforts at conflict resolution in general. It is important that the therapist not lose sight of the individuality of his black client. A number of writers have erred in the direction of believing that in black clients individualized ego development is impeded by, and subordinate to the traumatic experiences of the group. Writing from this perspective, Kennedy (1952) described black clients in general as indiscriminately hostile and expressed the belief that the primary source of neurosis in blacks is the long-standing frustration each experiences in relation to his wish to be white.

The white therapist in his transactions with his black clients must make every effort to eliminate bias and stereotypy from his perception of his client. He must also examine the possible counter-transference gratification he may derive from working with black Counter-transference motives which frequently impede progress in the treatment of black clients include (a) the need for a power role, (b) the need for affection, (c) the need to enlarge the scope of social experiences, (d) the need to expiate racial guilt (Sattler, 1970), and (e) the need to seek vicarious gratification through the sexual and aggressive activities of black clients.

While effective psychotherapy with black clients requires dealing with intense feelings about race and experiences of discrimination, the white therapist must avoid the pitfall of attempting to treat the "Negro problem" and losing sight of the difficulties of his individual client (Heine, 1950). And if the white therapist is also a member of a minority group which has been the subject of discrimination he must be careful to avoid the paternalism implied in suggesting that blacks should follow the examples of his own group if they are to be more successful in advancing the group's socioeconomic status. If the white therapist gets "hung-up" on issues of race, the therapy will have only limited effectiveness. It is the primary task of the therapist to encourage the development of a strong working alliance between himself and his client. He contributes to this "by his consistent emphasis on understanding and insight, by his continued analysis of the resistances, and by his compassionate, empathic, straightforward, and nonjudgmental attitudes" (Greensom, 1967).

BLACK THERAPIST—WHITE CLIENT
Client Variables

Very little has been reported in the literature on the parameters and dynamics of psychotherapeutic interaction when the therapist is black and the client white. There are many reasons for this. Perhaps most important among these reasons is the fact that it has only been in recent years that a significant number of blacks have entered the field. From the limited literature that exists on the experiences of black therapists in the treatment of white clients it is clear that the color of the therapist plays an important role in determining the contents of the relationship. Curry (1964a) has noted that when the therapist is black his skin color alone can elicit fantasies and symbolic processes in white clients which may have profound effects upon the process of therapy. He suggests that in the treatment of white clients the black therapist will have not only to deal with standard resistance and transference phenomena, but must also be prepared to deal with culturally conditioned resistances stimulated by the fact that he is black.

A number of writers (Curry, 1964a; Hamilton, 1966; Sterba, 1947; and Rodgers, 1955) have pointed out the symbolic associations which cluster around the colors black and white in our western culture. White is most often associated with cleanliness, divinity, illumination, purity, goodness, awareness, life, knowledge, and heaven; while black is associated with the mysterious, the exotic, the savage and with dirt, sin, badness, inferiority, darkness, sleep, death, emotional abandon, feces, man's fallen state, evil, ignorance, the unconscious, power, magic, libido, hades, Judas and Satan. Psychoanalysts dealing with the fantasies of white clients about blacks have noted the frequency to which such fantasies disclose an unconscious identification between the Negro, especially the Negro male, and the oedipal father (Sterba, 1947; Rodgers, 1955), the unwanted sibling (Sterba, 1947), the phallic-sadistic rapist (Rodgers, 1955), and the indulging uncritical mammy (Grier, 1967). These observations stand up and can be documented in the associations, fantasies and dreams produced by white clients in treatment with black therapists. It is important to note, however, that these culturally conditioned pre-formed transference tendencies may, if properly handled and interpreted, act as a catalyst to the discovery and working through of deeply entrenched neurotic attitudes more rapidly than would be the case with a white therapist (Grier, 1967).

Not infrequently a white client will prefer a black therapist because of certain past or present experiences with blacks or because of particular personality problems or dispositions. Young whites in the midst of anti-establishment rebellion may prefer a black therapist because of identification with blacks in terms of the insults and oppression they have experienced from the system. This kind of identification was illustrated in an article that appeared in a popular magazine under the title "The Student as Nigger." Others may feel more comfortable and secure in discussing their problems with blacks because they fear less the possibility of their secrets filtering back into the community through the indiscretions of the therapist. Some may seek out a black therapist because they are too ashamed to discuss certain topics with white therapists.

An example of this is the white female client who has engaged in sexual activities with black men. In these cases the black therapist may be especially prone to experience difficulty in the handling of transference and counter-transference phenomena. Overall, it might be stated that white clients under forty years of age have less difficulty accepting black therapists than their older counterparts.

The specific ways in which white clients will relate the blackness of their therapists will prove consistently to follow reaction patterns typical of their modes of coping and defending in diverse areas of living. Oral dependent clients may relate to the black therapist as an idealized maternal object who has limitless supplies of love and oral gratification to bestow. Narcissistic-seductive female clients may be inclined to see a black male therapist as unable to resist the amorous advances of a white woman and will directly or indirectly invite a sexual affair. Clients subject to secretiveness and shame will closely guard disclosing to family and peers that the therapist is black. Clients with problems of sibling rivalry will fantasy themselves not only as the black therapist's favorite client, but also as his only white client. In my own experiences white female clients may react to the discovery that the black therapist has other white patients with jealousy, rage, and conversion symptoms. On the other hand, white clients whose difficulties include tendencies to verbalize or act-out hostile destructive impulses may attack the black therapist in racial terms. They may engage in extensive tirades against blacks, excluding the therapist, of course, or make direct or indirect remarks about the therapist's "uppity" status by accusing him of fantasizing himself a black Jesus or dubbing him "Booker T. Freud" (Curry, 1964b). With white male clients it is not at all unusual for the black therapist to find a reluctance to disclose material that might indicate oedipal competition. White male clients who have had sexual affairs with black females or who have visited black prostitutes seem characteristically to delay revealing these facts until late in the therapy. Often white male clients who have had no such experiences will, at the point when the oedipal transference becomes prominent, begin to express fantasies and desires of having affairs with black females. White female clients in the midst of the oedipal transference will demonstrate longings for and expectations of sexual gratification from the black male therapist.

It has been my experience that a prominent preoccupation of white clients who enter into psychotherapeutic relationships with black therapists is the fear that the therapist will detect in them conscious or unconscious racism. And because of this fear white clients may avoid the discussion of any association, fantasy, or dream which they believe might disclose the existence of negative racial attitudes. These clients may become enraged at the slightest suggestion of the therapist that their material discloses an attempt to express or avoid feelings they are experiencing which relate to the subject of race. This type of sensitivity was demonstrated by a white female client who actually gave little evidence of harboring racist attitudes. During a particular psychoanalytic session in which she discussed facism and Hitler's extermination of Jews she repeatedly asked: "Am I not seeing something?" When the therapist translated this question into "Am I a Nazi or something?" it became clear that she feared that the therapist would interpret her discussion of facism as evidence of a hidden racist attitude.

In some instances white clients may abruptly refrain from voicing legitimate complaints about the conditions with which they are forced to cope. When questioned about this, they may express feelings of guilt, stating to the black therapist: "I really have no right to complain about my situation when you and your people have suffered so much more" (Curry, 1964b). The black therapist must expose this kind of oversolicitousness as resistance if a thorough examination of the client's difficulties is to continue.

Some white clients deal with the interracial aspects of the relationship by denying the blackness of the therapist. An example of this tendency is seen in a letter Curry, (1964b) received from one of his white clients stating: "The longer I worked with you the whiter you became." Such statements may be either positive or derogatory. They may indicate that, for the white client, the awareness of racial differences declined during the course of psychotherapy or they may represent accusation that the black therapist has forgotten his roots and has adopted attitudes kindred to those common to the white bigot. A young white woman who entered analysis at the suggestion of her sister—who later joined the John Birch Society—had since late adolescence thoroughly repudiated the idea of obtaining social or sexual gratification within her own groups and spent most of her time pursuing black lovers and establishing herself in black social cliques. During her analysis she met a young black professional whom she decided to marry. When the therapist suggested that her plans be delayed until the possible neurotic aspects of her decision could be examined and, if present, resolved, she accused the therapist of being as racist as her parents and siding with them in believing that an interracial marriage is of necessity an expression of psychopathology.

Transference phenomena in the white clients of black therapists are particularly fascinating. On the basis of my familiarity with the literature of psychotherapy and from my own professional experience, I am inclined to believe that recognizable transference phenomena may present themselves more rapidly in white clients when the therapist is black. This is particularly true in the occurrence of dreams in which the therapist appears undisguised. Also because of racial differences, displaced transference phenomena are more readily recognizable in dreams involving blacks or emphasizing color incongruities. With one white male client suffering from chronic schizophrenic deterioration the first signs of a significant remission in his symptoms coincided with a change in the content of his somatic delusion after several months of treatment with a black therapist. In an almost incidental manner he reported to the therapist that he no longer believed that what had lodged itself in his nose and caused his confusion was a white crystal. He had become convinced then that it was a black cinder. This proved to be an indication that through respiratory introjection the client had incorporated the black therapist into his psychological life and established a workable transference relationship that would make possible, for the first time in many years, his discharge from the back wards of a chronic psychiatric hospital.

Therapist Variables

So far we have focused on client variables in the black therapist-white client relationship. We must turn now to the psychosocial responses of black therapists to interracial therapeutic situations. Obviously, the black therapist will enter treatment relationships with white clients wondering whether he will be accepted by his client, and, if so, the extent to which racial differences will complicate what is to transpire. Where the black therapist has anxieties about his ability to attract and maintain a white clientele, he may be particularly prone to ingratiating behavior, the gratification of transference wishes, and "acting white." In some cases he may be so conflicted about his black identity that he may subtly convert the therapeutic situation into one in which the white client through reassurance and admiration ends up treating the therapist's neurotic reactions to being black (Curry, 1964b). Or he may be so angry and resentful of racial conditions in the nation that he exhibit the "crow-Jim phenomenon" (Curry, 1964b) wherein he practices reverse racism by requiring of his white clients the strictest adherence to the rules of abstinence and by ruthlessly demanding that they face certain anxiety producing conflicts before they are adequately prepared to do so. Curry (1964b) has described the crow-Jim phenomenon as a situation in which animosity, hostility and bitterness toward whites is experienced by blacks along with a predisposition to injure and discriminate against them. Yet, there is evidence (Seward, 1956) which indicates that blacks may be particularly effective in work with clients of different ethnic backgrounds than their own.

As in any interracial therapeutic situation, the black therapist is no less required to rid himself of racial hang-ups than whites if he is to be effective in helping his clients. He must deal with racial material in therapeutic situations in a straightforward, objective manner and avoid any inclination to identify individual white clients with whites in general or the negative and oppressive features of our system.

Therapist Variables

Calnek (1970) has written about some of the special difficulties that may develop when black therapists treat black clients. Among the major sources of difficulty he lists such factors as tendencies in the therapist to deny identification with blacks or to overidentify with them, differential responsiveness to passive versus assertive black clients, class and status differences between therapist and client, and tendencies in upwardly mobile black therapists to view therapeutic work with blacks as low status work and to prefer a white clientele. Sattler (1970) has suggested that in some cases, due to intragroup tension and hostility, black therapists may exhibit less tolerance and understanding of black clients than some white therapists. On the other hand, Sattler (1970) suggests that black clients prefer and work better with black therapists; that black therapists may offer black clients more freedom of expression and an opportunity for deeper identification with black ideals (Seward, 1956), and that black therapists may have an important influence upon the development of a healthier ego-ideal in black clients (Kennedy, 1952).

When the black therapist has intense, unresolved feelings about his own blackness, he may make it difficult for his black clients to deal with their own attitudes about race on their own terms. The black therapist who is strongly identified with conservative-traditional trends in black-white relationships may prefer black clients who are passive, resigned and masochistic and may reject the more aggressive, militant black client. At the opposite pole are black therapists who are themselves inclined toward militancy and are prone to verbalize resentment toward the white establishment and those blacks who either aspire to or actually possess important positions in that establishment. These therapists will show preference for the more militant client and will be inclined to chastize, lecture or reject the more passive, docile black client (Calnek, 1970).

But not all blacks are troubled by their blackness. Some have achieved an effective resolution of their feelings about being black.

When this is true of the black therapist he is likely to be able to be of considerable assistance to the black client who needs to internalize more effective ways of coping with the racial issues and patterns of discrimination which have complicated his efforts at successfully adapting to internal and external sources of conflict.

Client Variables

The black client who enters a psychotherapeutic relationship with a black therapist may exhibit considerable anxiety about the therapist's ability to understand his difficulties or to empathize with his view of reality. There may be a tendency to see the therapist's educational attainments and professional status as evidence of identification with whites and rejection of the ways of blacks. In these circumstances the black client may accuse the black therapist of being an "Uncle Tom."

Black clients who themselves reject blackness may, through the projection of their own self-hatred, manifest intense, overt hostility towards their black therapist. The more militant black client on the other hand may accuse the black therapist of having sold out to the white man, of being incapable of understanding the black experience, and of trying to convert blacks to the standards and life styles of whites.

Black therapists treating black clients must be prepared to experience many of the same tests by blacks that white therapists are put through. And it is as important in the treatment of black clients as it is in the treatment of white clients that black therapists have come to terms with their own feelings about being black in a society which, at deep unconscious levels, considers blacks dirty, unattractive, primitive, and inferior.

CONCLUSIONS

The long history of misunderstanding, hostility, and conflict among the races in the United States has had a deep and distorting effect on the system of ideation and fantasy that are likely to function in interracial relationships. Even in those individuals who experience very little conscious racism, it is likely that some racial stereotypes will continue to exist at unconscious levels of mentation and will gain subtle expression in behavior and thought. How else could it be, considering the nature and history of our socioeconomic system?

That stereotypic thinking is difficult to exclude from even our highest intellectual efforts is demonstrated in the frequency with which articles on the psychosocial aspects of race, appearing in research and professional journals, manifest methodological contamination due to a failure to adequately control for ethnocentric experimenter bias. Articles appearing in the literature of psychotherapy have been particularly prone to these kinds of errors because psychotherapy is "a relatively new discipline which has not yet standardized its concepts, theories and procedures" (Doob, 1965). Nor have training centers given necessary attention to assisting developing professionals in recognizing, understanding, and resolving the more subtle forms that undesirable attitudes concerning race may take in therapeutic relationships where skin color becomes an important variable.

When we examine psychotherapeutic relationships in forms such as white therapist-black client, black therapist-white client, or black therapist-black client, it is apparent that the topic of race will occupy a place of importance and must be dealt with straightforwardly. Its impact upon the therapeutic process itself will vary with the attitudes and personality organizations of both therapist and client. In this paper I have attempted to discuss some of the more frequent sources of difficulty observed in inter and intraracial psychotherapy, as well as some specific forms racial conflict and anxiety may take in client and therapist in varying racial combinations. Once these barriers to effective psychotherapy have been dealt with and overcome the contents and efficacy of therapeutic communication should differ in no important way from that which characterizes psychotherapy where issues of race do not exist.

REFERENCES

ADAMS, W. A. The Negro Patient in Psychiatric Treatment. *American Journal of Orthopsychiatry*, 1950, **20**, 305-310.

BENDER, L., Behavior problems in Negro Children, *Psychiatry*, 1939, **2**, 213.

CALNEK, M. Racial factors in the Countertransference: The Black Therapist and the Black Patient. *American Journal of Orthopsychiatry*, 1970, **40**, 39-46.

CURRY, A. Myth, Transference and the Black Therapist. *Psychoanalytic Review*, 1964a, **51**, 7-14.

CURRY, A. The Negro Worker and the White Client. *Social Casework*, 1964b, **45**, 131-136.

DOOB, L. W. Psychology. In Lystad, R. A. (Ed.), *The African World: A Survey of Social Research*. New York: Praeger, 1965.

GREENSON, R. R. *The Technique and Practice of Psychoanalysis*. Vol. I, New York: International Universities Press, 1967.

GRIER, W. H. When the Therapist is Negro: Some Effects on the Treatment Process. *American Journal of Psychiatry*, 1967, **123**, 1587-1592.

GRIER, W. H. & COBBS, P. *Black Rage*. New York: Basic Books, 1968.

HAMILTON, J. Some Dynamics of Anti-Negro Prejudice. *Psychoanalytic Review*, 1966, **53**, 5-15.

HEINE, R. W. The Negro Patient in Psychotherapy, *Journal of Clinical Psychology*, 1950, **16**, 373-376.

HOLLINGSHEAD, A. B. & REDLICH, F. C. *Social Class and Mental Illness: A Community Study*. New York: Wiley, 1958.

HUNTER, D. M. & BABCOCK, C. G. Some Aspects of the Intrapsychic Structure of Certain American Negroes as Viewed in the Intercultural Dynamic. In W. Muensterberger & S. Axelrad (Eds.). *The Psychoanalytic Study of Society*, Vol. IV, New York: International Universities Press, 1967.

KARDINER, A. & OVESEY, L. *The Mark of Oppression*. New York: Norton, 1951.

KENNEDY, J. A. Problems Posed in the Analysis of Negro Patients. *Psychiatry*, 1952, **15**, 313-327.

KLINEBERG, O. *Characteristics of the American Negro*. New York: Harper, 1944.

RODGERS, T. C. The Evolution of an Active Anti-Negro Racist. In W. Muensterberger & S. Axelrod (Eds.). *The Psychoanalytic Study of Society*. Vol. I, New York: International Universities Press, 1955.

ROSEN, H. & FRANK, J. D. Negroes in Psychotherapy. *American Journal of Psychiatry*, 1962, 119, 456-460.

ROSENTHAL, R. *Experimenter Effects in Behavioral Research*. New York: Appleton-Century Crofts, 1966.

SATTLER, J. M. Racial "Experimenter Effects" in Experimentation, Testing, Interviewing and Psychotherapy. *Psychological Bulletin*. 1970, **73**, 137-160.

SEWARD, G. *Psychotherapy and Cultural Conflict*. New York: Ronald Press, 1956.

SOMMERS, U. S. An Experiment in Group Psychotherapy with Members of Mixed Minority Groups. *International Journal of Group Psychotherapy*, 1953, **3**, 254-269.

ST. CLAIR, H. R. Psychiatric Interview Experience with Negroes. *American Journal of Psychiatry*, 1951, **108**, 113-119.

STERBA, R. Some Psychological Factors in Negro Race Hatred and in Anti-Negro Riots. *Psychoanalysis and the Social Sciences,* 1947, **1,** 411-427.

THOMAS, A. Pseudo-transference Reactions Due to Cultural Stereotyping. *American Journal of Orthopsychiatry,* 1962, **32,** 894-900.

WAITE, R. The Negro Patient and Clinical Theory. *Journal of Consulting and Clinical Psychology,* 1968, **32,** 427-433.

WILSON, D. C. & LANTZ, E. M. Effect of Culture Change on the Negro Race in Virginia. *American Journal of Psychiatry,* 1957, **114,** 25.

YAMAMOTO, J., JAMES, O. C., BLOOMBAUM, M., & HATTEM, J. Racial Factors in Patient Selection. *American Journal of Psychiatry,* 1967, **124,** 630-636.

The Human Potential Movement and Black Unity: Counseling Blacks in Groups

Ivory L. Toldson

The quest among Blacks today is for unity. Unity is rightfully recognized as an essential in the Black liberation movement. There are still factors within the Black ranks that hinder the coming together of Black people. The notion that Blacks are hard on Blacks is still evident. It becomes redundant to enumerate these factors since Black people are well aware of them. Collectively, these factors create a counter-force to Black liberation. Unity is a must. But there is a peculiar dimension growing out of the Black liberation movement that blocks unity.

Those who are most vehemently calling for unity are in many instances insensitive to Black behavior and in some cases are psychically troubled individuals (Cobbs & Grier 1972). The antecedents of the cry for unity too often are "act as I do," "be like me," "join my camp." Often such cries are met with stiff resistance. Black people have lived in this country by making special adaptations and adjustments to oppression. We have developed a cultural suspiciousness that is in the interest of continued existence. Our behavioral responses to racism and oppression are not the same however similar our experiences may be. One must ask then: Does Black consciousness preclude exactness in expression or idiosyncratic responses? No. Far too often Blackness is assessed in terms of who can say the worst thing about whitey in the loudest voice. Included in this group are Blacks who have not won the revolution within themselves. Consequently, they are rendered ineffective in the struggle. While at the apex of their scream of "I'm Black and proud," they spur their followers on blindly and persecute those who do not follow. Thus many Blacks are protectively positioning themselves between the masses of people and the imminent threat of the enemy. This is as counter-revolutionary as Uncle Tomism. But worse, conflict develops between factions within the Black ranks.

A noted scholar has theorized about this question: Must Blacks be enemies of Blacks? Fanon (1963) has ingeniously shown how oppressed people turn upon themselves when they feel too weak to fight the oppressor. The dynamics involved are outstandingly clear; but that's not enough. Means must be explored to begin

Ivory L. Toldson is Assistant Professor of Psychology and Educational Psychology, Department of Counselor Education and Counseling Psychology, Temple University, Philadelphia, Pennsylvania.

JOURNAL OF NON-WHITE CONCERNS, 1973, Vol. 1, No. 2, pp. 69-76.

diverting Black hostilities and frustrations and energies from their usual course of self-destruction. The search must continue for creative and positive ways of channeling this force toward the goal of Black liberation. Let us pursue another challenge to Black unity: the question of Black individualism.

The fact that Black Americans have a kind of "hustling" mentality is often ignored or labeled individualism. The survival instinct does not function solely in Blacks who exist at the poverty level, but permeates the personalities of Blacks as a people, particularly those whose heritage is traceable to poverty conditions. This is manifested in the hustling attitude of Blacks in intellectual and bourgeois circles. It is this group that constitutes the fortress of Black nationalist ideology (Allen 1970). What we see are "field niggers" who have escaped servitude and are "making it." This "making it" in the system is often derogatorily referred to as "individualism." The question becomes, how can Black people develop a cooperative, hustling mental set more closely aligned with the collective goals of the Black masses, rather than how do we eliminate Black individualism, which in more instances than not is functional. In other words, do the non-fitting parts of the puzzle need to be maneuvered or displaced? I think the former. The holes in the Black unity puzzle evidence too many displacements of Black soldiers within our ranks. This fraticidal tendency has to be overcome. Bear in mind that individual hustling is central to Black personhood (a state of mind), which is inextricably interwoven with manhood. Black manhood receives considerable attention in the political arena. Equal attention should be directed toward the personal development of Black people within the framework of a collective Black identity. That is, more energy should be directed toward the establishment of a cooperative mental set in the minds of Black folks.

The struggle is a racial struggle. Blackness goes across and beyond such categorical divisions as class, political ideology, and religious affiliations. Is there a place and praiseworthy function for all Blacks in changing the course of our destiny? Yes. A realization of this will come only through an acceptance of and respect for our uniqueness as individuals within the boundary of the collective uniqueness of Black people as a nation. When Black individualism transcends the collective uniqueness of Black folks it becomes dysfunctional—a kind of bewildering opposition to Black liberation. Dysfunctional individualism does exist within the Black ranks and needs to be dealt with in therapeutic ways.

In the foregoing, an attempt has been made to identify some of the obstacles impeding Black unity. Basically these are seen as conflicts within groups evolving from what appear to be differences in political ideologies, which are visibly observed in different behavioral responses among Blacks to racism and oppression. These conflicts are spurred on by the capitalistic exploitation of the poor. A stem-off from these suppositions is seen in the issue of Black individualism. Does the human potential movement have any answers to the question of Black unity? Possibly, but we must be aware of where the movement is coming from and what it's into.

THE HUMAN POTENTIAL MOVEMENT

What is the movement all about? We live in a world that is becoming increasingly automated and computerized. Accompanying this occurrence is a peculiar transformation in human relationships. Man's environmental responses are becoming man-to-machine responses, resulting in a frightening reduction of man-to-man responses. The consequences of this pattern are troubling. Affective behavior is in a state of atrophy and cognition is prevailing at levels bordering on robotness. This is displayed in the callousness and asinine rationalization voiced for the continuing sacrifice of human life and the perpetration of human cruelty, as in a war in which few people are aware of the pain of its victims. The supposition here is that progress in science and technology seems to be correlated with social upheaval and social distancing. Out of this apparent reality the human potential movement has grown. Its purpose is to revive man's affective behavior—to make him a whole person again.

The movement is a rather perplexing, terrifying, and yet intriguing force that is being felt in American institutions and among lay persons. Using such labels as sensitivity training, encounter groups, personal growth groups, sensory awareness sessions, T groups, and many other such terms, the movement is spreading. The participants (usually small groups of 6 to 15 people) are exhorted to get in touch with their feelings and to live in the here-and-now. The goals of the group are trust, intimacy, self-awareness, self-acceptance, and acceptance of others within the context of human participation. The catalysts are self-disclosure and honesty in the immediacy of the moment as the group process develops. Exercises—some are more appropriately labeled gadgets and gimmicks—are used to generate every possible human feeling. The risk is to try to "be the feelings" as they are felt, as opposed to the conventional way of suppressing, denying, or neutralizing feelings. The movement is being co-opted into the American mainstream. It is causing as many different reactions among persons and institutions as the varied forms in which it appears. The movement ranges from a panacea for our social ills to a communistic inspired method of brainwashing, and its impact is being felt.

THE HUMAN POTENTIAL MOVEMENT AND BLACK EXCLUSION

In its genesis, the movement contained an appealing facet. There was something revolutionary about it, even though it was largely white. It was attacking social systems with full force. But the capitalistic giant is invading this force. In doing so the system is enlarging itself with more of its own evil.

The human potential movement was conceived out of and matured to address an American dilemma (e.g., alienation, psychological truncation, existential frustration, etc.) that is largely a white dilemma. A few psychologically integrated humanists, surrounded by a larger number of neurotically driven affection seekers, finally admitted that the ill-fated system that sought to dehumanize its Black and poor constituents was in fact dehumanizing and creating sickness in its sponsors and advocates. The humanists proclaimed they would make the "well, weller." The hardened reality was the need to make the "sick, well." The space age has a counterpart—the sick age.

The hard sell campaign for group psychotherapy is evident (Kurhn & Crinella 1969). From classical group psychotherapy to religious conversions, millions of Americans have participated in the movement. Growth centers have grown like cancerous tissue. With Esalen as the prototype, the movement has become infected with the same diseases as all other American institutions—racism and capitalism.

The movement, at its very inception, was in the interest of deterring psychological morbidity among white people. The movement's tangential involvement with Black people occurred only in the interest of the health of white people. Black participation has been largely limited to interracial encounter groups or workshops in human relations. What are they like? In such groups, the Blacks vent their hostilities by telling it like it is, usually at the invitation of the whites who display an invisible sign that reads "Kick me—I'm liberal." After it's all over, the situation remains the same for Blacks, while the whites salvage some sense of guilt assuagement by allowing themselves to be punished by the Blacks. Blacks who have participated in encounter groups are almost always middle class, which furthers the guilt assuagement process for whites. The Blacks generally serve as guinea pigs for the whites by providing for them their first real contact with Black people. These clean-cut, educated Blacks, however militant, are socialized at least in part by white institutions and provide the far-removed whites with inaccurate data about Black people. The whites are seemingly pleased to be in the presence of the all-American Black people, not so much because they really like them or respect them, but because guilty reaction to terms such as racism, oppression, discrimination, prejudice, and exploitation is removed due to the contradictory evidence presented by the presence of the Blacks who made it in the system. The notions that "The rest of them could make it too if they weren't so lazy and dumb," and "If they were more like you people (the Blacks present)," are substantiated in the minds of the whites, dispelling the feeling that they are contributors to Black oppression.

The movement is pathological in another way—the dollar. Group leaders have become vulturous and are sucking on the blood of "group addicts" and sick people. Growth centers have solidly established themselves as entrepreneurs. Fees vary but are generally high. In addition, the market is being flooded with tapes, films, records, books, packaged therapy, and other items that carry astronomical prices. This capitalistic dimension further decreases the chance for Black participation, granted that the movement has little to offer the masses at this point in its metamorphosis. Are there salvageable elements in the movement for Blacks who are trying to unite?

THE HUMAN POTENTIAL MOVEMENT AND BLACK UNITY

To look at the human potential movement as it relates to Black unity demands a regression to the cultural milieu out of which both forces have grown. The human potential movement has grown out of a technologically advancing society that has created material comfort for white people. Unforeseen outgrowths of this have been alienation, lack of intimacy in interpersonal relationships, existential frustrations, and related concerns. The hypothesis here is that as man makes living easier for man (through automation and computerization), he removes himself further from nature and diminishes his contact with other humans. There is a diminution of the human dimension in human beings; the seeming irreversibility of this trend gave birth to the human potential movement. The movement quickly armed itself and was engaging in war against the system. At this juncture, it became compatible with the Black liberation movement, although they were of different origins.

Black unity, the anchor of Black liberation, also grew out of a technologically advancing society that created social and economic gloom for Black people. This is due mainly to the element of racism embedded in the American mainstream. This element only becomes active, through violent repression, when people of color think about entering the mainstream. The intended outgrowths of the system's treatment of Blacks are poverty, illiteracy, cultural unawareness, intra-racial strife and divisiveness, and broken spirits too weak to fight off the violent forces of unfair and unjust America. There is one aspect of Blackness that has not capitulated; it is tougher than the military, the national guard, and the police brigade combined. The human dimension in Black folks is still very much apparent. No amount of disease, illiteracy, joblessness, or bullets can make it acquiesce. Black humanness does not respond to decadent forces fomented by the system. Sometimes it lies dormant in order for Blacks to cope, but it is always there, ready to burst in full bloom when circumstances permit. Humanness is inextricably interwoven with the survival instinct. This is unforeseen in the system's perpetration of cruelty against Black people. It was this very humanness that spearheaded Blacks to strive for unity and to go to war against the system to achieve liberation.

To make the human potential movement applicable to Black unity, the revolutionary flavor of the movement must be revived. The movement must deal with the disease with which it is infected, but so must the Black unity movement. The rudiment of the problem of Black unity is Black identity in a collective sense. Blacks are interested in self-determination, self-sufficiency, and self-revolution (warring within oneself between the suppressed Blackness and the whiteness imposed by society). The human potential movement concerns itself with the liberation of humanness within humans. Black humanness is not in need of liberation, but of awakening, and can be used as a catalyst to advance Black unity. Both movements are group struggles; both involve group work—one largely white, one Black. At this point, I will discuss how achieving a sense of collective Black

161

identity, through utilizing skills peculiar to the human potential movement, can serve as a positive force to unite Blacks.

COLLECTIVE BLACK IDENTITY AND BLACK UNITY

It is my contention that a sense of collective Black identity can be achieved in "Black identity groups." The first consideration in working with Blacks in groups is that the process, including goals and techniques, should embrace the principles of Black liberation and respond to the naturalness of Black folks. The naturalness of Black people has been stifled and choked by Western life. To get a clearer picture of the innate heritage of African people in America, one only has to observe the tribal tendencies of African people on the African continent. Breetveld (1972), in an interview with African psychiatrist Thomas Lambo, learned this: "African culture is based on a warm, stable, cohesive social unit. The whole emphasis of child rearing is to teach the young that they are an organic part of that unit, to give them a deep-rooted feeling of belonging [p. 4]." The infant from birth enjoys the security of the extended family. Lambo continued: "Reality for the African is found in the soul, not objects. The aim of life is not to master oneself, or outer things, but to accept a life of harmony with other beings on a spiritual scale . . . [p. 5]." This clearly expresses the doctrine of collective Black identity and the naturalness of African people in America. It's a kind of human-affective orientation toward life. Middle class America has derogatorily dubbed this feature "emotionalism"—we call it *Soul*. Western life has not changed these ancestral imprints, but to a degree has suppressed them, particularly as relates to Black identity in a collective sense.

BLACK IDENTITY GROUPS

Black identity is an imperative for optimal Black mental health. Cobbs and Grier (1972) theorize as follows:

Blackness has had an exciting effect on Black America. . . . It has stimulated a reversal of feelings about self, and where one had felt a shrunken half-shell, with black awareness the body fills out and a man feels genuinely proud of himself. Attitudes shift from self-denigration to expansive superiority; men and women shed an old identity and with it the wretchedness previously associated with color.

Blackness has the effect of penetrating and shattering the pressure bearing down on and distorting black lives. It allows blacks to cleanse themselves of fear, and, in one act, remove not only intimidations of immediate hostility, but also all ceilings, permitting freedom to move as far and fast as one's wits will allow [p. 17].

Inherent in this theorizing is the essentiality of Black identity groups. These groups are interested in revitalizing Black people with the spirit and health of Blackness and enabling us to work more constructively for the social betterment of our people. We must recognize that our slave adaptations to Western life and the oppression, subjugation, and degradation of African people in America has fostered spurious identities in Black folks. Many Blacks, at least in part, have had to adopt the white life style. This was the price one paid to live in materialistic comfort. Furthermore, it was impossible to muster feelings of self-worth when your reference group was viewed with intense scorn. This enhanced the process of realignment with the dominant culture. Realigning one's identity base with another race does not end the search for identity. Circumstances have driven many Blacks to attempt identification with the larger culture only to find themselves in a state of limbo—black skin, white mask land—asking: Who am I? Where do I fit in? At last an answer is available. A true identity base for Blacks can never be found in white culture. The spiritual dimension that bonds Black people together can find similar ties with no other people. Black people must restore their spiritual allegiance to Black people. Collective Black identity must be our ultimate reference point. A clear sense of where one comes from is vital to a clear sense of where one is going.

A true sense of being is arrived at through the fusion of two processes, which occur in Black identity groups. Beisser (1971) explains it this way: "In order to find self in relationship to a group, an individual moves between polar positions of being like and unlike others, through the processes of dedifferentiation and differentiation [p. 135]." The former is an intense quest for sameness between an individual and a group, whereas the latter involves an intense quest for uniqueness. In group work with Blacks, the focus should be on those things that join us as a people, particularly in the beginning phase of the group process. A true sense of sameness, of belonging, must be collectively developed. As it grows, the bonding process intensifies. Functional individualism budding within this developed framework of Blackness becomes a healthy occurrence.

Group skills generated from the human potential movement and newly developed skills must be adapted to Black life style and cultural phenomena. Art, history, literature, music, Black expression through physical activity—all are fertile areas from which appropriate group skills can be cultivated, always embracing political, social, and economic realities. With imagination and creativity, working with Blacks in groups with the intent of arriving at a feeling of group Black identity can enhance the cause of Black unity.

Black identity groups offer the following possibilities:

1. An opportunity to solidly restructure or to refine an appropriate identity base.
2. An opportunity to define one's own strengths and talents, e.g., uniqueness, anchored in an appropriate identity base.
3. An opportunity to become more genuinely and spiritually involved with Black brothers and sisters and oneself.
4. A chance to integrate one's cultural heritage into a true, healthy way of being.
5. A chance to help develop constructive proposals and strategies to more expeditiously uplift Black people.

To emerge victorious, we must align ourselves with each other. Nathan Hare (1970) underscores this thought: "In the mobilization of our full resources for black liberation, we must bear in mind that we are all oppressed and that our history has made soldiers of every oppressed individual. We are all soldiers . . . [p. 5]." Just now, at this moment, I feel a strange, pleasurable sense of being-Black.

REFERENCES

Allen, R. L. *Black awakening in capitalist America*. Garden City, N.Y.: Doubleday & Company, 1970.

Beisser, A. R. Identity formation within groups. *Journal of Humanistic Psychology*, 1971, *11*, 133-135.

Breetveld, J. P. A brief conversation with Thomas Lambo. *Psychology Today*, 1972, *5*(9), 62-65.

Cobbs, P., & Grier, W. Black psychology. *Contact*, 1972, *3*(2), 15-27.

Fanon, F. *The wretched of the earth*. New York: Grove Press, Inc., 1963.

Hare, N. We are all soldiers. *Black Scholar*, 1970, *2*(3), 2-5.

Kurhn, J. L., & Crinella, F. M. Sensitivity training: Interpersonal "overkill" and other problems. *American Journal of Psychiatry*, 1969, *126*, 840-844.

Life skills:
Structured counseling
for the disadvantaged

WINTHROP R. ADKINS

The difficult life problems of disadvantaged adults and adolescents are not easily resolved through traditional unstructured counseling methods. The Life Skills counseling program provides a structured means of helping disadvantaged groups acquire the necessary experience, knowledge, and skill to cope effectively with the psychosocial aspects of personal development, parenthood, and citizenship. Life Skills counseling employs a life problem-derived curriculum and a four-stage learning model which integrates counseling and teaching functions as it facilitates problem-solving through inductive and deductive modes of inquiry and application.

THE MULTIPLE PROBLEMS of disadvantaged adolescents and adults, which make it difficult for them to take full advantage of their emerging training and employment opportunities, have been frequently described in the literature (Gordon, 1969; Harrington, 1962; Riessman, 1962). Some progress has been made in devising meaningful programs to teach vocational and basic reading and mathematics skills (U.S. Department of Labor, 1969). There has not, however, been a concomitant advance in finding ways to help disadvantaged students and workers learn the life skills—the psychological and social skills for mastering the interrelated problems in living encountered in training, on the job, in the home, and in the community.

Although virtually every training and employment program for the disadvantaged has employed counselors to help

students and workers deal more effectively with their problems in living, the relatively high percentage of premature terminations attributable to various psychosocial problems (U.S. Bureau of the Budget, 1969) attests to the fact that counseling programs are not yet coping effectively enough with the needs of disadvantaged clients. One reason why counselors have not been more successful is that the personal problems faced by their clients are numerous and complex. Another is that counselors often lack the appropriate experience, preparation, and understanding of their clients (Gordon, 1964; Trueblood, 1960). However, perhaps an even more basic reason is that, lacking more effective tools, counselors have relied heavily on nonstructured discussion methods in individual or group counseling as the primary means for helping to resolve difficulties and make appropriate plans.

The traditional counseling interview and even modern sensitivity training methods, structured by the client's problems as they unfold and by the techniques of the counselor, were developed

WINTHROP R. ADKINS is Associate Professor of Psychology and Education at Teachers College, Columbia University, in New York City.

The Life Skills program was initially developed by the author with the assistance of Robert Wolsch and Sidney Rosenberg, formerly at Training Resources for Youth, Inc., Brooklyn, New York.

PERSONNEL AND GUIDANCE JOURNAL, 1970, Vol. 49, pp. 108-116.

primarily with middle-class clients coming from highly organized communities. These people presumably possess a reasonable amount of knowledge and familiarity with the resources and demands of their environment (Strodbeck, 1964). The disadvantaged client, however, frequently comes from a disorganized community, has few dependable family, school, and community resources, and has had little opportunity to learn about his interests and abilities and the requirements of training and employment. There are distinct limits on the effectiveness of nonstructured discussion as a means of helping him to acquire the considerable new experience, knowledge, and skill necessary to cope with his problems and make meaningful choices, as Amos and Grambs (1968) suggest.

A NEED FOR NEW METHODS

A number of observations of traditional individual and group counseling sessions with black disadvantaged adolescents bear out these limitations. It was found in a vocational training program (Adkins, 1966; Adkins & Wynne, 1966) that:

1. Trainees found it difficult to sustain focused discussion on any one topic, but instead kept flitting from problem to problem with insufficient attention or effort on any one. When counselors helped to structure their sessions with pre-prepared leads, materials, and exercises on specific common personal problems, trainees were able to focus effectively, make progress, and attend to their other training tasks.

2. Group discussion frequently revealed a great deal of shared ignorance. Patently false concepts and facts were uncontested by all but the counselor. The group appeared to have little access to new knowledge that would challenge their misconceptions about important areas of their lives. The counselor's efforts to get them to collect evidence which put in question their own facts

and assumptions were much more successful.

3. Counselors reported that the majority of their clients had very similar problems and that they noticed a great deal of repetition in their own behavior in working with different clients and different groups. It was apparent that a more efficient way of handling these common problems would be desirable.

4. Most of the "emotional" problems of trainees had large cognitive and intellectual components and, in effect, were largely problems of not having sufficient facts, sound knowledge and categories to define them, information about resources, and the ability to frame alternative courses of action. Frustration over an accumulation of unresolved problems produced negative emotions such as fear, guilt, and anger which cumulatively led to patterns of withdrawal, apathy, aggressive acting-out, or feelings of alienation. Yet when problems were analyzed into tasks, rather than dealt with holistically, trainees experienced needed success in dealing with them. This experience had the effect of supplanting negative emotional reactions with positive ones and encouraging renewed attack on other problems.

5. Words and concepts used by clients, and even black counselors, were not based on common experiential referents. Lacking common experiences, words simply meant different things, not easily explained by words alone. Trainees appeared to be eager for experiences in which they could see, hear, and otherwise sense new activities, settings, and tasks. They seemed to trust knowledge gained through direct experience and mistrust ideas expressed verbally or in writing unless related to their experiences.

6. Many of the trainees acted as if "talk is cheap" and either saw group sessions as stages on which to perform or became apathetic with prolonged discussion unless it led to action. When talk was

either a prelude to action or a reflection of past action, focused interest remained high and trainees seemed to benefit.

7. Like most adolescents, trainees had effective and rewarding relationships with their peers and responded well to peer-group learning activities. They seemed most open to learning if the peer group and the counselor encouraged them to express their own ideas about the issue or task at hand and if they appeared to value what the trainees said.

These observations suggested that a different kind of counseling program could be designed which would help disadvantaged clients minimize their weaknesses and take full advantage of their strengths. Could we not collect and categorize the common problems of trainees and deal with them more efficiently? Could we not first take advantage of their preference for solving problems and for obtaining knowledge inductively from experience and then gradually introduce them to other means of learning about themselves and their opportunities? Could we not, in effect, reach our counseling goals better if we considered the problems of our trainees as our *curriculum* and employed a variety of teaching as well as counseling methods? Why not a curriculum for counseling?

DESIGN REQUIREMENTS

On the basis of these and other observations it was felt that the program should meet the following design requirements:
1. It should be life problem-centered and be capable of adaptation to a wide variety of problems related to living and working in the city.
2. It should build upon the knowledge and skill they already possess and provide a means for improving problem-solving skills while demonstrating the utility of new knowledge gained by reading, study, and research as well as by experience and discussion.
3. It should take advantage of their

good peer relations by maximizing group activities in areas of common concern, and yet it should provide for personal needs through individual counseling.

These initial observations and design requirements for a structured counseling program led to the development of a Life Skills program at Training Resources for Youth (Adkins, Rosenberg, & Sharar, 1965), a large, comprehensive, experimental training project for disadvantaged adolescents living in Bedford-Stuyvesant. In the succeeding years I have continued the development of Life Skills, concepts and operations with black, white, and Indian populations both in the U.S. and Canada (Adkins & Rosenberg, 1969). The process of curriculum design and the learning model described in this article represent the most recent version of that development.

THE DESIGN OF A PROBLEM-CENTERED CURRICULUM

The syllabus for the Life Skills curriculum is based on the problems the trainees are currently facing and those they will encounter as they progress through training to actual employment.

The problems for the most recent syllabus were collected by working with counselors and other staff familiar with disadvantaged clients in order to make a crude task analysis of current counseling problems and the major psychological and social skill requirements of employment and personal development in the context of work, family, and community. Numerous individual problems resulting from this were then analyzed, combined, and categorized into some 50 common life problems which were in turn clustered together under five major track headings representing composite objectives. They are: Developing Oneself and Relating to Others; Managing a Career; Managing Home and Family Responsibilities; Managing Leisure Time; and Exercising Community Rights, Opportunities, and Responsibilities. The Life problems provide the basis for the design of curriculum units. The representative curriculum unit headings in TABLE 1 illustrate the range of simple and complex problems which must be resolved to demonstrate competence on a given curriculum track. Because the curriculum is developed from the actual problems faced by trainees, motivation is greatly enhanced and the dangers of irrelevance and designer bias greatly reduced.

The Life Skills curriculum is designed to be used in small groups of about 10 trainees who are concurrently enrolled in basic education, vocational education, or on-the-job training programs. Each group is led by a specially trained Life Skills counselor who is thoroughly familiar with the trainees and the instructional and counseling requirements of the learning model. Group meetings are followed up by regular individual counseling sessions and trainees spend about two hours each day in the Life Skills program.

THE STRUCTURED FOUR-STAGE MODEL

Effective counselors and teachers engage in a number of different processes in implementing their goals. If these proc-esses were made explicit, they could define a series of distinct sequential roles for learners and educators which would help to clarify the expected behavior of both and be relatively easily learned. The four stages of the model—Stimulus, Evocation, Objective Inquiry, and Application—through which a Life Skills learning sequence progresses are designed explicitly to enhance motivation, to demonstrate the value of past learning, to guide exploration, and to apply knowledge usefully. In addition the process provides a model for problem-solving. Each lesson is planned on the basis of the four stages. The goal is to increase knowledge about oneself and about ways in which to cope with one's environment, and to facilitate planning and action based on this greater knowledge. A fundamental notion is that experience followed by reflection, followed by goal-setting, followed by further exploration, reflection, and so forth, in the process of implementing goals is an effective means for encouraging self-induced behavioral change. The four-stage model, described in TABLE 2, which was adapted from the work of Wolsch (1969) and revised with the assistance of Rosenberg (Adkins & Rosenberg, 1969), indicates how this is accomplished.

TABLE 1

Major Curriculum Tracks and Representative Units

Tracks	Representative Units
Developing Oneself and Relating to Others	Dealing with parental rejection; identifying one's interests and abilities; proper diet
Managing a Career	Interviews, tests, and application blanks; relating to one's boss; pay-check deductions
Managing Home and Family Responsibilities	Becoming a father; meeting needs of wives; budgeting and buying
Managing Leisure Time	Planning one's time; changing mood and pace through recreation; participative vs. spectator activities
Exercising Community Rights, Opportunities, and Responsibilities	How organizations function; dealing with discrimination; finding one's way around the city

TABLE 2
Overview of the Four-Stage Life Skills Model

	Stimulus	Evocation	Objective Inquiry	Application
OBJECTIVES	• focus attention of group • stimulate group to respond	• evoke responses from all group members • demonstrate knowledge already acquired and dignify the learner • enhance group rapport • categorize group knowledge • raise curiosity	• aid inquiry into what is known by others • help find and use resources • help discover new sources of knowledge • help test current assumptions about knowledge	• apply knowledge to aspects of problems to acquire skills • broaden experience • feel success in coping effectively
	Stimulator	**Evocateur**	**Resource person**	**Shaper and coach**
ROLE OF LIFE SKILLS COUNSELOR*	• prepare and present stimulus	• ask questions and lead discussion to elicit what group already knows • record group responses • help group categorize knowledge and raise questions	• suggest sources of knowledge • provide resources • assist learners in using resources and making presentations • conduct discussions to assimilate what learned	• help define and select problem • provide initial projects • help learners to frame and carry out own projects
ROLE OF LEARNER	• respond to stimulus	• discuss what each knows and feels about problem	• make inquiries to obtain knowledge using multimedia kit • present findings to group	• define, select, and carry out individual, team, and group projects
MATERIALS FOR LESSONS	• films, clippings, pictures, stories, etc. with high emotional impact	• blackboard, tape recorder, mimeograph	• multimedia kit of pamphlets, films, recordings, suggested trips	• selected prepared projects and suggested project types
DURATION	• until discussion starts	• as long as group can still produce ideas and is interested	• as long as group wants to know what others know and what is knowable	• as long as project takes or until interest wanes

* In addition to the above, he conducts regular individual counseling sessions at various times.

Stage I: Stimulus

The Life Skills learning sequence begins with a provocative classroom encounter with a selected problem. As the name implies, the objective is to stimulate the interest of the learners in a common topic and thus create readiness for group discussion. A second purpose is to provide immediate content for initiating discussion. The Life Skills counselor (LSC) selects a highly controversial or emotionally laden aspect of the problem and presents it in the form of a film (either fully presented or stopped at an exciting point) or a picture, a tape recording, or a news clipping, or tells a story of a particularly pertinent experience. This initial stimulus may be external (from the LSC) or internal (from the group itself). The LSC's main role is to select and plan the stimulus, convene the group, and insure that the stimulus is effectively presented for maximum impact. His enthusiasm and involvement are most important. The desired outcome is that the group will be pensive, agitated, intrigued, or amused, and will be ready—even raring—to talk about the problem they have just experienced. Depending on the unit chosen, the LSC might present a videotape of a black youth being fired from his job, or have a trainee describe his feelings about the recent birth of his baby, or show a film depicting a narcotics addict suffering from withdrawal symptoms.

Stage II: Evocation

Once the discussion is initiated, the objective is to evoke from each of the group members what he, based upon his own experiences, knows about the problem. The main intent is to help the trainee become aware of how much he and others already know about the problem and thereby dignify him as a learner. Other purposes are to encourage the free expression of ideas and feelings on a focused topic in a supportive, nonjudg-mental atmosphere, and to provide a living illustration of basic epistemological issues and the multiple sources of knowledge now utilized by the group (experiencing, finding out from a self-proclaimed or culture-proclaimed authority, observing, reading, counting, listening, etc.). By judicious questioning, comparing, and reflecting, the LSC attempts to keep a lively discussion going about the topic. It is most important that he be receptive and that he set a tone similar to that of brainstorming sessions, by insisting that all have the opportunity to speak and that there be group respect for each person's contribution.

During the discussion the LSC also acts as a recorder by writing the ideas, words, phrases, or images on the blackboard or a flip chart in the original form in which they are expressed. He may fill boards on all sides of the room as he attempts to exhaust the knowledge of the group on the subject. He liberally dispenses verbal rewards for effort in the manner of an art teacher attempting to get students to express themselves freely on a blank canvas. Recordings on the blackboard tends to give the contributions of the group a semi-permanent status insted of allowing the comments to disappear immediately after utterance. Members feel that they have been heard and that their ideas have value for subsequent analysis and discussion.

When the boards are filled, the topic is exhausted, or interest begins to lag, the LSC asks the group to identify ideas that "go together" or that are contradictory, or that they agree with or dispute. The intent in this phase of the Evocation stage is to categorize the output of the discussion and to raise interest in finding out more about the topic in order to follow up associations or resolve contradictions. If the LSC also mimeographs the categorized knowledge of the group and hands it back as "curriculum material," the trainees tend to feel pride in what they as a group know and have constructed. Having been given an opportunity to describe what they *know* about a topic, they can psychologically afford to admit what they do *not know*. The novel concept of "I have been a learner" seems to translate into "I am a learner" and leads to curiosity and additional inquiry.

Stage III: Objective Inquiry

Having probed the limits of their own knowledge, the major objective of this stage is to encourage and assist members of the group to explore a variety of other sources of knowledge about the problem. After identifying what the major questions of interest are, and what new knowledge is needed, the group is led to assign its members tasks for obtaining information. The LSC shifts his role from question-asker and recorder to resource person and question-answerer. He assists teams and small groups of learners to make full use of the specially prepared multimedia kits. These kits are cardboard boxes containing pre-selected films, filmstrips, pamphlets, books, pictures, tests, maps, lists of lectures, addresses of libraries, cards listing suggested field trips to agencies, places of employment or points of interest, persons to talk with, things to count, subjects to research, and additional sources of information.

Although the multimedia kits take a somewhat long time to construct in advance, they are extremely useful in minimizing the information search problem for the learner and can be tailor-made for the particular needs of the group. With a small materials development staff, individual items on a whole range of likely problems can be assembled. Curriculum materials and video and audio recordings made by other groups can also be included.

After the teams of learners have found information relevant to their assignment both outside and inside the classroom, the LSC helps them use it to plan their presentations as experts on a subject before the whole group. Initially the LSC leads the group presentation session, but he gradually shifts the responsibility for such sessions to individuals in the group. As groups become more familiar with the process of searching out relevant information, they become less dependent on the multimedia kits and the LSC and can discover their own sources of information. In the process of completing their tasks, trainees learn how to operate projectors, find books in the library, plan trips, improve their reading and discussion skills, carry out simple research, take tests, talk with experts such as doctors, lawyers, and employers, interview others, prepare presentations, analyze results, and hopefully to think more clearly. The desired outcome is that they will not only obtain useful information about a specific problem but also have a variety of new experiences and learn the basic skills of inquiry and resource identification.

Stage IV: Application

It is not enough to obtain, present, and discuss information, since it is likely to be forgotten if not put to use. The main objective of this stage, therefore, is to demonstrate the utility of knowledge by providing opportunities to apply what has been learned to real life problems, under either real or simulated conditions. The group surveys its accumulated knowledge and selects one or several aspects of the problem it is interested in acting upon. The LSC shifts his role from resource person to coach. His main task is to help trainees frame projects they can carry out with some success. If the subject of the unit is selecting an occupation, for example, an appropriate project for an early lesson might be to make an inventory of one's interests and abilities based on information and categories gained in the Evocation and Objective.Inquiry stages. If the subject of the unit is "making your emotions work for you" and the lesson deals with controlling one's anger, the project might be to role-play techniques of reperception and delayed response learned in the Objective Inquiry stage to a simulated anger situation. If the subject of the unit is the role of a father in a family, the project might be to tutor a younger child in some skill. If the subject of the unit is presenting oneself effectively to others, the project might be to make a videotape of a job interview conducted with a cooperating employer using new knowledge about verbal and nonverbal communication. Initial projects should, of course, be relatively simple, but with experience much more complicated projects such as planning to start a laundromat business, or managing a voter registration campaign, or locating and renting an apartment can be undertaken. The desirable outcome is that group members will be able to carry out projects which help them to solve their own life problems with a minimal help from the LSC.

FLEXIBILITY OF OPERATIONS

When projects are completed, the four-stage model for the learning sequence is recycled. If the next lesson is an extension of the lesson just completed, it is possible that the Stimulus stage can be eliminated. If the group elects to move on to a different unit, then of course the new lesson begins with a Stimulus as described. The four-stage model can be employed flexibly. Cycling through all four stages may take several sessions or be completed in one session. The sequence of stages can be shifted when appropriate. The stages may be explicitly explained to trainees and adhered to strictly by the group, or they may be used more informally by the LSC as a guide. The units selected may focus on one area in depth, such as gaining employment or coping with problems of health or marriage, or may deal in less depth with a broad range of problems,

such as suggested in this article. The problem-centered Life Skills program may form the core of an entire training center curriculum integrated with more conventional classroom treatments of subjects at advanced levels, or it may be used on a more limited basis to deal with the most pressing life problems faced by learners at school or at work. In all cases, it is recommended that individual counseling be regularly employed to supplement group activities and to facilitate reflection and goal-setting.

There is reason to believe that the Life Skills program may have certain advantages over other didactic and counseling approaches. In developing units one is forced to make an explicit study and analysis of the actual problems trainees are experiencing as they negotiate their social environment and the tasks these imply. These must be stated in terms of specific behavioral objectives. Rigorous thinking is required to identify what will stimulate the trainees, what they are already likely to know, what resources are needed to help them find it out for themselves, and, most important, how they can concretely apply what they have learned in order to realize success and progress in solving problems. Moreover, in conducting a Life Skills lesson, the LSC must pay attention to a variety of important aspects of learning which are frequently omitted in many counseling and teaching situations. As a result of these features and the fact the curriculum units themselves are derived from the actual life problems important to the trainees, motivation for learning is usually high.

STAFF REQUIREMENTS

The skills of individuals from various fields have been employed in *designing* Life Skills lessons and units. Interestingly enough, staff with counseling backgrounds and without special training can cope very effectively with the Evocation stages, but surprisingly poorly with Objective Inquiry and Application stages. Teachers tend to be good initially at thinking about Objective Inquiry, but poor at Evocation and Application. Some of the most provocative Stimulus stages have been suggested by salesmen, and some of the most realistic Application projects designed by job developers and placement specialists.

In *conducting* Life Skills units and lessons, staff with counseling and teaching backgrounds have been most frequently used as LSC's, although there has been some experimentation with paraprofessionals. With special training in the operation of the four stages of the Life Skills model and with practice, LSC's become adept at thinking operationally and conducting lessons. They report that they find the four-stage sequence very helpful in structuring their various roles and preparing for lessons.

Development of the Life Skills program is continuing. The initial program designed to help urban black adolescents in New York City is now being refined and adapted for use with Indian adults in rural Canada. Second-generation programs will explore the implications of the Life Skills approach for other populations, both disadvantaged and middle-class, and in industrial, educational, and community center contexts.

REFERENCES

Adkins, W. R. Counseling in the inner city: Life Skills education. Paper presented at the APGA convention, Washington, D. C., 1966.

Adkins, W. R., & Rosenberg, S. *Theory and operations of the Life Skills program.* Privately produced videotape, 1969.

Adkins, W. R., Rosenberg, S., & Sharar, P. *Training resources for youth proposal.* A comprehensive operational plan for a demonstration-research training center for disadvantaged youth. New York: Training Resources for Youth, Inc., 1965.

Adkins, W. R., & Wynne, J. D. *Final report of the YMCA youth and work project.* Contract 24-64, Department of Labor. New York: YMCA of Greater New York, 1966.

Amos, W. E., & Grambs, J. *Counseling the disadvantaged youth.* Englewood Cliffs, N. J.: Prentice Hall, 1968.

Gordon, E. W. Counseling socially disadvantaged children. In F. Reissman et al. (Eds.), *Mental health of the poor.* Glencoe, Ill.: Free Press, 1964.

Gordon, J. E. Counseling the disadvantaged boy. In W. E. Amos and J. Grambs (Eds.), *Counseling the disadvantaged youth.* Englewood Cliffs, N. J.: Prentice Hall, 1969.

Harrington, M. *The other America.* New York: Macmillan, 1962.

Reissman, F. *The culturally deprived child.* New York: Harper & Row, 1962.

Strodbeck, F. L. The hidden curriculum of the middle class home in Hunnicutt. In C. William (Ed.), *Urban education and cultural deprivations.* Syracuse, N. Y.: Syracuse University Press, 1964.

Trueblood, D. L. The role of the counselor in the guidance of Negro students. *Harvard Educational Review,* 1960, *30,* 252–269.

U.S. Bureau of the Budget. *Study of the programs of the U.S. Office of Economic Opportunity.* Washington, D.C.: U.S. Government Printing Office, 1969.

U.S. Department of Labor. *Manpower report of the President.* Washington, D.C.: U.S. Government Printing Office, 1969.

Wolsch, R. Poetic composition in the elementary school: A handbook for teachers. Unpublished doctoral dissertation, Teachers College, Columbia University, 1969.

Psychological education for racial awareness

NORMA JEAN ANDERSON

BARBARA LOVE

Norma Jean Anderson is Assistant Dean for Graduate Affairs and Professor in the Human Relations Center at the University of Massachusetts—Amherst. Barbara Love is Assistant Professor in the Urban Education Center at the same institution. This is a shortened version of a larger series of exercises. The full manuscript may be obtained from the authors.

Counselors must concern themselves with societal problems that frequently subvert the effectiveness of their programs. Significant among these problems is the issue of racism. While counselors have recognized the various ways that racism affects people in the United States today, they have been at a loss in prescribing ways to reorient themselves and their roles within institutions to deal with such social problems as racism.

One of the ways counselors might begin this process is by helping black and other minority children develop a sense of pride and by helping white children develop increased racial understanding. Recent educational research has documented the correlation between level of pride in self and pupil academic performance. The "Black is Beautiful" movement is concerned with helping the black child develop a more positive self-concept. Note, for instance, how Barbara Buckner Wright expresses herself in her poem "Black." [1]

I am a Negro ———
    And I am ashamed.
Chemicals in my hair to make it other than what
    it is,
Bleaches on my skin to make it more . . . non-
    black,

Cosmetics on my face to be like the "other"
Why must I try to be other than what I am?
The French say they are French,
    from France,
The Irish say they are Irish,
    from Ireland,
The Italians say they are Italian,
    from Italy.
And I say I am Negro ———
    from where?
Is there a Negro land? The French, Irish, Italians
    all have a culture and heritage.
What is My land? Where are My people? My
    culture? My heritage?
I am Negro ———
    And I am ashamed.
Who GAVE me this name?
"Slaves and dogs are named by their masters . . .
    Free men name themselves"[2]
Must I be other than What I am?

I am Black. This is a source of pride.
My hair is short and finely curled.
My skin is deep-hued, from brown to black.
My eyes are large, open to the world.
My lips are thick, giving resonance to my words.
My nose is broad to breathe freely the air.
My heritage is my experience *in* America . . .
    although not *of* it;
Free from my pretense; open to truth
Seeking freedom that all life may be free

I am Black, America has cause to be proud.

---

[1] The poem "Black" is reprinted with permission from *Let's Work Together*, by Nathan Wright, Hawthorn Books, 1968.
[2] Ron Karenga, *The Quotable Karenga.*

PERSONNEL AND GUIDANCE JOURNAL, 1973, Vol. 51, pp. 666-670.

Until recently, school systems have failed all minority students by not portraying minority role models in positions of authority and by not integrating minority history and culture into the curriculums of the schools. An additional failure has been demonstrated by teachers, counselors, and administrators who are not prepared to deal with a minority constituency. Needless to say, these same errors are compounded and continued in offices, agencies, and other work and living settings. Knowing about the history and culture of minority groups and being sensitive to how racism functions in all institutions of society is important for all counselors, be they in the heart of the inner city or in the outskirts of suburbia. Understanding has not moved much beyond a superficial level, and skill development appears to be nonexistent.

Changing society so that it does accept the responsibility of preparing all to live comfortably and fully in a multicultural society is the responsibility of all those who are a part of the institution. School counselors, however, have a special function to perform, for they have contact with both students and teachers. This means that the role of the counselor should be redefined and expanded and that counselors should assume responsibility for making efforts to increase positive human relations and fostering development of a multicultural view of the world. Of particular importance is the counselor's new role in curriculum development and inservice teacher training.

Counselors are in a unique position to know when there is a need to devote some special attention to dealing with the issues of self-concept and intercultural understanding. The counselor may be the focal point for getting an entire school to begin rethinking its goals, philosophy, and practices. There are some strategies that a counselor can use to get students started in this direction. One such strategy is a student workshop that is scheduled into the school day,

such as the racism workshop described in this article. While designed for a school setting, many of these exercises have equal validity for colleges, employment agencies, and industrial settings. The general objectives of the workshop are (a) to help black and other minority children develop a sense of pride; (b) to help white children develop increased racial understanding; (c) to help all children develop a beginning knowledge of social, anthropological, and biological facts regarding human nature, culture, and race; and (d) to help all children acquire an understanding of the steps that can be taken to overcome racism and be able to relate to them verbally and adapt them into the actions of themselves and others.

ACTIVITIES AND INVESTIGATIONS

Activity 1: Racist Attitudes

Racism is the attitude that one race is innately superior to others; it is the basis of most intergroup friction. Racism is caused by cultural influences and results in varying degrees of negative or undemocratic behavior toward minorities, often with horrible consequences to the total society. The nature, extent, and intensity of racist attitudes among a group needs to be determined in order that steps can be taken to change them.

Pretest the students to determine their attitudes toward minority groups and their understanding of the problems raised by belonging to one or the other of these groups. Direct the group activities in this unit toward meeting the ignorance, misinformation, fears, and suspicions they cite.

Ask open-ended questions. These will stimulate highly thoughtful creative writing and will reveal negative attitudes based on stereotypes. You can use 10 or 15 minutes beforehand as a warm-up period, telling of your own experiences and feelings and asking students to talk about theirs. Then put the test questions on the board, asking each student to choose one question to write on. Assure the students that only you will read their papers. Examples of open-ended questions or sentences:

1. To my mind, races ought/ought not to be segregated because . . . .
2. I am/am not afraid of people whose skin color is not the same as my own because . . . .
3. I went to a party for blacks and whites, which turned out to be a bad/good experience because . . . .
4. When I think about (blacks, whites, Chinese, Jews) I see . . . .

Keep an anecdotal record of what individuals say and do during the course of the workshop. Study these records for evidence of changes in attitudes and actions.

Activity 2: Sources and Forms of Racism

Racism is learned from observation and emulation of the attitudes of parents, peers, and others children admire as they grow up. Racism results from overgeneralization—forming general attitudes without sufficient evidence, prejudging without the facts or in spite of the facts. Racism stereotypes people, attributing to individuals general characteristics, usually objectionable, of the group to which they seem to belong. Stereotyped thinking is often used to defame a person through rumor and hearsay. The concepts of observation, emulation, overgeneralization, stereotyping, and defamation may be written down on paper and handed out or placed on the blackboard to structure the beginning point for this activity.

Much behavior that reveals racism is in the form of verbal aggression, such as through rumors, jokes, doggerel, accusations, teasing, threats, and name-calling. Have students list and describe, from their own experience or knowledge, these and other ways that racism is learned.

Activity 3: Overcoming Racism

Racism is the result of ignorance concerning the nature of race. The scientific facts concerning the nature of race can frequently help to alleviate attitudes of racism. For example, there is no genetic superiority of any one race over another; all people are of the same species, and their observable differences are determined largely by environment and culture. When communication can be established between the majority and the minority, understanding and appreciation can ensue.

Have group members consider their attitudes toward the concept of race. Open-ended questions can be devised that fit the particular situation and that will not unduly disrupt the class. Special care should be taken if the class is nearly equally divided between black and white students. Discuss some of the reasons for the apparent differences between races. Do people really differ because of race? Why do many people tend to accept stereotypes about other people, never bothering to investigate? Why do so many stereotypes sound reasonable?

Roleplay a situation involving racism. For example, consider two mothers in a supermarket who have their children with them. As they chat, their children play. A little girl of another race steps up to play with them. Let the roleplayers act out alternate endings of this experience. Discuss the experience. How did the mothers feel? What influence did the mothers have on their children? What happened to the little girl of another race who wanted to play?

Have students work in groups, using dictionaries to look up definitions and discussing meanings of words and terms used in studying racism. A popular exercise is to have students brainstorm words and ideas they associate with key words. Have group discussions. Assign each group one human category, such as Frenchmen, Englishmen, Chinese,

Women, Men, Teachers, Parents, Politicians, and so on. Have them discuss the characteristics of their category of people. Show the students that they often think in stereotypical patterns.

CULMINATION AND EVALUATION

Since one of the primary objectives of this unit is to try to effect a positive change in attitudes toward minorities and toward racism in general, it is important to evaluate attitudes at the end of the workshop. Reuse the tests and other devices that were initially used to discover the students' racist attitudes. A comparison of the two results for each student would show what change, if any, took place. Keep a record of the nature of ethnic and racial makeup of conversation circles that form in succeeding group activities. Note whether the subject matter has any effect on the makeup of the groups when they are formed voluntarily.

SUPPLEMENTARY ACTIVITIES

The following suggestions are only a few of the means the counselor can use to evaluate the workshop. Each counselor will have other activities for student development and will want to expand these techniques. The counselor should adapt the evaluation to the particular group being worked with and use the evaluation as a reinforcement device.

- Have students write an essay or short story depicting what they think the ideal society should or would be like in terms of the relationship between racial, ethnic, and other societal groups.

- Ask that poems, essays, stories, and plays written by students be read to the class by the authors.

- Appoint a play committee to present a skit for an assembly, such as an excerpt from Duberman's *In White America* (1964) or an original play that has been developed in class. Students from other schools could be invited to play some of the roles if your school is not integrated.

- Ask students to hand in suggestions as to what the school system should do to help in the development of human rights. Discuss the suggestions.

- Have students check out their own neighborhood and city and write a report on the state of open society in their neighborhood and city.

- Ask the group to develop a series of techniques that could be used by its own members or others to eliminate racism. The group should specify the area they are developing techniques for (schools, industry, housing, etc.)

- Have a bulletin board committee work on different contributions to American culture—examples of paintings, sculptures, inventions, and medicine—made by members of various cultural groups.

- The United States has been described as a "melting pot." Have students prepare a speech to convince an audience that this is or is not the case.

- Ask each student to imagine being a black American arguing before the U.S. Supreme Court for the right to live in any section of the city. Ask students to use the Constitution and write an argument to convince the court.

Resources for use with this workshop may be obtained from a variety of sources. The counselor might make a very profitable excursion to the local library and check for books, films, filmstrips, pamphlets, and photograph and record collections on Negro history and culture, minority affairs, and civil rights. A conversation with the librarian may produce much material for the counselor to use in this workshop and ongoing activities. The librarian may be willing to keep an eye out for new materials coming into the library on the subject, and once the librarian becomes a part of such a program, new orders for library materials are more likely to include material with that focus. Some useful books include Bontemps (1963), David (1968), Katz (1968), Malcolm X (1964), Plaski and Brown (1967), Schulz (1969), and Wright (1968).

The counselor may also wish to contact national human relations and activist organizations that prepare bibliographies and publish related materials, distributed on request or for a nominal fee. Such organizations include the Anti-Defamation League of B'nai B'rith, Foundation for Change, the Center for Urban Education, and the Center for Humanistic Education at the School of Education, University of Massachusetts —Amherst.

After completing the workshop, the counselor may decide to organize a series of ongoing groups aimed at achieving racial awareness. The counselor will also find ways of sharing ideas and techniques with teachers in the school. Only when all those who have responsibility for the education of youngsters accept the need for education for racial awareness and become actively involved in that process can we hope for the final elimination of racism in this society.

REFERENCES

Autobiography of Malcolm X. New York: Grove Press, 1964.

Bontemps, A. *American Negro poetry.* New York: Hill & Wang, 1963.

David, J. *Growing up black.* New York: William Morrow, 1968.

Duberman, M. B. *In white America.* New York: New American Library, 1964.

Katz, W. L. *Teacher's guide to American Negro history.* New York: Quadrangle Books, 1968.

Plaski, H., & Brown, R., Jr. *The Negro almanac.* New York: Bellwether, 1967.

Schulz, D. A. *Coming up black.* Englewood Cliffs, N.J.: Prentice-Hall, 1969.

Wright, N., Jr. *Let's work together.* New York: Hawthorn Books, 1968.

Cultural Factors in
Group Counseling and Interaction

EDWARD KANESHIGE

The University of Hawaii has a student population that is somewhat unique in American colleges and universities. When the enrollment is broken down into various ethnic categories, statistics show that the majority of students are of Asian-American background. This is not surprising, since more than half the population of Hawaii is nonwhite. However, statistics on student use of the university's counseling services, which are provided on a nonfee, voluntary basis to the entire student body, show that the proportion of nonwhite (primarily Asian-American) students who use the services is considerably less. One of the prime reasons for this lack of acceptance and use of counseling services is the inherent conflict between the values of Asian-Americans and the values that are implicit in the counseling process.

Although different orientations in counseling place emphasis on different methods and techniques that are most likely to bring about success, the various methods appear to be in general agreement about the desired outcomes. Counseling emphasizes the individual worth of each person and his growth toward greater maturity. This may pose problems for the individual's family and friends, but generally, where there is a conflict, the growth of the individual is considered to be of greatest importance. Understanding the emotional aspect of one's behavior and motivations is an-other characteristic of counseling. Counselees are encouraged to be expressive of their emotions rather than stifle them. Since counseling is a verbal activity, the full and open expression of feelings, problems, conflicts, etc., is a necessary condition.

The values and goals of group counseling are similar to, if not identical with, those of individual counseling. Although each client must be aware of other group members, he is basically working toward his own self-understanding, growth, and maturity. The usual expectation is that one learns more when he is focusing directly on understanding his own dynamics and behavior, but it is possible that significant learning also occurs when one is attempting to aid another individual in understanding his dynamics and behavior.

Most counselors and psychologists accept these goals rather naturally, and they are frequently unaware that the conditions and goals of group counseling run counter to some of the values of their clients. They may not have examined the possibility that some of their fundamental beliefs and premises in counseling are actually contrary to the cultural heritage of some individuals they counsel. Asian-American students encounter a number of conflicts as they participate in the group counseling process—which has been recommended to them as a way of resolving their conflicts.

PERSONNEL AND GUIDANCE JOURNAL, 1972, Vol. 51, pp. 407-412.

CULTURAL PATTERNS IN GROUP COUNSELING

Let us first examine some of the conditions, goals, and techniques of group counseling as they relate to the values of one Asian-American group, Japanese-Americans, and then go on to see how the differences in cultural patterns emerge in group interactions.

Will Power

One of the first conflicts that the Japanese-American student faces is his accepting the fact that he has a problem he cannot adequately overcome by himself. This is not as easy as it may seem, since his culture views personal problems and shortcomings as being due to a lack of resolve and determination by the individual. The Japanese-American client finds it difficult to admit that he has a problem when he knows he will be told that he hasn't tried hard enough. His culture believes that understanding one's motivations may be important but that the primary cause of human failure is insufficient will power.

Consequently, this client sees that taking his problems to a counselor cannot solve the conflict and that the only hope he has is to try harder. If the problem persists and continues to cause pain and unhappiness, he develops a fatalistic attitude and bears the burden in stoic fashion. It is therefore not surprising that he somatizes many emotional problems and, if he does bring them to a counseling center, it is only after considerable time and pain.

Nonconfrontation

In many group counseling formats there is only a minimum of structure and direction. The group leader may start each session off, but much of the content and focus is voluntarily initiated and pursued by individual group members. A group member is expected not only to share of himself and his personal concerns but also to become actively involved in the dynamics and problems of other members. To be involved means not only to empathize and be supportive but also to be open and to confront others who are self-deceptive or unable to accept their ability to contribute to a problem's resolution.

The Japanese group member is deterred from directly confronting other group members because he has been taught that it is impolite to put people on the spot; that it is presumptuous on his part to be assertive; and that the group leader is the most knowledgeable person and all should therefore defer to his greater wisdom and judgment. So he finds it difficult to make his share of comments and questions, even when he feels that he has a valid contribution to make.

Humility

A related factor in the degree of participation is the issue of humility. Japanese are taught to be self-effacing because their culture values humility and modesty. "Don't be a show-off or engage in any behavior that smacks of being a braggart" is a common admonition. An example of the way this value works is found in the elementary schools. The teacher asks anyone who knows the answer to a problem or question to raise his hand. She is certain that the problem is not overly difficult and that there are some children who know the answer. However, she is greeted with what appears to be complete nonresponsiveness. No hands go up. No one wants to be a show-off, even though many would enjoy praise and recognition. Similarly, in a counseling group the Japanese client struggles with his desire to volunteer comments and suggestions because of the gnawing feeling that to do so would label him a show-off.

Shame

Another prime value of the Japanese culture is to not bring shame to the family

name. The Japanese individual is encouraged to perform deeds that will bring honor to the family, but his failure to attain positive public recognition is not a major consequence. On the other hand, bringing dishonor to the family name is of such importance that family members are repeatedly admonished against performing deeds that could bring disgrace to the family. The Japanese feel that family problems and conflicts are to be resolved within the family circle and that the only image that can be publicly displayed is a socially acceptable and consistent one. Therefore, the admission and display of personal inadequacy, even in a counseling group, is a sign of familial defect, and this brings shame to the family.

Related to this is the Japanese concept that the individual is of minimal importance as compared to the importance of the family. The individual exists and is important only in relation to his group. Thus, the public exposure of family conflicts in the process of resolving individual conflicts and eventually achieving self-fulfillment is an unacceptable display of selfishness and exaggerated, self-importance. Reaction and punishment generally follow swiftly.

The existence of these conflicting values for the Japanese group is not unique. Every minority ethnic group experiences value conflicts to some extent.

Additional problems are created, however, when other group members and the counselor misunderstand or misinterpret the Japanese client's seeming lack of effort to help himself. Being judged as not trying or not wanting to improve because he doesn't ask for help or can't talk about his problems compounds the problems that he has. And to cry out at this unfair judgment seems futile, since it does not alleviate the problem.

CULTURAL PATTERNS IN GROUP INTERACTION

Let us now examine the ways in which the differences in cultural values and patterns show up in interactions among group members from Japanese and Caucasian-Western backgrounds. Four values or patterns of behavior—verbal participation, emotional expression, avoidance of conflict, and acceptance of authority—have been selected to illustrate these differences.

Verbal Participation

Verbal participation is the extent to which an individual verbally participates in the group. Although there are individual differences among members of the same nationality group, anyone who has lived in Hawaii for any length of time would generally agree that Caucasians talk more than Japanese do. It is for this reason that, in the schools, Japa-

181

nese students are urged, challenged, and encouraged to participate more in classroom discussions, while their Caucasian classmates are gently restrained and encouraged to let their relatively nonverbal fellow students say more.

Let us examine how the verbal participation pattern operates in a group situation. In a group composed of teachers working on improving their self-understanding and their interrelationships, the following exchange took place between a highly verbal Caucasian teacher and a Japanese teacher:

Caucasian Teacher: I don't feel that it's really fair for you local [Japanese] teachers to remain silent and force us [Caucasian teachers] to carry the ball in our discussion with the principal. I feel that it's important that someone speak up for us teachers; but since no one will, I feel that I have to take the responsibility, even though I would prefer not to.

Japanese Teacher: Gee, that's really interesting. What I was thinking while you were talking was that I hoped you would realize that you were talking too much and that you were monopolizing the time. I didn't want to say so, because I felt that it would be impolite for me to do so. Also, I kinda felt that you had a need to talk and be recognized by the group, so I felt that we should be tolerant and understanding of you. Actually, I felt that we were the ones who were behaving responsibly by not speaking out and complaining about your excessive verbalization.

In pursuing this exchange, it became clear that there was a wide difference in opinion as to what talking and silence meant and whether one behavior was more desirable than the other. The Caucasian position seemed to be that (a) a responsible person talks so that something can be accomplished; (b) silence does not accomplish anything; (c) a person who is quiet is either not very bright or does not have any ideas. On the other hand, the Japanese position appeared to be that (a) it is better to be quiet than to ramble on and say nothing or say something that is not well thought out; (b) the talkative person doesn't think very much because he is too busy talking; (c) the talkative person is essentially an attention seeking, narcissistic individual. The Japanese cultural pattern is to be quiet and listen to others who have more wisdom than you do; the Caucasian tradition is to exercise your initiative and responsibility by talking. If you are uncertain about whether or not to say something, the Japanese view is to remain silent; the Caucasian view is to say it anyway.

Emotional Expression

Emotional expression is defined here as the extent to which an individual reveals his inner feelings to others. It is closely related to, but not the same as, verbal participation.

In most situations the Japanese person tends to remain nonexpressive. He has been raised since childhood not to show his emotions. Thus, although he may be moved by what is occurring in the group, he is almost instinctively restrained from revealing his concern, and his facial expression remains passive. The Caucasian, whose upbringing has nurtured emotional expression, interprets this behavior as demonstrating a lack of feeling about what is transpiring. One Caucasian characterized this behavior as a sign of noncaring, and it brought forth this exclamation from him: "Doesn't this have any effect on you? Don't you care at all?" An individual who is unaffected by another person's suffering and pain is considered almost nonhuman and frequently becomes the focus of anger.

Thus the Caucasian view seems to be that (a) emotional expression is good; (b) the individual who is emotionally expressive is mature and accepting of himself. The Japanese view appears to be that (a) emotional expression is a sign of immaturity; (b) one should strive for adult behavior, and emotional restraint is one example of this.

Avoidance of Conflict

The Japanese culture values the individual who subordinates himself. The individual who sacrifices himself to avoid conflict even when his position may be justified is frequently looked upon with commendation. The individual who insists on his way, even when justified, is often looked upon with disapproval and is frequently condemned. In a verbal dispute, then, the Japanese individual tends to disengage himself from the argument, even when he is convinced that his position has more validity than that of the other person.

Acceptance of Authority

Japanese children are taught very early in life that they are the least worthy and the least knowledgeable and that to be presumptuous is a cardinal sin. They are taught to speak only when absolutely certain, and even then only with extreme modesty. In groups, this type of upbringing is evidenced in the extent to which the Japanese individual wants the goals of the group sessions to be clearly described and specified and his subsequent willingness to stay with the original goals. When it appears that the group is deviating from the original goal, the Japanese individual attempts to get the group back to its original goal. The Caucasian individual sees this conforming behavior as unnecessary and even undesirable and would prefer that the group have the freedom to move in more creative ways. The Japanese person sees this kind of free-flowing behavior as another mark of immaturity and a lack of personal discipline. Imposing rules and regulations is therefore seen as a deprivation of freedom from one viewpoint and as a stimulator of freedom from the other.

THE COUNSELOR'S ROLE

An individual's cultural heritage influences his attitudes and behavior in his daily life. It also influences his acceptance of counseling as a desirable method of increasing his self-understanding and self-worth. Even when he accepts the goals and methods of counseling, however, he may find that his personal values and beliefs are in conflict with them. It is important that counselors understand and recognize the existence of these potential conflicts and that they *do not judge the Asian-American client from the Western-white value orientation.* To do so would hinder or stop the progress of counseling and possibly create even more conflicts for some individuals.

In group counseling, the counselor can work toward (a) helping the Asian-American client overcome the cultural restrictions that hamper his emotional growth and (b) helping other group members grow in their understanding and acceptance of minority group members. The group counselor can do this in a number of ways.

1. He can encourage the Asian-American client to be a more verbal participant by providing a group climate that is supportive and nonthreatening.

2. He can demonstrate that he understands the uniqueness of the Asian-American by verbalizing some of the cultural value differences and by sensitively recognizing the internal struggle that the Asian-American faces in expressing himself.

3. He can aid the verbally "nonexpressive" and "nonaggressive" Asian-American client who is struggling to express his feelings by minimizing interruptions by other group members. When two group members try to speak at the same time, he can tactfully restrain the more talkative one and encourage the one who has more difficulty in expressing himself.

4. He can reassure the Asian-American client and all group members of the confidentiality in the counseling process.

5. He can try to improve the accuracy of the interpretations made by group members by pointing out and clarifying what is happening, as in the following example:

Client #1 (Caucasian): I don't see it the same way that you do. I think you're wrong. [He proceeds to describe his views.]

Client #2 (Japanese): [no response]

Counselor (to Client #2): Do you feel that your understanding of the situation was wrong and that Client #1's interpretation was right?

Client #2: No. I still feel I was right, and I think that Client #1's explanation doesn't make sense at all.

Counselor: How come you didn't say that?

Client #2: I didn't want to hurt his feelings, and besides, it isn't worth the hassle.

Counselor: It's important that you do express your feelings both for yourself, so you can be understood, and for the others, so that their perceptions can be more accurate.

6. He can challenge aggressive assertions, and critical statements made to Asian-American clients by their Caucasian counterparts where he feels that the assertions are only partially accurate. Where he might ordinarily wait for the attacked person to defend himself, the counselor may have to recognize that the "passive" Asian-American client may not defend himself because of his cultural inhibitions. The counselor's actively stepping in and commenting on the statements and behaviors would be important in improving the understanding of what is happening.

7. He must recognize that he is being a model for all group members, but especially so for Asian-Americans, who value authority. His tone of voice and manner of interaction with each group member are unconsciously and sometimes consciously noted and may do much to encourage or stifle verbal expressiveness.

8. He can help the group process by alerting group members to listen more carefully and to consider the observed behavior from the standpoint of the person being observed rather than that of the observer. "What does it mean to you?" and "What do you think it means to Client X?" are questions that might stimulate group members to think beyond the usual interpretations.

9. He can help the Asian-American client recognize that he is not necessarily denying his cultural identity if he does not always act consistently with his values. The client can be helped to recognize that he can rationally choose to change his pattern of behavior because the new behavior is more in keeping with the kind of person he wants to be and not necessarily because it is merely conforming to society's codes. For example, he may decide to change his behavior when he understands that his quiet, unassuming, nonassertive behavior is being read by non-Asians as inarticulate, conforming, and obsequious.

In summary, the group counselor can help the Asian-American client to be more expressive in communicating his feelings and thoughts to the group without negating his cultural values. The counselor can work with other group members in creating an atmosphere that increases the possibility that each individual will be accepted regardless of his background and values. Counseling can be more than therapeutic; it can also be rewardingly educational.

RECOMMENDED READING

Burrows, E. G. *Hawaiian Americans: An account of the mingling of Japanese, Chinese, Polynesian, and American cultures.* Hamden, Conn.: Archon Books, 1970.

Fullmer, D. Characteristics of Hawaii youth. *Hawaii Personnel and Guidance Association Journal,* 1971, *1,* 76–78.

Kitano, H. H. L. *The evolution of a subculture.* Englewood Cliffs, N. J.: Prentice-Hall, 1969.

LaViolette, F. E. *Americans of Japanese ancestry.* Toronto, Canada: The Canadian Institute of International Affairs, 1945.

Okimoto, D. I. *American in disguise.* New York: Walker/Weatherhill, 1971.

Patterson, C. H. *Theories of counseling and psychotherapy.* New York: Harper & Row, 1966.

Smith, B. *Americans from Japan.* Philadelphia: J. B. Lippincott, 1948.

Sue, D. W., & Sue, S. Counseling Chinese-Americans. *Personnel and Guidance Journal,* 1972, *50,* 637–644.

CHAPTER V

GROUP PROCEDURES WITH ADULTS AND SPECIAL COUNSELING PROBLEMS

THE THEME-CENTERED INTERACTIONAL METHOD

Group Therapists as Group Educators

by

Ruth C. Cohn*

Roots and Purpose

Group therapists are challenged by a world which needs improvement in education and communication. There is pressure from inside and outside of our profession to enlarge our scope of activities and to share our knowledge and experience with individuals and groups which can profit from our experience and skills. In the last few years, many community action programs have faltered not only for lack of funds or for political reasons but also because of a lack of skilled group leaders. Without specialized training as consultants to communities, group therapists often have felt puzzled or harassed facing situations where the job required modifications of their therapeutic skills. Meanwhile Growth Potential Centers are opening up all over the country encountering the public's needs with the help of professionals and paraprofessionals whose training rarely provides them with the specific skills groupleading requires.

The theme-centered interactional workshop method has been designed and practiced to fill this gap in our profession. It is primarily applicable to small groups which share a common interest and which are conducted by a professional group therapist. However, it's principles have also been used in leading convention audiences up to

*This is an enlarged and modified version of a paper with the same title read at the Convention of the American Group Psychotherapy Association, Jan. 1970.

JOURNAL OF GROUP PSYCHOANALYSIS AND PROCESS, Winter 1969-70, pp. 19-36.

500 people and in large conflict groups.* And the method in modified version has been helpful for teachers, organizers, clergy, paraprofessionals, etc.

This paper endeavors to put forth some of the basic principles and techniques of the theme-centered interactional workshop method for professional group therapists.

The theme-centered interactional workshop is an offspring of group therapy and psychoanalytic theory. Many years ago this author became fascinated by the fact that most group therapy patients described their therapy as "the most important learning experience of my life," while so many students in academic settings seemed to count the days until their escape to freedom. The question arose whether it was the theme of group therapy — "I want to feel and function better" — which made the difference between living learning and dead learning? The emphasis on self rather than on external themes? Or was there something specifically alive in the method of group therapy itself? Would it be possible to introduce into other learning situations those elements of the group therapy model which promoted the participants' passionate involvement?

Group therapy relates to and respects the feelings of each individual. The heaviness in someone's breathing, his quickened heartbeat, his tears or joyfulness become the group's concern. Feelings are respected as man's inalienable right — whether they relate to his realistic or illusionary vision of this world. The structure and atmosphere of the group therapy setting encourages the expression of emotions and the validation and deepening of communication which are the root of the passionate involvement of group therapy patients — hardly paralleled in classrooms and seminars. Could one create

*Amer. Assoc. for Humanist Psychology, (AAHP) 1969
Am Psychol. Assoc., (APA) 1969
Deutsche Assoziation fur Gruppentherapie and Gruppendynamik
(DAGG) 1969 — Pontiac State Hospital, Mich. 1969

educational settings which would allow teachers and students to experience and exchange feelings in the classroom and yet to remain related to the theme under study?

Most schools of psychotherapy share respect for feelings, for resistance and avoidance patterns. Freudian conceptualization differentiates between those feelings which promote progress and integration, and others which resist insight and change. Almost always the work on feelings which indicate resistance takes precedence over the work on content. The therapeutic process is therefore slow, but solidly rooted in non-cluttered ground. In gestalt therapy theory, emphasis is placed on feelings which the patient tries to avoid: the process of learning to accept and to bear his feelings is seen as curative and clearing up "unfinished business." In experiential group therapy, the authenticity of feelings is seen as the core of therapy and worthwhile living. In comparing psychotherapeutic and other learning groups it became obvious that personality characteristics and feelings were not sufficiently honored in any other educational or communicative setting. Knowledge in schools could probably be gained more efficiently if anxiety, preoccupation and avoidance patterns would be dealt with prior to the requirement of learning content. Such methods would distinctly differ from classroom methods where unobtrusive disturbances were either disregarded or authoritatively "dismissed," while openly disruptive students were sent out of the room, suspended, expelled, or in desperation put into the care of a psychotherapist. Teachers have certainly not been trained to take time and interest to reassure themselves of the continued attentiveness of their students and the group's cohesion around the theme under discussion. Even less would a teacher work on his own resistances against teaching – be it a momentary aversion or preoccupation, anger against the establishment, rejection of students or a deep-seated anxiety about exposing himself.

The first theme-centered interactional workshop was conducted by this author in 1955 with students in a private psychoanalytic training group. (1961) The method borrowed from group therapy the respect for resistances and the explicit concern with feelings as an important ingredient of all learning. However, in contrast to psychotherapy, feelings were not considered the main theme to be explored but were accepted as an important element of all learning processes which had to be taken into consideration and sometimes given more attention. The main theme that prevailed was the topic under study. Yet when any individual's feelings became so disturbing to him as to interfere with his participation, attention was given to the disturbance. The rule soon became "disturbances take precedence." This rule corresponded to the psychoanalytic maxim of giving precedence to resistance. The results of these private training workshops were convincing and stimulated colleagues to encourage the author to modify the method for applications in industry and agencies for improved communication.* It was a relatively small step to convert the training into a general educational and communication method which was then named the Theme-Centered Interactional Workshop.

Philosophy and Structure

The Theme-Centered Interactional Method has a firm structure which is based on a holistic and humanist philosophy. Man is seen as a psychobiological unit and, as such, experiencing himself as both autonomous (making choices – determining) and conditioned (being determined and perishable). Man is also a social being, and as such, interdependent and in the steady flow of give-and-take with things and people. Growth occurs as people become more aware and more effective in using their autonomy and interdependence. We mature as our choices become more and more realistic and relevant to our own fulfillment in this world, and the reality of human bondage which ties each individual's own fulfillment to the fulfillment of all others. A person who makes choices by default (e.g., through apathy) or by distortion (e.g., by transference) learns to shed these immature ways

---

* William Zielonka, Ph.D.
  Sol Rosenberg, Ph.D., Peoria State Hospital, Ill., 1962.

and develops realism about his autonomy and interdependence. (A person who makes choices by "doing what he feels like" without consideration of the environment or interpersonal relationships is autistic rather than autonomous.) This philosophy is expressed in the Theme-Centered Interactional Workshop rules for participants and groupleaders. The stringent structure of the method is usually not apparent to the novice (as the discipline of meaningful free verse is not discernable to the layman) yet it is the stable directedness through philosophy and rules which primarily differentiates the Theme-Centered Interactional Workshop from free group process groups.

External yet important arrangements concern the specificity of time and space. Workshop series may take place in five or ten two-hour or continuous weekly sessions, a week-end, a week, in a group leader's office, a school, business place, etc. Each series centers around a theme.

Theme

The theme must be specific to the group's needs or interests (e.g., intra-organizational relationships, a research or activity project, or a psychological or interpersonal conflict theme such as "The Therapeutic Milieu — toward a Team approach in a Hospital" or "Bridging Gaps between Parents, Teachers and Administration" or "Challenge of Change" etc.

The content and working of the theme is important, e.g., the theme "Conflict" has a negative hypnotic effect on a group and is likely to keep the participants in conflict, while "Conflict Management" suggests work toward constructive resolutions. A workshop on "Writer's Block" never came off the ground while others called "Freeing Creativity in Writing" were successful. Themes may be neutral for research groups but they should imply active choices for activity groups. A workshop is likely to fail when participants are put into a negative mood by words like "Problems in Raising Children" or "Disturbances in Handling Money."

189

The Theme-Centered Interactional Workshop can be graphically seen as a triangle in a globe.

The *triangle* presents the workshop setting which is organized in awareness of dealing with the three basic factors of all interactional groups:

1) The individual: I,

2) The group: We,

3) The theme: It.

The *globe* designates the environment in which the workshop takes place: time, location, make-up of the group and the auspices under which the workshop series takes place. The Theme-Centered Interactional Method gives equal importance to the three basic points of the triangle and their relationships, and keeps the "globe" in mind. The richness of this simple structure is evident if one visualizes the complicated structure of the "I" as a psychobiological unit, of the "We" as the interrelatedness of the group's members, and the theme as the infinite combination of concrete and abstract factors. (The theme, whether it concerns people, matter or theories is always an "It" — an object. The experienced "You" becomes a "We", the observed "You," a "Thing").*

The leader's role is to be the guardian of the method. He structures the group according to time, place, and environment ("the globe") and he promotes dynamic balancing of the triad factors which include his own "I" — his own subjective participation.

---

*This ability to "thing" people (a concept coined by George Bach) appears to me as the greatest stumbling block in our achieving social progress. When people are "It" or "They", I do not identify with them as if "They" were "I's" (Like me). They are then "Things" I may not give a damn about, can shoot at or let starve.

The group leader's initial attention is geared to the "globe" — time, place and circumstances. He estimates the required time by the participants' backgrounds, the volume of the task or object of study, and the group's financial pressures. The location is equally important, in terms of attention to psychological factors involved (such as what this room is generally used for) and seating arrangements, avoidance of outside interferences, noise, etc. (There is horror in a workshop experience in a non-air-conditioned, one-way-vision screen room on a hot summer day.) Attention to the auspices under which the series takes place includes the hierachy in the organization: who governs the setting, who pays the bill, who is factually and/or emotionally involved in sponsoring the program and who opposes it. (These aspects in planning resemble the considerations of child therapists who need the parents' cooperation if they are to treat the child successfully.)

The circumstances also include the questions whether participants are a "captive" group (as in prisons, or less literally so, in situations where participation is an obligation to the work place — teachers in schools, staffs of hospitals, groups of counselees, etc.), or whether the participants voluntarily enroll for an announced workshop, or ask a group leader to organize a workshop for them. Any confusion about time, place, and especially the auspices under which the workshop takes place undermines successful work. Once a workshop is in process, the attention to the "globe" recedes, and the leader focuses on the triangle of individual, group and theme. In this work, however, as in any other therapeutic or educational endeavor, the spirit of what is being done as well as the personality of the group leader is essential for process and outcome. Techniques are nothing but "sounding brass and tinkling cymbals", unless they are used by a group leader who combines his knowledge with personal warmth and a constructive social philosophy. However, even these personality facets can be trained and are not in most instances genetic destiny or immovably fixated at an early age. (1968)

The theme-centered interactional workshop method puts the basic holistic principles into practical use by giving equal attention to the somatepsychic and spiritual aspects of the individual, (I), the group (We), and the theme (It). The balance between I, We and It is never perfect but must shift in a dynamic forward direction. The group process results from shifting balance the way a bicycle pitches because of the rider's shifting his weight from pedal to pedal. If perfect balance were ever achieved, the process would come to an end. The group leader's job is to employ his weight always toward the "un-used pedal," that is from "I" to "We", from "theme" to "I", from "We" to "theme", etc. He has to be sensitive to appropriate timing. Intervening too early or too late has an equally stifling effect on the group process — whether he neglects or over-protects an individual, goes along with unrelated group interaction or remains with a theme while group cohesion gets lost. It is important to maintain group cohesion. This is established when all participants — in whatever unique individual ways — are rallying around a sub-theme:

In a workshop on "Black and White America and I," George was upset about people's indolence. He was close to tears. If the leader did not react to George and try to re-direct the group's attention to other issues, he would perpetuate and cement George's feelings about people's aloofness and in fact promote indolence in the group (or elicit the group's wrath against himself). If he went deeply into an analysis of George's life or of the group's stirred-up feelings, he would conduct a therapy group and sacrifice the theme under discussion. As it was, in this instance the leader encouraged George to express his emotions, and George, in turn, responded with memories of childhood deprivations. He remembered in tears that he had to move away from his home town as a little boy shortly after having been threatened by blindness. During his illness he had experienced support from friends whom he had to lose forever by leaving town. The participants were moved by George's story and his angry and sorrowful tears; they also confronted him with his irrational holding onto a feeling of isolation and deprivation. As soon as the emotional climate permitted it, the group leader related George's experience to the theme of the study: "Black and White America and I." There were many bridges: Aloofness, indolence, uprootedness, reactions to other people's pain, rightful demands, etc.

Dynamic balancing means observing correct timing with regard to the emotional and intellectual needs of individuals, the total group, and their willingness to work with the theme. (Timing in an interactional workshop can be compared to timing in dream interpretations in classical analysis. If the dreamer is allowed to continue with free associations indefinitely, the possibility of understanding the dream is lost. If his associations are cut off too soon, the frame of reference in which the dream can be interpreted will be insufficient.)

The emphasis on equal awareness for the triangle "I, We, and It", signifies the theme-centered interactional method. Academic teaching and round table discussions concentrate primarily on the "It" (the theme aspect), classical therapy on the "I" (individual) and group therapy and encounter groups on the "We-and-I" (the group). Both T-groups and the theme-centered interactional group adhere to the "I-We-It" structure but differ in shading through their historical bases: T-groups were derived from field theory, sociology, group dynamics and primary interest in organizations; the theme-centered interactional method was conceived on the basis of psychoanalytic therapy, group therapy, group dynamics, and primary interest in education.

Techniques and Ground Rules

In the first session of a workshop series, special care is given to promote the holistic spirit within the structure of "the triangle in the globe." The leader is geáred to sensitizing the participants toward recognizing their autonomy and interdependence.

Introductory techniques serve the purpose of establishing the importance of being "I", being part, and working on a theme in a group climate which promotes awareness, compassion and cooperativeness and the sense of the importance of the here-and-now. Such techniques require careful anticipatory considerations about the respective workshop — its purpose and goal, the likely expectancies and anxiety levels of the participants, and their educational and emotional level, etc.

A frequently effective initial procedure for well motivated groups (those where members contract individually rather than organizational or conflict groups) is the request for a prolonged silence. The leader gives successively, and with several minutes between each of the three steps, the following instructions to the participants:

1. To *think* about the theme and to *remember* experiences related to it.

2. To be aware of experiences and feelings, perceptions and sensations in the *present group*.

3. To direct attention to a specifically *designed task* which relates to the given theme. (The leader always carefully prepares this task ahead of time so as to include in it the participant's immediate experience to the given theme.) This is essential. The living-learning hypothesis proposes that all learning proceeds centrally in the here-and-now, which encompasses centrifugally the past and the future. The more explicitly the here-and-now can be used in the task, the more interesting becomes the studied theme.

Example: Theme: Training Intuition.

Auspices: Voluntary group. The leader asks for a relaxed silence with closed eyes.

1. Please think about these concepts: "training and intuition." Have you ever put these words together before? What do they mean to you? Did these words make you sign up for this workshop? Think about what you have been calling intuition and what you have read about it. Do you think it is inborn as a unique gift that only some people have, or does everybody have a talent for intuition that we might train? Please be silent and think about the concept of "training intuition."

2. Please open your eyes. How do you feel to be in this room with a group of strangers and to be challenged to think about "training intuition?" How do you feel right now — do you feel easy, uneasy, excited, bored — what does your stomach say?

3. Choose one person in this room whom you don't know. Think of something you would like to tell this person which might be of importance to him (her) and to you.

These instructions are given with several minutes of silence for each individual instruction — the first one to induce thinking with personal involvement, the second to promote awareness of sensations and feelings, and the third one to connect thoughts and feelings to a task related to the theme. To say something important to a person whom I don't know — which turns out to be true — means to be intuitive. The alternative is to be in error.

After the introduction, the leader puts forth intermittently and with considered timing the ground rules which are directed toward promoting personal interaction between the group members around the theme, and to encourage each person's awareness of his autonomy and interdependence.

1. Let us *give to this group and get from this group whatever each of you and I want to give and to get* here in this session in terms of ourselves, others and the theme. (This

195

rule encourages the autonomous choice of giving and getting in the interdependence with others. The following rules give more specific instructions in the same spirit and goal-directedness.)

2. *Be the chairman of yourself:* speak up or be silent as you want to. (This rule does not say "when you feel like it" but "when you want to." This encourages every participant to be his own *chairman with his own needs and agenda and with the needs of the group in mind.* Whenever all group members achieve personal chairmanship, the group leader — who is chairman of himself as well as the chairman of the total group — can temporarily relax his overall function and act only in the role of a "participant-chairman.")

3. *Only one person can speak at a time.* When several people speak up at the same time — they shall talk to each other. (In various ways, this rule leads to important interaction between group members who must talk out or fight out who holds the floor. Incidents of conflict as well as "side-conversations" which are against the rule become important facets of the inter-actional theme-centered process.)

4. *If you are bored, angry, in pain, preoccupied or unable to participate in any way, bring it to the group. (Disturbances take precedence* because the disturbed group member is "absent" and he and the group lose out if a link is missing. Each individual and therefore the total group achieve more for themselves and the penetration of the theme if all participants in their unique ways are simultaneously involved with themselves, each other and the theme. This ground rule is occasionally abused. A group member may report any minute annoyance and emotion as a "disturbance." The disruption of the group by such surplus communications and their meaning for the incessant speaker will then be picked up as the essential sub-theme for this moment.)

5. *State yourself* "per I", and not "per We." ("We" is either a summation of all "I's" for which group validation is needed, or a fictional generalization which usually serves to avoid autonomous choice and responsibility.)*

6. *Statements are usually preferable to questions.* (Questions often are hiding places and are limiting. Corresponding personal statements are more revealing and stimulate others. Example: Question of group member: "What do you think about giving kids too much freedom?" Group Leader: "I do not relate well to such generalized questions. Please make the statement you based your question on!" Group Member: "My kids didn't turn out well – I think I spoiled them.")

7. Be aware of *messages from your body and of bodily expressions of others.* (This rule is an aid to preventing intellectualization and in promoting awareness of other aspects of people's personalities and perceptivity. Physical awareness is an important experience in itself as well as a potent tool for recognizing feelings.)

Directives for Group Therapists Functioning as Theme-Centered Interactional Leaders

The group leader's technical directives are implicit in his task of keeping dynamic balance of the triangle – individual, group and theme. While the educator and discussion leader are more likely to

---

*Impersonal speech characterizes evasiveness and lack of awareness of personal responsibility. The "We" and "It" spirit is, however, so commonly accepted as for instance to make acceptance of this paper in this Journal conditional on changing the writer's style from "I" to "It". This Journal's editor, however, graciously suggested I state my viewpoint in a footnote. The Theme-Centered Interactional Method rests upon the conviction that the "We"-experience is based upon each individual participant's "I"-experience. Correspondingly: The more personal a writer expresses himself – not only as an abstract intellect but as a full blooded person, the more likely will the reader respond to the experiences and thoughts of the writer. The theme serves as the bridge from person to person.

over-emphasize theme versus individual and group, the group therapist as group leader has to make a deliberate effort to see that the theme is given its due. His training and experience guide him toward professional intuition for individual needs and group interactional processes. He now has to learn to give equal emphasis to the given theme or task. (This shift in emphasis parallels a situation in which an architect, a master of building residential houses, has to add a new dimension of his vision if he engages in city planning.)

1. *The theme is treated as a connecting link to which each individual and the group relate.* (Individual and group members are encouraged to react to the theme in their own unique ways — cognitively, emotionally, as total personalities. How do I react, feel, think, in relation to the theme — what are my experiences with "Challenge of Communication", "Understanding Modern Poetry", "Improving Communication Between Staff Members," etc.) Undoubtedly, the penetration of a theme in a personal way can and does often lead not only toward the expected and promoted personal growth, but also toward therapeutic processes within the groping personality. But, methodologically, this aspect is incidental. Group cohesion is promoted by concentrating on the theme rather than by eliciting emotional responses and reactions between group members. Emotional responses are considered to be important and are recognized as such. They may be linked to the theme or discussed as joyful or disturbing experiences. However, in contrast to group therapy, personal and interpersonal reactions are not pursued as the major theme (unless the given theme of study or the task happens to coincide with these inter-group reactions).

2. *Transference distortions are only explored when they are either relevant for the theme or interfere with the individual's or group participation.* (Example: A participant complains about the group leader's paying less attention to

him than to others. The group leader responds with concern about this person's feelings. This may include empathy, his personal reactions or generalized interpretation. The group often wants to help and "therapize" the troubled group member, and the group leader may go along with this as long as the emotions about the incident are strong: as soon as possible he leads to another sub-theme ("stepping on another pedal").

3. The *Group atmosphere has to be accepting* and basically non-critical if the theme is to be in balance as a partner in the triad. (If the group climate were basically negative — especially in the beginning — participants would have a hard time working on any other theme than their hurt feelings, rage, taking sides, etc. If the group leader himself were to be critical and rejecting in the beginning of a series, theme-centered interaction would either not take place or remain on a personally uninvolved level. It is preferable that the group leader, in the beginning of a workshop, react to every statement, including hostility by group members towards himself or others, in a receptive way. He may reflect what has been said with Rogerian skill or add something to what has been stated in an illustrative or supplementary spirit. He may encounter statements with his own thoughts and feelings — even negative ones — if he makes it clear that he accepts his own as well as other people's hostility as normal components of living. This interactive procedure gives group members the experience that each person's feelings and opinions are respected as their way of being — which may include desire for change. Once all feelings and thoughts are accepted as an integral part of people, hostility, affection, sexual desires or rejections, criticism, etc., can be much more easily assimilated by the group. As soon as a positive group climate is established, the group leader becomes less active, and a free flow of interaction in the group takes place.)

Example: Group Member: "I feel I don't want to be in with the group and I don't want to be out either. I'm just on the fringe and I'm very angry about this." Group Leader: "Try to permit yourself to be on the fringe. Just be on the fringe without torturing yourself." Group Member (at end of session): "I felt so good being in by being out and not feeling guilty. Later on, I was with it and enjoyed that too."

4. *All rules given* to the participants *pertain equally to the group leader* who is at his best if he follows the rules given to the participants. (This includes specifically the rule of not asking questions (although exceptions are necessary) as well as the rule of bringing up emotional disturbances if they prevent him from being a full participant. If a group leader states his conflict or deep emotions of whatever kind, this is usually helpful to the group, while keeping disturbances under cover almost invariably leads to some lack of group cohesion. This is especially true if conflicts between co-leaders are not acknowledged.)

5. *The group leader keeps in mind his function of balancing between "I-We-It"* and selects from his own experiences, thoughts and feelings those for open communication which he deems helpful for the dynamics of the balancing process. If the group has turned over-intellectual, he may state his own feelings. If the group emotes without concern for the theme, or intellectual connections, he may give some of his thoughts or interpret the emotional flow of the group. Many other techniques of shifting the weight within the triangle are useful; e.g., brief summaries of what has just happened or generalizations or interpretations serving as closure of a sub-theme, and leading the group to shifting the balance toward another topic. (Interpretations in psychotherapy and in interactional groups are useful for cementing achievements and insights; they are out of place and harmful prior to a completed process or experience.)

6. Deeper *pathology of group members are not coped with as therapeutic problems*. All persons' statements are observed under the aspect of the here-and-now of theme, the individual and the group. (The group leader can in many ways accept paranoid, depressive, withdrawn or overbearing behavior with full respect for this group member's feelings and thoughts. He can also respect the various group reactions toward the disturbed person. Participation of a pre-psychotic person is rarely dangerous for this group member himself because of the supportive attitude of the workshop atmosphere; he may, however, produce some strain for the group leader and the group. Rarely and only under accidental circumstances or the group leader's misjudgement, will an acute psychotic episode be prompted by an interactional workshop – less likely than in daily life. The "globe" – the given circumstances – must give the group conductor the lead, whether he can or should exclude a severely disturbed group member for his own or the group's sake. In community groups, this is often not possible nor desirable.)

7. There are, however, times when it is possible and worthwhile to deal with a temporary acute disturbance of a group member with the help of *shortcut therapeutic techniques*. (Such techniques may include brief existential encounter, role playing, gestalt therapy, vertical interventions, working on bodily tensions, playing a pertinent interactional game, promoting feedback, etc. Whatever techniques are used, it is the respect for each person's inalienable right to being what he is at any given moment which must be transparent to the group. The "nihil nocere" (never harm the patient) maxim is the most important guideline for any therapeutic intervention on the "I"-line of the "I-We-It" triangle in the community theme-centered interactional workshop.)

The theme-centered interactional workshop has been used in classrooms (from mathematics to poetry), recreational centers (with adolescent and adult group leaders), with hospital staffs, business management, with black and white groups, social agencies, migrant teachers, school boards, community centers, etc. Teachers have their classes in the direction of living-learning groups. Further theoretical work on exact modifications of this method for non-therapist group leaders is in process.* Group therapists are likely to remain prominent teachers of a method which we hope will increasingly interest larger educational and community organizations.

REFERENCES

1. Cohn, Ruth C.: "A Group-Therapeutic Workshop on Counter-transference," *Int. J. Gr. Psychother.*, Vol. XI, July, 1961.

2. Cohn, Ruth C.: "Group Therapeutic Techniques as Educational Means in the Training of Psychoanalysts," in *Group Psychotherapy Today.* Basel and New York: S. Karger, 1965, pp. 48-58. (See also: H. Strean, "The Personal Impact of Group Training," *Loc. Cit.* pp. 33-38.

3. Cohn, Ruth C.: "From Couch to Circle to Community," in *Group Therapy*, Dr. Hendrik Ruitenbeck, Ed., New York Atherton Press, 1969.

4. Cohn, Ruth C.: "Training Intuition" in *Ways of Growth*, Herbert Otto, ed. D. Grossmann, N.Y., 1968.

*The theme-centered interactional method is studied, practiced and taught at the Workshop Institute for Living-Learning (W.I.L.L.), New York City.

THE CONSCIOUSNESS-RAISING GROUP
AS A MODEL FOR THERAPY WITH WOMEN

ANNETTE M. BRODSKY

By now, almost everyone is familiar with a sense of growing unrest among women with many of their traditional sex role stereotypes. There is no evidence that women are more like each other psychologically than men are like each other. In fact, the bulk of evidence on gender role differences points out that the differences between individuals of each sex are greater than differences between men and women (Mischel, 1966). Yet, for a woman in particular, her sex determines to a large degree her future roles in life, dictating limitations on the options for her development, regardless of intellect, activity level, or physical and emotional capacity (Epstein, 1970; Amundsen, 1971). This role confinement has been psychologically frustrating to many women and is a major basis for identification as feminists of many of the therapists on the Feminist Therapist Roster of the Association for Women in Psychology (Brodsky, 1972). Epidemiological studies (Gurin et al., 1960; Chesler, 1971) reveal that women complain more of nervousness, impending breakdown, and attempts at suicide (and they are beginning to achieve this goal more often). They are more frequently seen in therapy, and more likely to be hospitalized for their mental disorders. As Chesler (1971) points out, women are the most "treated" category in our society. The Task Force on Family Law and Policy (1968) concluded that the married woman, in the traditional feminine role of housewife, has the most difficulty psychologically, and the discrepancy between married women and other groups increases with the years of marriage. Bart (1971) noted that depression in middle-aged women was most likely to occur when there was an overly strong commitment to the

mother role so that other forms of individual identity were lacking when the children left home.

Directing women into narrowly confined roles is a long socialization process that starts with the toys and books of young children that encourage specific social models that differentiate instrumental and expressive tools of development (Bardwick, 1971). The realization that women are not to make a significant impact upon the world, that their role in life is not only different from that of their brothers, but qualitatively inferior in terms of the rewards of the society in which they live, occurs in vivid and demonstrable form by high school years. Horner (1970) demonstrates dramatic evidence of the suppression of self-esteem and self-actualization in adolescent girls. The motive to avoid success becomes a powerful inhibition on the academic achievement of girls. The fears of loss of femininity associated with being competitive, the social disapproval of intellectual females, and the actual denial in bright women that a woman is capable of high levels of achievement, were all themes repeatedly related in projective stories of Horner's subjects. Sixty-five per cent of the sample of females, compared to less than ten per cent of the males, showed this phenomenon of avoiding success.

The identity crisis is perhaps most noted in the married, middle-class women who have been over-educated and under utilized. The gulf separating the life style of the upper-middle class housewife and her mate is perhaps wider than any other strata in our society. By definition these women are happy. They have husbands, families, and household help. Why don't they feel fulfilled? Freidan (1963) refers to the uneasiness and

PSYCHOTHERAPY: THEORY, RESEARCH AND PRACTICE, 1973, Vol. 10, pp. 24-29.

disillusionment of the bored middle-class housewives as the "problem that had no name." These women continued to live out their proscribed roles in spite of vague, undefined needs for more variability and needs for more opportunity to reveal individual talents that were often not consonant with the roles of "kinder, kuche, and kirche" (children, kitchen, and church).

With the re-awakening of the feminist movement in the 60's, women began to investigate the problem with no name. Bird (1968) discovered what women in the working world suspected, but dared not voice aloud. That is, when a woman leaves the stereotyped roles, she fights a battle of subtle and often blatant discrimination and resentment. The battle is a lonely one for those who can overcome the initial fears of loss of femininity, social disapproval and disdain of men and women alike for daring to compete in the male domain.

Consciousness-raising (C-R) groups grew out of both the sense of restless constraint noted by Freidan and the awareness of being different and alone noted by Bird. These feelings were finally exposed as a common occurrence and C-R groups developed a very important aspect of the women's movement, the awareness of women that others shared these same self-doubts.

The small group structure of the women's movement was ideally suited to the exploration of personal identity issues. The technique of heightening self-awareness by comparing personal experiences was as basic to the continuance and solidarity of the movement as any other tactic. Women found themselves eliciting and freely giving support to other group members who often were asserting themselves as individuals for the first time in their lives. They gained strength from members who confronted others, and they learned to ask for their own individual rights to adopt new roles and express new behaviors.

The individual changes that occurred in the context of C-R groups were unique from many therapeutic techniques that women had previously experienced. Many C-R group members had previously been in therapy

(Newton & Walton, 1971). Many others had considered the entire mental health profession as implying illness and abnormality and had no contact with individual or group experiences until they joined a C-R group.

By education and training, women had been encouraged to be conformists and passive. In their traditional roles, they had been isolated from each other and from events in the larger political and economic world beyond their narrowly confined psychological space. The C-R group offered a sense of closeness or intimacy with other women as opposed to a media-produced sense of competition and alienation from each other. The development of the concept of sisterhood arose as a shared understanding of the unique problems of being a woman in a man's world.

Movement women (Allen, 1971) and professionals (Newton & Walton, 1971) have begun to study consciousness-raising groups for their perspectives on the social movement, and on exploration of new life styles. The present analysis focuses on the psychological impact, with particular reference to the issue of identity crises. In terms of contrast with therapy groups, the C-R group starts with the assumption that the environment, rather than intrapsychic dynamics, plays a major role in the difficulties of the individuals. The medical model of abnormal behavior based on biological, innate causes is not acceptable to these groups. They are struggling to redefine these very concepts that have been seen as assigning women to a helpless patient role, destined as victims of their biological nature to behave in certain ways (Weisstein, 1969; Chesler, 1971).

Women in C-R groups do not react in traditional female interaction patterns that are commonly seen in all-female therapy groups. For example, ask a therapist who has dealt with all-female groups of mothers of patients, institutional groups, etc. The typical response is that women are catty, aggressive, competitive, and much tougher on each other for digressions, than they are toward men.

In C-R groups, women are confronted with acting as individuals. They are encouraged to examine their uniqueness apart from their roles toward others such as wife, mother, or secretary. It appears easier for a woman to reveal taboo subjects and feelings such as not liking the caring of young children, wishing one had never married, feeling more intelligent than one's boss or husband, or being tired of boosting his self-esteem at the expense of her own. Finding that not only are these feelings not abnormal, but common experiences among other women, can have an almost religious conversion reaction in some women (Newton & Walton, 1971).

A sense of trust in other women and a closeness based on common problems that arise from external sources as well as internal deficiencies, serves to bind the groups into continuing, relatively stable units. The attrition rate for the groups I and my colleagues have encountered as well as those studied by Newton & Walton (1971) appear to be lower than those of typical voluntary therapy groups, or sensitivity groups. They appear to move to an intimacy stage rapidly and maintain a strong loyalty. Dropouts occur early, often due to conflict with male relationships that are threatened by changes in dependency behaviors.

The therapeutic processes that occur in these groups are akin to assertive training, personal growth groups, achievement-oriented training or simply self-development groups. In assertive training, the key technique seems to involve the role models provided by other group members. Women as models are more convincing than male authoritarian leaders for whom the assertive role is a cultural expectation. Likewise, achievement needs are raised more readily in an all-woman group. The identification with other women who achieve is more real than transference to a model outside the situation of direct discrimination experiences. In this sense, like Synanon, Recovery, Inc., or Alcoholics Anonymous, in C-R groups some experienced members give strength to the neophyte.

I have seen faculty women return to long forgotten dissertations and take advanced courses, and housewives who have confronted their husbands for more rights or domestic help. Others went through divorces from marriages that had been security traps, and childless women stood up for their right to refuse to have children simply because others thought they should.

One difficulty with the groups comes at a stage when the women try to transfer their new found behaviors outside the group. In a parallel fashion to the sensitivity group member who expects others outside the group to respond as positively as the group, C-R group members often find that the group understands, but the outside world does not change to correspond with the groups' level of awareness. It is at this stage that women tend to become angry with their employers, lovers, and old friends for continuing to act in chauvinistic, stereotyped patterns. A new response from a woman may be either ignored, misunderstood, patronizingly laughed at, or invoke a threatened retaliatory confrontation. Unlike the individual in a more traditional assertive training situation, these women are behaving often in new ways that society usually does not condone. In frustration, women may overreact and as a result, provoke just the response they fear to get. For example, loud demands for better treatment on the job by a previously meek woman may well meet with a backlash response leading to termination of her entire job.

This type of frustration often leads to a period of depression, either of individuals or the group as a whole. They feel that while they can become aware of their situation and make individual changes, they cannot make much of an impact on the outside world. There is little outside reinforcement to carry on their motivation. At this later dropout stage, the faculty woman gets pregnant instead of completing her dissertation, the potential divorcée decides that security is more important after all, the frustrated housewife announces that "Joe thinks this group is making me unhappy and he wants me to quit," or the graduate student can not find time because she is up nights typing her boyfriend's thesis.

If these regressive tendencies are weathered by the group, the most crucial, and often the most effective, stage of the group experience develops. The women plan to actively alter the environment in a realistic manner to make it more compatible with the developing growth needs of the members. The direction of the group turns from personal, individual solutions (except for occasional booster-shot sessions as the need arises) to some sort of group action. Actions that groups may take vary according to talents, age and needs. They might consist of organized protests, political lobbying, educational programs, or missionary goals of helping to organize other groups to expand the population of the enlightened. The C-R group works to give a sense of social as well as personal worth to the members, and as a by-product, serves to help modify an environment insensitive to the needs of an increasingly growing population of restless women.

The premise of this paper is that the C-R groups of the women's movement have implications for the treatment of identity problems of women in therapy. The following ways are suggested possibilities for transferring the C-R groups dynamics to use in individual therapy. First, in working with women on identity issues, therapists should be aware of the increasingly wider range of valid goals for healthy functioning of women in terms of roles and personality traits (Maccoby, 1971). For example, exuberance should not be interpreted as aggression because the behavior occurs in a female. Second, a good therapist is aware of the reality of the female patient's situation. Many factors are beyond her control. She cannot realistically expect to attain achievement comparable to a man, unless she has greater intellectual and/or motivational abilities. Discrimination does exist (Amundsen, 1971; Bernard, 1971; Astin, 1969; Epstein, 1970; Bird 1968, etc.). Because of this discrimination, the importance of encouragement through assertive training and independence from others, including the therapist, is paramount to counteract the many years of discouragement through subtle, cultural mores. The therapist can serve as supporter and believer in the patient's competence through the regressive, dropout stages and finally, in the face of individual frustrations he or she can recognize the need for some direct an meaningful activity related to improvemen of the societal situations.

Working with women's C-R groups offer a number of insights to a therapist for th particular problems women face in trying t resolve the difficulties of living in a worl that revolves around men's work. For ex ample, those women who report patterns o intrusive male behavior often appear to b oversensitive to slights and minor brushoffs C-R group experiences help women to confirm the reality of such slights, rather than den their existence or pass them off as projec tions. For a man, such incidents can b overlooked as exceptional, and not integrate into the broader experience of being taker seriously and accepted as a thinking in dividual. For a woman, the experience is mor a rule, than an exception (unless she is a exceptional woman). Her sensitivity to suc slights comes out of an awareness of th situation, and a concomitant frustration i being unable to defend herself in the situatio without appearing pompous, uppity, or para noid.

The accumulation of experiences of bein interrupted in conversations, having he opinions ignored or not taken seriously ca severely affect a woman's feelings of com petence and self-worth. Her desire to be as sertive, or to make an impact on the environ ment is continuously weakened by this lacl of affirmation of her self by others.

There are therapists who maintain tha women who act insecure or inferior in suc situations are doing so in order to get second ary gains from such postures (using feminin wiles) and her verbalizations of a desir for independence or responsibility are no genuine. Such therapists probably do no understand that without role models or en couragement from the environment, thes women have no real choice in not accepting the only reality they have been indoctrinate to believe about the capabilities of their sex

Other major themes that some therapist are apt to misjudge or overlook when dealing with women clients can be briefly mentione here. Unaware therapists still tend to conside marriage uncritically as a solution fo women's problems without realizing that, like with men, divorce or no marriage may often present the best available alternative for the individual. When a woman proposes such a solution, the therapist may become more concerned with her non-traditional life style than with her personal feelings in living out such a style.

Some therapists also automatically assume that a woman's career is secondary to her mate's career. The conflict over "having it both ways," by wanting a career and family is still seen as the wife's burden, not the husband's also. Unusual patterns of division of household tasks, child care, etc. are no longer stigmas that label individuals as deviant. Therapists have been guilty of producing iatrogenic disorders in women who felt comfortable with what they were doing until the therapist suggested that they were selfish, unreasonable, or pointed out how no one expected them to accomplish so much and they would be loved and accepted without this unrealistic drive to compete.

Perhaps related to the foregoing is the frustration women have experienced with therapists who can empathize readily with a man who is stifled by a clinging, nagging wife, but who interprets the same complaint from a woman as her being cold and unfeeling for not responding affectionately to an insecure, demanding husband. The crucial issue surrounding such misunderstandings is an unconscious tendency for many therapists to have a double standard for men and women in mental health and adjustment (Broverman, et al., 1970). This attitude restricts their capacity to allow their clients a free expression of the various available roles. Women, after all, have needs for self-esteem, independence, expression of anger and aggression; and men have needs for security, affection and expression of fear and sorrow. While, at present, men may have more diverse models in our society for the development of an adequate masculine role, women's models have been restricted for the most part to housewives or the more narrow traditional feminine occupations.

Perhaps the strongest message to be seen from the success of these C-R groups is that women are capable of using other women as models. Identification of women with role models of their own sex has been largely limited to the traditional homemaker roles or the feminine occupations such as teaching and nursing. The acceptance of more varied roles and personality traits in women will help to integrate a larger portion of women into the "mentally healthy" categories.

Until this happens to a greater extent, perhaps,.as Chesler (1971) suggests only women should be therapists for other women. On the other hand, if therapists must have the same experiences as their patients in order to help them, we would be a sorry lot indeed. The important lesson for clinicians, male and female alike, is to make a particular effort to study the facts and reasoning behind the women's movement. We help neurotics, psychotics, children, handicapped, any group of which we are not a member by keeping educated with the current literature written by those in close touch with large numbers of that particular population. In the same vein, any male therapist who has not kept abreast of current theory and issues relating to women, is treating from a position of ignorance. The sample of women in his personal life does not provide sufficient clinical data or theory on which to base therapy. Women have a great need today for allies in their struggles to alter a constricting environment. Legal and political allies are not sufficient. Understanding, enlightened therapists are necessary if we want to avoid psychological casualties of today's transitional cultural changes.

REFERENCES

ALLEN, P. *The small group in women's liberation.* New York: Times Change Press, 1971.

AMUNDSEN, K. *The silenced majority: Women and American democracy.* Englewood Cliffs, New Jersey: Prentice Hall, 1971.

ASTIN, H. *The woman doctorate in America.* Hartford: Russell Sage Foundation, 1969.

BARDWICK, J., & DOUVAN, E. Ambivalence: The socialization of women. In V. Gornick & B. Moran (Eds.), *Woman in sexist society: Studies in power and powerlessness.* New York: Basic Books, 1971, 147-159.

BART, P. Depression in middle-aged women. In V.

Gornick & B. Moran (Eds.), *Woman in sexist society: Studies in power and powerlessness.* New York: Basic Books, 1971, 99-117.

BERNARD, J. *Women and the public interest.* New York: Aldine-Atherton, 1971.

BIRD, C. *Born female: The high cost of keeping women down.* New York: McKay, 1968.

BRODSKY, A. (Ed.) *Feminist therapist roster of the Association for Women in Psychology.* Pittsburgh: KNOW, Inc., 1972.

BROVERMAN, I. K., BROVERMAN, D. M., CLARKSON, F., ROSENKRANTS, P. & VOGEL, S. R. Sex-role stereotypes and clinical judgments of mental health. *Journal of Consulting Psychology,* 1970, 34, 1-7.

CHESLER, P. Patient and patriarch: Women in the psychotherapeutic relationship. In V. Gornick & B. Moran (Eds.), *Woman in sexist society: Studies in power and powerlessness.* New York: Basic Books, 1971, 251-275.

EPSTEIN, C. *Woman's place: Options and limits in professional careers.* Berkeley: California Press, 1970.

FRIEDAN, B. *The feminine mystique.* New York: Dell, 1963.

GURIN, G., VEROFF, J., & FELD, S. *Americans view their mental health.* New York: Basic Books, 1960.

HORNER, M. Femininity and successful achievement A basic inconsistency. In J. Bardwick, *Feminine personality and conflict.* Belmont, Calif: Brooks/ Cole, 1970, 45-76.

MACCOBY, E. Sex differences and their implications for sex roles. Paper presented at American Psychological Association, Sept. 1971, Washington D. C.

MISCHEL, W. A social-learning view of sex differences in behavior. In E. Maccoby, *The development of sex differences.* Stanford: Stanford University Press, 1966, 56-81.

NEWTON, E., & WALTON, S. The personal is political: Consciousness-raising and personal change in the women's liberation movement. In B. G. Schoepf (Chw), *Anthropologists look at the study of women.* Symposium presented at the American Anthropological Association, November 19, 1971.

REEVES, N. *Womankind: Beyond the stereotypes.* New York: Aldine-Atherton, 1971.

Report of the Task Force on Family Law and Policy to the Citizen's Advisory Council on the Status of Women, Washington, D. C., 1968.

WEISSTEIN, N. Kinder, kuche, kirche as scientific law: Psychology constructs the female. *Motive,* 1969, 29, 6-7.

COGNITIVE MANIPULATIONS WITH DELINQUENT ADOLESCENTS
IN GROUP THERAPY[1]

HERBERT HARARI

The present paper was prompted by the observations of the writer, a social psychologist acting as a consultant for a psychiatrically-oriented community mental health clinic in California. The observations focused primarily on practices of individual and group therapy with adolescents, especially with youngsters who had shown chronic delinquent behavior patterns with sociopathic overtones (lying, stealing, runaway, truancy, drug dependence, gang fights, etc.).

Close contact and consultations with a large segment of clinical personnel (psychiatrists, psychologists, and social workers) over a four-year period lead this writer to believe that the practices in the community mental health clinic in this study reflected a stereotyped notion of group therapy as a cathartic instrument. Accordingly, the "ideal" therapy group was expected to be marked by intense transferences, ventilated hostilities, outpourings of affection, reliving of sibling rivalries, etc. Adherence to this experiential stereotype became increasingly prevalent with the new popularity of quasi-therapeutic approaches such as sensitivity training and encounter groups (rather than the topic-bound approach within the framework of traditional group dynamics which had marked earlier T-group practices). What finally emerged was a complex practice which can best be described as "emotional-affective-cathartic" in nature, rather than "intellectual-cognitive-rational."

The cognitive-affective dichotomy is introduced here even though it is granted that in order to achieve effective group therapy one neither can nor should discount the affective aspects of interpersonal interactions. The major contention of this paper, however, is that the *systematic* application to group therapy of cognitively-derived principles which are traditionally part of social psychology, can largely enhance the former.

Balance Models of Interpersonal Cognition

Social psychologists have given a great deal of attention to the processes involved in interpersonal perception and cognition. Most of the research in this area has been generated by various "balance" theories (e.g., Festinger, 1957; Heider, 1958; Newcomb, 1961; Osgood & Tannenbaum, 1955), of which one (Heider's) will be briefly described later on. As a rule, investigation of interpersonal perception variables follows an approach which explores the manner in which congruence of attitudes, judgments, and inferences attributed to other people and their actions become determinants of one's perception of or attraction to another. This type of research has been limited almost exclusively to the social-personality-developmental areas in psychology and published in journals dealing with those areas. The clinical literature, according to a recent extensive review (Maselli & Altrocchi, 1969), has remained remarkably disinterested in explicit theories or findings in the area of perceptual inferences and attribution, despite the fact that their implications are abundant in clinical lore and writings (e.g., the attribution of hostile and nonhostile intent to others).

One of the better known balance theories is based on Heider's *p-o-x* model of interpersonal perception. Briefly, its analysis is focused on the cognitive field consisting of *p* (the perceiver), *o* (another person or persons), and *x* (usually an impersonal entity such as an act, event, etc.). Also included are the affective

[1] The author wishes to express his appreciation to William Baak, Chief of Psychiatric Services, Children and Adolescent Division, Community Mental Health of San Diego for his assistance.

PSYCHOTHERAPY: THEORY, RESEARCH AND PRACTICE, 1972, Vol. 9, pp. 303-307.

209

TABLE 1

Situation	*p-o-x* Pattern*	Description
Type I Balanced	*p*L*o*, *o*C*x*, *p*L*x*	Perceiver (p) likes other person (o) who causes what p ceiver likes (x).
Type II Balanced	*p*L*o*, *o*-C*x*, *p*-L*x*	Perceiver (p) likes other person (o) who does not cause w perceiver dislikes (x).
Type III Balanced	*p*-L*o*, *o*C*x*, *p*-L*x*	Perceiver (p) dislikes other person (o) who causes what p ceiver dislikes (x).
Type IV Balanced	*p*-L*o*, *o*-C*x*, *p*L*x*	Perceiver (p) dislikes other person (o) who does not ca what perceiver likes (x).
Type V Imbalanced	*p*L*o*, *o*C*x*, *p*-L*x*	Perceiver (p) likes other person (o) who causes what p ceiver dislikes (x).
Type VI Imbalanced	*p*L*o*, *o*-C*x*, *p*L*x*	Perceiver (p) likes other person (o) who does not cause w perceiver likes (x).
Type VII Imbalanced	*p*-L*o*, *o*C*x*, *p*L*x*	Perceiver (p) dislikes other person (o) who causes what p ceiver likes (x).
Type VIII Imbalanced	*p*-L*o*, *o*-C*x*, *p*-L*x*	Perceiver (p) dislikes other person (o) who does not ca what perceiver dislikes (x).

* o = other person or persons (group).

components of liking (L) or disliking (-L) toward the other person (*o*), or toward the event (*x*); and the cognitive components of causation (C) or non-causation (-C) of the event (*x*) by the other person (*o*). All this makes it possible to generate eight interpersonal situations of which four are balanced (tension-free) and four are imbalanced (tension-inducing) to the perceiver. The eight situations are listed and described in Table 1.

Given these eight interpersonal situations, Heider further postulates that (a) there is a tendency for cognitive units to achieve balance, and (b) if no balance exists, the state of imbalance will give rise to tensions and forces to restore balance. For example, if I (*p*) perceive my enemy (*o*) as committing an act (*x*) which I like, I experience tension (Type VII). To relieve the tension I may perceive my enemy in a new light, as a friend (Type I); or deny that he committed the positive act (Type IV); or perceive the act as negative (Type III). Similar perceptual manipulations occur in other imbalanced situations such as when my enemy does not do what I dislike (Type VIII), when my friend does what I dis-

like (Type V), or when my friend does not what I like (Type VI).

What could theoretical models such Heider's mean to the practicing clinician? pointed out by Simon & Newell (1963), th retical models have considerable heuris value, which should be of interest to clinicia in any case. Moreover, consider the patie therapist relationship from the patient's po of view. The patient enters the situation w certain expectations about therapy and the pists. The therapist, willingly or unwilling provides the patient with continuous cognit inputs by means of cues (verbal, facial, tor etc.) from which the patient infers confirm tion or repudiation of his expectations. T patient's interpretation of how his expec tions are being met will in turn have an eff on his attitude and behavior toward the the pist, which in turn will have an effect on chartered process of therapy and event prognosis. Obtaining information about patient's cognitive assessment of a given tient-therapist relationship could thus be considerable value.

An experimental study (Harari, 19

found that in comparison to the normal adolescent, the delinquent patient experiences more discomfort and tension when he expects to be helped but perceives the therapist as being *powerless* to do so; or when he does not expect to be helped and perceives a *power* display by the therapist. The perception of the therapist's moral obligation or lack of it to help the patient, was of little consequence to the patient. In all cases, balance was regained by patients changing their attitudes towards the therapist.

Applying Balance Models to Group Therapy

If one stipulates that affection and trust to the therapeutic agent (therapist and/or group) is the *sine qua non* for successful therapy with these youngsters, then any expectation of help on their part must be met by directive, structured, "powerful" behavior by the therapeutic agent, or he may lose the patient's affection. While such behavior may be premature in the case where the young patient does not expect help or shows an initial dislike for the therapeutic agent, it by no means suggests a non-directive approach to the problem. Cues which essentially convey to the patient that the therapist is at most an aid, since the patient must pull himself up by his own bootstraps, were found to be detrimental to psychotherapy. Delinquent adolescents, at least, simply do not respond favorably to this kind of approach.

Once the general orientation of "directiveness" was established for the therapists, it became possible to introduce some quasi-standard preliminary operations to delinquent adolescents assigned to group therapy. The first step included the assessment of a wide array of patients' expectations concerning the therapist and the group they were about to enter. As expected, direct questioning yielded useful, but not always reliable information. Many of the patients were forced to come to the clinic and undergo therapy by probationary court order which sometimes obscured their real expectations. Furthermore, the assessment of patients' expectations by too much direct questioning sometimes involved the risk of premature confrontation, which is especially detrimental to psychotherapy with adolescents. The second procedural step thus included the additional presentation of Heider's eight interpersonal situations, and questioning the patient of his reaction to them (e.g., "What would you have done in this case?"). The questioning was done by simply substituting the p, o, and x components listed in Table 1 with descriptive, real-life terminology. The therapists at the clinic had considerable leeway in creating these situations, as long as they followed the basic paradigm of the p-o-x model. The situations were to be relevant to the patients' milieu and couched in appropriate terminology (Harari, 1967; 1971).

As a third step, the Survey of Interpersonal Values, or SIV (Gordon, 1960) was frequently administered to the patients. Apart from being an excellent measure of interpersonal values, it also served as a useful predictor for adolescents' cognitive responses to interpersonal situations. The following Type VII imbalanced situation can serve as an example: "Eric dislikes Lonny very much. But Lonny is a big shot in the group who helps Eric achieve what Eric wants—to win the election as vice-president of the club." Adolescents who according to the SIV showed high support-seeking tendencies tended to respond to the question "What does Eric think now?" with a change of attitude toward the other person ("Lonny is a nice guy after all"); adolescents with high SIV scores on recognition-seeking responded with a change. of perception of the other's action ("Lonny did not help to win the elections"); adolescents with high SIV score on independent behavior responded with a change of attitude toward the event ("Lonny did not want to get elected anyway"); etc. (Harari, 1967).

Cognitive Manipulations: Two Illustrative Examples

Phil and Alan were typical of the adolescents routinely assigned to the clinic for group therapy. Phil was a thin, tense, somewhat hysterical 15-year-old delinquent boy who came to the clinic as a result of a mandatory court order, a fact which he repeatedly mentioned when he protested that he neither expected nor wanted help, that he did not intend to expose himself to any group "capping" sessions, and that he neither liked nor trusted "shrink" therapists and groups. Alan, a stocky, passive-aggressive, somewhat withdrawn 16-year-old boy whose sociopathic behavior pattern (truancy, shop-lifting, drug dependence, etc.) had been diagnosed as part of an adolescent adjustment reaction, also indicated that he neither liked nor trusted therapists and groups. This pattern of dislike and mistrust was quite typical of most of the delinquent adolescents assigned to the clinic. Alan, however, was brought in by his parents rather than by court order. Moreover, while he remained silent on the issue of self exposure to the group, Alan clearly indicated that he expected therapy to be of some help to him.

Such routine and familiar information can be meaningfully augmented with analyses of patients' responses to Heider's eight p-o-x situations. For example, Phil was most upset by this Type VII situation, when asked how a boy called Gary felt: "Gary hates Bill, thinks he is a creep. Gary also wants to be on the football team. He finds out that Bill goes around telling everybody that he, Gary, will make a fine football player and should be on the team." Alan, on the other hand, was most upset by Steve's situation in the following Type VI hypothetical situation: "As manager of the basketball team, Tom can influence the coach about which member should go on a field trip the team is about to take. Steve, a friend of Tom, wants to go, but he finds out that Tom had not said a word about him to the coach."

Of even greater interest were the cognitive modes of balance restoration by Phil and Alan to the respective situations. Phil simply denied that Bill was indeed doing nice things for Gary. In other words, Phil regained balance by reverting to a Type IV perception i.e., by denying his initial perception of the other's action. Alan, on the other hand, suggested that Steve never wanted to go on that field trip in the first place. Alan thus regained balance by reverting to a Type II perception, i.e., by changing his initial attitude toward the event.

SIV profiles of Phil and Alan were consistent with their respective modes of balance-seeking and could have served as predictors. Phil, who scored high on the value of recognition-seeking (91st percentile) could be expected to deny credit to others for committing

a positive act. Alan, who scored high on t value of support-seeking (89th percenti could be expected to sacrifice his initial at tude in order to save a friendship.

Once the patients' cognitive responses p-o-x situations were assessed, it became fea ble to plan for the "ideal" therapy situati *Cognitively speaking, such a situation is m likely to be a Type I balanced situation.* Wh p = patient, o = therapist and/or group, a x = an event that o either causes or not, v few individuals indeed would experience i balance when they perceive a friendly therap and/or group committing positive acts.

How could liking for the group (pLo) instilled in Phil? He disliked the group (p-l and wanted no help (p-Lx). The therap could induce the group—explicitly or imp itly, but above all skillfully—to convey Phil that it was about to help him with problems. The result would be a Type VII uation (p-Lo, oCx, p-Lx) which is balanc but would maintain Phil's dislike for group. If, on the other hand, the given cue Phil would indicate that the group was not ing to help him, imbalance via Type VIII si ation (p-Lo, o-Cx, p-Lx) would occur. In t case, to regain balance Phil would most lik have to continuously assert that the group a attempting to help him, a tiresome struggle deed.

Since Phil had to attend therapy sessi because of a court order, it was possible maintain a cognitive struggle in him for qu a while. Whenever he sneeringly insis "You're trying to 'help' me to turn strai aren't you?", the group and therapist sponded with polite but firm denials. It s became evident that Phil had to do someth about his obviously ambivalent perception what the group was doing to him. One way Phil to regain balance could have been to mit that he expected and wanted the grou help him. In that case a Type IV balanced uation (p-Lo, o-Cx, pLx) would emerge, sion-free for Phil, but again not necessa conducive to successful therapy. Fortunat recognition-seeking individuals such as I find it very difficult to admit changes initially-held attitudes. What was more lik to occur, and did in fact happen, was that I would attempt to regain balance by grudgi changing his affect toward the group. In that case a Type II balanced situation would emerge: "The group is 'all right' because it does what *I* want it to do—it offers no help."

As expected, Phil gradually ceased his sarcastic remarks about the group's futile attempts to help him. At the same time, he began to indicate that the group was "all right." Gradually, his balance-seeking attempts became so flexible that he even admitted changes in his initial attitudes. For example, by the 10th session he openly acknowledged that the group made him feel comfortably "loose" when he discussed his own problems. In *p-o-x* terminology, this was the first of the anticipated "ideal" Type I therapy situations (pLo, oCx, pLx, with x = self exposure). Phil responded positively to many other such group situations throughout the seven months prior to successful termination of therapy.

Alan's case invited an entirely different approach. He disliked the group (p-Lo), but unlike Phil, he expected to be helped (pLx). If the therapist and the group were to convey to him the same cues as to Phil, namely that they are not helping him, a Type IV balanced situation (p-Lo, o-Cx, pLx) would emerge. Once again, while this may reduce Alan's tension, it is far from the desired Type I "ideal" situation. A more productive approach would be to indicate to Alan that he can and will be helped by the group. The ensuing situation, Type VII (p-Lo, oCx, pLx) would be an imbalanced one. Support-seeking individuals such as Alan, however, tend to solve such situations by changing their attitude toward the other person(s) from dislike (p-Lo) to liking (pLo). Moreover, if the message to the patient is clear that the group has the *power* to help, most delinquent adolescents will have a

positive change in attitude toward *p* (Harari, 1967; 1971). Accordingly, Alan was given to understand from the very moment that he attended sessions that he can expect to get help from the group, and that the group can in fact help him. It took no more than five sessions for Alan to achieve the desired Type I balanced situation, i.e., liking the group (pLo), expecting help (pLx), and perceiving the group as giving help (oCx).

In summary, the procedures described here made it possible to derive some systematic generalizations from patients' expectations concerning the patient-therapist and/or patient-group relationships. Even more important, it provided guidelines for the dispensation of different cues to the individuals undergoing group therapy.

REFERENCES

FESTINGER, L. *A theory of cognitive dissonance.* Evanston, Ill.: Row & Peterson, 1957.

GORDON, L. V. *Survey of interpersonal values.* Chicago, Ill.: Science Research Associates, Inc., 1960.

HARARI, H. An experimental evaluation of Heider's balance theory with respect to situational and predispositional variables. *Journal of Social Psychology,* 1967, **73**, 177-189.

HARARI, H. Interpersonal models in psychotherapy and counseling: a social-psychological analysis of a clinical problem. *Journal of Abnormal Psychology,* 1971, **78**, 127-133.

HEIDER, F. *The psychology of interpersonal relations.* New York: Wiley, 1958.

MASELLI, M. D., & ALTROCCHI, J. Attribution of intent. *Psychological Bulletin,* 1969, **71**, 445-454.

NEWCOMB, T. *The acquaintance process.* New York: Holt, Rinehart, & Winston, 1961.

OSGOOD, C. E., & TANNENBAUM, P. H. The principle of congruity in the prediction of attitude change. *Psychological Review,* 1955, **62**, 42-55.

SIMON, H. A., & NEWELL, A. Models: their uses and limitations. In E. P. Hollander & R. C. Hunt (Eds.), *Current perspectives in social psychology.* New York: Oxford University Press, 1963.

PSYCHOANALYTIC TREATMENT OF SEVERELY DISTURBED JUVENILE DELINQUENTS IN A THERAPY GROUP

Girard Franklin, Ph.D.
Wallace Nottage, M.S.S.W.

It HAS GENERALLY BEEN assumed that inveterate juvenile delinquents with severe character disorders are not amenable to intensive treatment aimed at accomplishing major personality changes. Previous work by Redl (1945), Slavson (1947), McCorkle et al. (1958), Eissler (1950), Schulman (1956) and others has suggested that this type of juvenile delinquent is only likely to respond favorably to supportive therapy that does not attempt to focus in depth on self-awareness.

We have found, however, by treating such seriously disturbed delinquents in psychoanalytic group therapy five times a week, where direct focus on personality exploration is explicit and consistently maintained from the outset, that it is possible to involve them successfully in deeply meaningful and highly productive understanding of themselves. The approach described here has been developed and implemented in a number of treatment centers operated by the New York State Division for Youth (Luger, 1964).

In our use of psychoanalytic group therapy the objective is to work

Dr. Franklin is Group Therapy Consultant, New York State Division for Youth, New York City.

Mr. Nottage formerly was Facilities Program Coordinator, New York State Division for Youth, and presently is Deputy Director of Probation for the Courts of the City of New York.

INTERNATIONAL JOURNAL OF GROUP PSYCHOTHERAPY, 1969, Vol. 19, pp. 165-175.

toward the maximum psychoanalytic goal of reconstruction of character structure in view of the severely disturbed life functioning of the youngsters treated. The specific population for which treatment is provided consists of adjudicated mid-adolescent delinquents whose extremely poor response to probation indicates that commitment to a state reformatory is inevitable. In their contacts with the probation officers, as in their contacts with all authority figures, various forms of apparently impenetrable resistances are manifested. Typical is the garrulous, quick-witted, seemingly friendly youth who deftly turns aside any focus on himself, bespeaking the shrewd, skilled "sharpie" who is easily able to talk himself out of any troublesome situation, as well as the openly defiant youth who readily admits to his delinquent behavior with no apparent remorse whatsoever, and who very aggressively proclaims, "Send me away. Do what you want, I don't give a shit. I do what I want and no one's gonna make me do anything I don't wanna do. I didn't ask to be on probation in the first place."

The extreme recalcitrance of these youths is equally reflected in their responses to a wide variety of community resources from which they have been unable to benefit. They seem to be completely unreachable and hopelessly incorrigible. In short, as one boy's probation officer put it, "This kid is destined to be shot down by the police or be behind bars for life." The severity of the boys' characterological difficulties is such that it appeared to us they could only be helped if they could be reached through a very direct, highly intensive treatment approach aimed at effecting very substantial changes in their personalities.

For the most part those boys who come into treatment are motivated entirely by the realization that otherwise they are destined for commitment to a penal institution, although occasionally there is also a momentary hopefulness for themselves generated by the enthusiasm of their probation officers. It is usual for a boy to choose treatment as the lesser of two evils rather than because of a motivation to change. Entering treatment is established as a condition of their probation, and they are made aware that refusal to do so will place them in serious jeopardy with the court. In some instances boys who drop out of treatment are immediately committed.

Although most of the youngsters often seriously contemplate breaking off treatment, especially during the early phase of analysis of their resistance to self-awareness, termination rarely occurs without the agreement of their therapist. Seldom do youngsters who have terminated treatment have to return to court because of further difficulty. In many instances youngsters have voluntarily sought and successfully utilized further help in the community after experiencing difficulties in carrying out their objectives. And occasionally it has been necessary for some to return for further intensive treatment. All of the youngsters have maintained contact with the therapist by letter or telephone, and many have made personal visits.

Special considerations in our decision to attempt psychoanalytic treatment of these youngsters in a group were dilution of intense hostility toward the therapist as an authority figure (Peck and Bellsmith, 1954), exposure of their characteristic difficulties of deep-seated distrust and fearfulness as manifested in transference responses to each other (Franklin, 1959), and vitally needed peer support of growth strivings at a time when intense, underlying passive-dependent longings threaten to overwhelm them (Fried, 1956).

In deciding on the frequency of the sessions, several considerations guided our thinking. The very low tolerance of delinquents for frustration and anxiety, coupled with their predilection for discharging tension through impulse behavior, suggested the desirability of intensive treatment on a daily basis. Especially in the early stages of treatment they need almost constant support and encouragement to be able to come to grips with the deeply rooted, intense feelings of worthlessness that generally lurk behind their persistent efforts to block off self-awareness. As expressed by one youngster, "I been coming in here night after night and arguing with you guys, but it's no use. All my big talk is bullshit. The truth is there's hardly a guy in here I'm not afraid of. It's so hard to admit what I really feel about myself. I been playing a game all these years of acting tough and smart when I really feel like shit. I'm scared when I fight and in spite of all my big talk I really feel stupid. I feel like I'm nothing inside."

At such times the respectful silence of his peers, if not their outright sharing of such feelings or expression of admiration for the courage of such honesty, greatly helps a youngster to hang on to an image of himself that is not devastating and alleviates his strong impulse to quit treatment.

The freedom to express feelings on a daily basis also greatly contributes to keeping tension down to therapeutically desirable proportions. The acceptance in the group of spontaneous outbursts makes it possible for feelings to be released without the consequences of retaliation or ridicule they deeply fear. "Blowing one's cool" is initially a source of great shame to them, primarily, we believe, because in fact they have such very poor control over their emotions and impulses when these are strongly aroused. The feeling of helplessness experienced at such times, and the ever-present possibility of being overwhelmed, is a major cause for the intense feelings of inadequacy present in these youngsters.

The release of feelings that gradually occurs has the dual value of helping them to know what their feelings are and to recognize their difficulties in coping with them. Cliff, a deeply sullen, uncommunicative youngster of formidable physical strength, had an easily aroused, uncontrollable temper that led to innumerable instances of his beating up almost anyone he became involved with, including teachers, parents, siblings, and peers. He was totally unaware of the intense anger in himself that was so obvious to the rest of the group. Even when it erupted in explosions of obscenities, threats of violence, and physical attacks, he insisted that he was not angry, until he finally realized that no one would take advantage of him during such episodes of loss of self-control. The weakness he experienced at such times made him feel very vulnerable to attacks from others, as well as deeply ashamed of his extreme crudity, which at this point was still the only way he was able to express what he was feeling.

The frequency of the sessions also has the great advantage of helping the group members to detect resistances in each other that often are employed with considerable skillfulness. For example, one boy, Eddie, appeared to be sincerely and earnestly trying to talk about himself. "I want to very much," he said, "but I just don't know how to begin." When pressured, his tears and look of pain aroused considerable sympathy from his peers: "Don't you see he's all upset? Let him take his time. He'll come around." When eventually it became clear to them that he was not going to come around and his behavior was perceived as resistance by the group, Eddie admitted he had enjoyed the game he'd been playing and had laughed to himself about how once again, as on many other occasions, he had been able to manipulate others successfully.

Daily sessions also have the value of being a strong, concrete indication to the boys that they are regarded as people worth spending that much time with. The frequency with which the therapist is willing to work with them is an important contribution to their involvement in therapy because it signifies to them his interest in them as well as his belief in their potential. It also reinforces their growing realization that their situation is a gravely serious matter and that they have come to a crucial point in their lives. The therapist tells them at the outset of treatment, "You are here on the recommendation of the court because of the problems you have had in the community. We are going to give you what may very well be your last chance to better understand yourself and your problems so that you can live in the community as a more mature person capable of making a worthwhile life for yourself." In this and many other ways during the course of treatment, the therapist stresses that he regards therapy as an opportunity they are very fortunate to have available to them.

We found that one of the most significant advantages of group therapy is the influence which these youngsters have on each other in stimulating their interest in observing and understanding themselves. Usually, when a boy enters treatment, he is disturbed by, but also intrigued with, the extremely frank expression of thoughts and feelings by his peers about themselves and each other. As one youngster in his third session put it, "I never heard guys talk like this before. At first I thought they were just ratting, but now I can understand that they're being honest about themselves and each other."

However, in spite of any initial positive reaction to the therapy group, these youngsters do not readily engage themselves personally in treatment, and, in fact, cannot because of the depth of their resistances. Here, again, group therapy proves to be of great value because the responsibility for participation can be shared with peers. This enables each youth to become involved in the therapeutic process at whatever pace is possible for him.

During this phase of treatment there are two particular advantages of the group. The satisfactions gained from the friendships the boys begin to develop help to sustain them in treatment while they are fighting as actively as they need to against self-awareness. These relationships also contribute greatly to a gradual development of accurate knowledge about themselves because of the importance each youngster attaches to the reaction of his peers.

When these youths become deeply involved in therapy, they are keenly perceptive about each other and highly adept in a vernacular rendering of their observations. At times, their alertness to the subtlest of defenses is remarkable and has great impact on even the most resistive youngster. Though often their initial reactions to comments about themselves from peers are characterized by fear and hurt, which they conceal behind hostile attacks, it becomes increasingly difficult for them to reject observations of people they know to be their friends. As they work through together their various fears of each other's reactions, there is nothing about themselves that they cannot bring out freely and constructively in the group.

Tony, a very muscular youth with a reputation for being a good fighter, had so badly beaten up a teacher and a policeman that they required hospitalization. He came from a family in which an older brother he greatly admired for his toughness and popularity with girls sharply contrasted with their passive ineffectual father who depended heavily on their aggressive, domineering mother. Tony finally revealed in the group, with much anxiety, "Before I came here I was giving blow jobs to my brother, and I would lock myself in the bathroom and jack off with my mother's bra and panties on." He spoke of this not simply for the sense of relief of getting it "off his chest" but also because of the feeling that at last here was a chance to understand what made him want to do these things.

The openness which makes sharing possible grows out of the trust they come to have that their peers will try to understand and help while continuing to respect each other. That they respond to each other in such positive ways instead of with their previously characteristic contempt or disgust can be mainly attributed to the youngsters talking about such experiences with their feelings of inner torment and suffering revealed, rather than masked, as before, behind a facade of toughness and cold indifference. Ray, who at first sat in complete silence following Tony's revelations, said, "Man, when I first heard Tony talking about these things, I thought, 'How could a guy do such things.' I felt like telling him he was disgusting. I didn't want to have anything to do with that nasty mother-fucker. But when I sat there watching Tony talking and crying, I couldn't help feeling sorry for him and feeling this guy's got a deep problem and needs help. He's in trouble and he's gotta bring that shit up in the group."

Their positive responses are strongly fostered by their awareness of the courage it takes for a boy to bring out problems which are extremely embarrassing to him. Roger, a "nervy guy" who would do anything on a dare, usually took the lead among his peers in delinquent acts which seemingly showed a great deal of courage. For some time he had been primarily concerned like the rest of his peers with making a good impression on the group. Finally, he broke through this defense. "Some of you guys may not want to have anything to do with me after this meeting. I care about what people think of me, but I can't let it stop me any more from talking about the things I feel inside of me. I know it's for my own good and it's gonna help me." He went on to talk about his desire for passive homosexual relationships, which up to that point had been concealed behind a tough exterior. "I keep saying how I'd like to screw that cat, but I've been lying. All I can think of is how I'd like him to do it to me. I want him to just hold me like a baby and make love to me."

In time it becomes easier for them to bring out their shame-laden impulses and actions because they come to see these in perspective as only a part of themselves or each other: "This doesn't mean I'm all bad, that I'm no fuckin' good." And, also, they gradually understand that what superficially appears to be crazy or disgusting stems from basic human feelings and desires which are present in everyone.

Those boys who can openly admit to their doubts and fears about themselves greatly encourage other youngsters to do the same. In fact, to be able to do so gradually comes to be a measure of strength among them. This represents a major turning point in treatment. As expressed by Ralph in talking about whether commitment to a penal institution was a less painful prospect than the anxiety aroused by facing oneself: "Sure, so I'm a little guy and don't fight so good, and those hard rocks up there can probably get to my ass, but that's just ass. You guys are getting into my head and fuckin' up my mind. Up there I know it's hard and you're locked up. But you mind your business and do what you're told, you finish your time, and you're home free. You don't have to think and talk about things you don't want to talk about that bother you." Thus, therapy comes to be seen as a very difficult challenge and is respected by them as a true test of their manliness rather than "an easy out."

Further incentive comes from their being deeply impressed by those youngsters who, having faced and worked on problems within themselves, have begun to show a calm and manly dignity based on a growing feeling of genuine self-confidence that is dramatically in contrast to the brash and patently superficial bravado prominent among newer members of the group. That those with whom they are so closely identified can achieve such a constructive outcome from their efforts to know themselves provides them with a concrete stimulus that greatly strengthens their determination to involve themselves more purposefully in treatment.

The many ways in which group therapy proves useful in helping to overcome resistances parallels the group's value in resolving distorted perceptions of others and consequent inappropriate behavior toward them. Through a constant process of comparing and evaluating their various perceptions of each other, they are able, in time, to attain a high degree of objectivity about the accuracy of their impressions and the appropriateness of their reactions to each other. Most of the youngsters rarely remain unaware for very long of distortions which occur among them. Not surprisingly, their perceptiveness is more true at first with regard to their distortions of each other than of the therapist. Their transferences to the therapist are more deeply entrenched and for a longer period of time appear more valid to them. But as a result of the insights and strengths they gain from working through their various distortions of each other, they eventually become better prepared to question the accuracy of their impressions of the therapist.

As their capacity to cope with interpersonal difficulties increases, they are able to experience affection, friendship, and even love toward each other and the therapist of an intensity which they have rarely, if ever, experienced before in past associations with others. Their previously intense underlying feelings of depression and despair are based to a considerable extent on the isolation and loneliness that come from an extreme lack of emotionally gratifying attachments to others.

Nat, who had a long history of extremely sadistic behavior, including vicious assults and destruction of property for the pleasure it gave him to watch others suffer, only permitted himself to be close to the animals he kept as pets. For many months he remained completely detached emotionally in the group, until very gradually he began to develop a friendship with another boy. In the session following a fight which had occurred between them (Nat had hit the other boy so hard that he fell and sustained a concussion for which he had to be hospitalized), Nat was asked how he felt about what had happened. He expressed some regret, but the others did not believe him because they had never known him to have concern for anybody. When they pressed him to admit that he was not really sorry, Nat broke into tears and revealed with intense anguish how badly he felt and that this was the first time he had really cared about anyone.

Bob, a tall, husky, 18-year-old, who, in addition to numerous burglaries, had stolen 43 cars during his long history of delinquency, initially called the therapist "the warden." His attitude toward the therapist was a sullen detachment covering thinly veiled feelings of hatred. Later, after Bob had permitted himself to become more closely involved with the therapist, he was much like a love-starved little boy who had found his long-lost daddy. He constantly wanted to engage in physical play with the therapist on a rough-housing level that would have been appropriate to a four-year-old boy, and he expressed an intense desire to be adopted by him.

Gradually, the nature of his relationship to the therapist changed until it ultimately developed into an abiding and profound love for him as a man he deeply cherished and respected but a person quite separate and different from himself. He openly and easily expressed his feelings and thoughts to the therapist and was genuinely open to and interested in the therapist's responses to what he had to say, without, however, looking to him to plan his life or solve his problems for him. Also, he was often able to be sensitive to, and considerate of, the therapist's feelings and needs, and at times he was quite helpful to him without sacrificing a due concern for his own needs and interests.

The evolvement of strong, close relationships with other group members and the therapist are deeply gratifying to these youngsters and undoubtedly are the most vital part of the therapeutic process. The experience of these relationships does much to bring the boys into conflict with their own antisocial attitudes and behavior and are in great measure responsible for the depth of their involvement in working toward personality changes. They become keenly aware of their own serious difficulties in being able to develop and maintain such relationships. Overcoming these obstacles within themselves comes to matter a great deal to them because they so strongly want to build lives for themselves in which deeply meaningful friendships are of central importance.

One further aspect of the value of group therapy for these youngsters is that the challenge posed by new group members closely resembles the problems which they face in their daily living situations. Their newly acquired positive strivings arouse intense antagonism both in new boys in the group and in former neighborhood companions. Ultimately, they are able to cope with these assaults constructively through achieving a realistic sense of self-worth and a greater awareness and understanding of the problems of others. Their increased capacity for positive reactions to conflicts with others is particularly apparent at first, of course, with group members, but gradually increases with peers and adults in their daily lives.

When they reach the point at which their ability to work out problems within themselves and to develop satisfying relationships with others are fairly well consolidated, they then feel sufficient self-assurance to attempt an adjustment in the community independent of the therapy group.

SUMMARY

We have attempted to describe various significant aspects of the therapy group which make it possible to utilize psychoanalytic treatment successfully with juvenile delinquents with severe character disorders. Of crucial importance is that treatment be on a five-times-a-week basis and that emphasis on self-understanding be consistently maintained from the outset. In particular, we have observed that the members of the group are of invaluable help to each other through their very presence, by their influence on each other in stimulating interest in self-understanding, by the similarity of their problems and their insights into them, by the support and encouragement they give to each other during times of great stress, by their skillful confrontation of resistances and their awareness of transferences, and through the salutary effects of the relationships which they develop with each other. We have concluded that seriously disturbed juvenile delinquents, who are so often regarded as untreatable, can accomplish major personality changes leading to successful adjustments as a result of intensive psychoanalytic group therapy.

REFERENCES

Eissler, K. R. (1950), Ego-Psychological Implications of the Psychoanalytic Treatment of Delinquents. *The Psychoanalytic Study of the Child*, 5:97-121. New York: International Universities Press.

Franklin, G. H. (1959), Group Psychotherapy with Delinquent Boys in a Training School Setting. *Internat. J. Psychother.*, 9:213-218.

Fried, E. (1956), Ego Emancipation of Adolescents through Group Therapy, *Internat. J. Psychother.*, 6:358-373.

Luger, M. (1964), Launching a New Program: Problems and Progress. *Syracuse Law Rev.*, 15:693-703.

McCorkle, L., Elias, A., and Bixby, F. (1958), *The Highfields Story*. New York: Henry Holt & Co.

Peck, H. B., and Bellsmith, V. (1954), *Treatment of the Delinquent Adolescent*. New York: Family Service Association of America.

Redl, F. (1945), The Psychology of Gang Formation and the Treatment of Juvenile Delinquents. *The Psychoanalytic Study of the Child*, 1:367-377. New York: International Universities Press.

Schulman, I. (1956), Delinquents. In: Slavson, S. R. (ed.), *The Fields of Group Psychotherapy*. New York: International Universities Press, pp. 196-213.

Slavson, S. R. (1947), *The Practice of Group Therapy*. New York: International Universities Press.

Experiences with an Older Adult Group at a Private Psychiatric Hospital

SANFORD FINKEL, M.D.
WILLIAM FILLMORE, M.A.

The Psychosomatic and Psychiatric Institute (P&PI) of Michael Reese Hospital is an 80-bed private psychiatric hospital consisting of five units, each with its own distinctive milieu. Units are not based on age groupings but on diagnostic consideration. At one extreme there is a maximum security unit; at the other, an open unit, which also functions as a night hospital. Geriatric patients are admitted to all units, although they cluster on the middle unit. This is also the largest unit—29 patients—and the unit where electroshock therapy is administered.

Group therapy was initiated in November, 1968. At that time group therapy and group programs existed for adolescents and young adults. Staff attention and interest centered on these groups, and the elderly appeared isolated and withdrawn.

Initial goals of the group were to increase contact among the geriatric patients who were socially isolated and to bring about increased understanding and verbalization of feelings, such as depression and anxiety, that are common in this population. Patients were told that the purpose of the group would be to discuss common or mutual concerns and interests but that the members would decide what these might be.

All patients over 65 on all units were expected to attend twice-weekly 30-minute group sessions. Membership was open-ended, and

JOURNAL OF GERIATIC PSYCHIATRY, 1971, Vol. 4, pp. 188-199.

patients were usually admitted to the group within one week of their admission to the hospital. Because of the rapid turnover of the elderly population, the group frequently reconstituted itself.

From November, 1968, until June, 1969, the geriatric population of the hospital ranged from three to 11 patients. All told, a total of 34 patients were involved—27 women and seven men. All units were represented, although only one patient from the most closed unit participated. Length of hospitalization varied from one to 14 weeks, the mean being 44 days.[1]

The aim of this paper is to establish the functions the group serves, to convey a flavor of the topics commonly discussed, and to show the shifts in attitudes of the therapists, all of whom were inexperienced in group work with the elderly.

REVIEW OF THE LITERATURE

Silver (1950) conducted inpatient group psychotherapy with 17 female patients 70 to 80 years old, all with diagnoses of senile psychoses. His results indicated improved morale for both patients and nurses. Schwartz and Goodman (1952) conducted group therapy with 19 obese, elderly, outpatient diabetics. Thirteen of them lost a significant amount of weight, and two were able to discontinue insulin. Linden (1953, 1955) treated a group of senile female patients with intensive group therapy over a period of two years. Forty-five per cent were ready to leave the hospital after an average of 54 hours of group therapy. Two-thirds of these were able to resume their customary activities. In the control group, consisting of patients not treated in groups, only 13 per cent were able to leave. Didactic talks, individual questioning, and goodnatured sarcasm were among Linden's therapeutic techniques.

Wolff (1963) carefully chose 110 older hospitalized patients. Fifty per cent were discharged within one year versus 18 per cent for a control group. He viewed group therapy as a treatment of choice for the elderly patient because it is "less alarming." Accept-

---

[1] The staff team included Dr. Sanford Finkel, a psychiatry resident; Mr. William Fillmore, a Social Group Worker, Mrs. Jessie Rugg of Adjunctive Therapy, and Mrs. Del Rosario of the Nursing Staff. Dr. Jerome Grunes provided overall supervision of the program, while Mr. Bernard Makowsky provided group work supervision.

ance by the group is more important than acceptance by the individual. In general, Wolff prefers a supportive, rather than an insight, approach. "The development of deep insight for elderly persons is frequently not only impossible but undesirable," he notes.

Klein, LeShan, and Furman (1966) have extensively and successfully applied group techniques on nonpsychiatric older people. Others have also studied the effects of group therapy with the institutionalized aged (Benaim, 1957; Rechtschaffen, 1959; Ross, 1959; Schwartz and Goodman, 1952; Wolk and Goldfarb, 1967). All are impressed with the improvement in mood and performance of the older adult, although all emphasize that their impressions are not substantiated by scientific data.

FUNCTIONS OF THE GROUP

Initially, the therapists wondered what function the group could serve. Many of the original patients were reluctant to come to the first meeting. Frequently, they would raise objections to association with other older adults. A 78-year-old female was told that the group was for patients over 65 years of age. Her reply was, "I'm not old. Ask Mrs. B, she's an old lady." (Mrs. B was 67.)

Another comment was, "I have nothing to say, so why should I come?" When the therapist pointed out that a patient could come and *listen,* the reply was, "O.K., but I'm not going to say anything." Yet, invariably most spoke up within the first 10 minutes of their first meeting. Even the initially silent, more regressed and depressed members were vocal after a few meetings. The great majority looked forward to the meetings and attended them regularly. Why and how did the patients benefit from the group? Staff members examined the hospital records and the notes of our meetings. Following is a summary of the functions the group serves. Of course, different patients benefit from the group in different ways, and the group does not serve all these functions for every patient.

1. *The group as a socializing agent.* Group discussion among the elderly has been shown to promote socialization (Benaim, 1957; Kalson, 1965; Linden, 1953; Ross, 1959; Schwartz and Goodman,

1952). In our group patients enjoy chatting (or arguing) with each other at the meetings. Conversations begun in the group are carried back to the units and vice-versa. No longer is the geriatric patient a hermit amidst the active patients and staff. The group shares many interests and problems which contribute to a feeling of belonging and identifying with peers. Moreover, we agree with Benaim (1957) that group psychotherapy facilitates the geriatric patient's adjustment to the hospital.

Mrs. I had a moderate organic brain syndrome with paranoid and depressive features. Before she joined the older adult group she was considered a social isolate on the unit. She resisted staff attempts to involve her in activities or conversation. During her first two meetings Mrs. I said nothing. When, 30 minutes before the meeting, we reminded her to attend, she put on clean clothes and makeup. At her third meeting she was willing to discuss her past, and at her fifth meeting she brought an elderly woman whom she introduced as a "nice new lady, who we'd like to get to know better." Mrs. I found a card partner in the group and was often seen initiating conversations with other geriatric patients on the unit.

To encourage the social aspect a weekly social hour was established during the ninth month of the program.

2. *The group as a medium for staff contact* (Linden, 1955). Geriatric patients feel unimportant. At P&PI this feeling was reinforced, for adolescent and young adult groups had existed for several years with a full-time social worker and activity therapists. The elderly have suffered innumerable losses, and one way to recoup them is to associate with "meaningful people," authority figures who have what they themselves do not—status, health, youth, and enthusiasm. Some patients lingered after the meetings and asked staff members questions or told them about problems. Eventually most of these patients were persuaded to bring these issues into the meeting, but some members continued to come mainly for their exclusive post-session staff interviews. During the meetings some members direct their questions and comments strictly to staff. Patients view the therapists as sources of encouragement. The mere fact that someone is interested in the geriatric patient increases his self-esteem. The results of the study of Nodine and associates (1967) suggest that

staff attention increases alertness, better performance, and even improved memory in the patient with organic brain syndrome. Both RNA-administered and placebo-treated groups of hospitalized senile patients "showed definite improvement in mental functioning from the attention they received during the study" (p. 1259).

3. *The group as a forum for problems and information.* Older adults frequently desire factual information. Forty per cent receive EST; patients want to know the side effects and prognosis. They also ask about other types of therapy. Staff and patients also provide information about employment and housing.

In the group the old patient can share his problems. That someone will listen to him, sympathize and help whenever possible he finds very reassuring. That other patients have similar difficulties and situations lessens his feelings of isolation.

Mrs. E was a 77-year-old who worked until she became depressed a few weeks prior to admission. Most staff and patients had difficulty tolerating her perpetual complaints. During the meetings we discovered that underlying her somatic complaints was a concern about her future—where she would stay and what she would do. Gradually the patient was able to discuss her primary concern rationally. The group discussed several alternatives, and, with the group's encouragement, she decided to move to Florida. Once she had come to a decision, satisfactory arrangements were made, and the patient improved.

4. *The group as a means of reality orientation* (Wolff, 1963). Although staff members empathize with patients who exhibit psychotic behavior or organicity, they point out reality in a noncondemning manner. Inappropriate behavior or irrational and jumbled speech is not ignored. Staff explains their meaning to the patient and other group members.

Mrs. P, an 82-year-old widow, came to P&PI from a home for the aged. She utilized the defense of compartmentalization to an extreme degree. In particular, she called patients by the wrong names. This disturbed the patients, who denied the incorrect identity. Mrs. P insisted that she was correct. After two sessions we were able to point out that patient Mr. F reminded her of Dr. S, her former employer, and that that was why she called him by that name. This was very reassuring to Mr. F. In time, Mrs. P correctly learned most of our names.

5. *The Group as a stimulus to motivation.* Many patients functioned better during and immediately following the meetings.

Mrs. G, a 79-year-old widow, from a nursing home, became confused and agitated following an operation for a broken hip. She was considered a difficult management problem on the ward, but was polite and verbal in the group. None of the nursing staff on her unit had ever seen her walk, although a few thought that she could. Following one meeting, she returned to the ward and walked down the halls pushing her wheelchair while the nurses looked on in amazement. Two weeks later she returned to the nursing home.

6. *The Group as a role provider.* The group provided a variety of opportunities for role fulfillment. Since the overall treatment strategy must in part involve helping the patient to find formerly useful roles or to establish new adaptive ones, the group proved an excellent adjunct to other forms of therapy. Patients who seemed to have the most successful group experience (as estimated by symptomatic improvement) were those who were able to establish a constructive role in the group.

Miss G, a 67-year-old, single social worker, was admitted with a psychotic depression with paranoid features. After several meetings in which she said very little she assumed the role of her prior occupation and frequently portrayed a social worker in tone of voice. Upon discharge she obtained work as a part-time social worker for a governmental agency. She functioned well in this position until she died of a stroke 10 months later.

Mrs. H, 76, was hospitalized in an acutely agitated state following the leg amputation of her sister with whom she lived. She had made a few acquaintances through the years but had never been considered an extrovert. Her two children, living in different cities, were not particularly close to her. Yet she was "everybody's helper" in the group. Any new patient would be oriented and comforted by Mrs. H. Later she extended these activities to younger patients on the unit. She was one of the hospital's most popular patients. Despite her initially poor prognosis, she was doing well seven months after discharge.

7. *The group as a diagnostic agent.* The group permitted diagnosis of the kind and extent of pathology not previously determined by the patient's therapist.

Mr. G, a 66-year-old married lawyer admitted with an agitated depression, was painfully aware of a recent partial loss of his cognitive ability. During his other three admissions he was hospitalized for two to three weeks with five to seven EST treatments. The plan was the same for this hospitalization. The patient attended his first meeting when three patients were attending their last. The latter were lighthearted, jovial, and relatively enthusiastic about discharge. Mr. G interrupted in a hostile manner and demanded that everybody stop talking about discharge or he would leave. As he spoke about his own situation, it became obvious that, despite his family, his work was the most important part of his life. Because of his organic changes he was no longer capable of performing satisfactorily. While Mr. G rambled on, none of the other patients said anything for the duration of the meeting. Staff members believed that the patient was a suicide risk and conveyed this discovery to his therapist. Mr. G was then transferred to a more closed unit and was hospitalized for several months before discharge. He did not participate in the group meetings for one month but later returned as an active member.

A few patients did not attend the group meetings. One depressed woman refused to sit in the same room with disoriented patients. Throughout the only meeting she attended, she reiterated anxiously, "Isn't it a shame what can happen to a person?" She would not further express her feelings, however. Interestingly, she attempted to influence other depressed members not to attend, but was unsuccessful. In general, depressed patients occasionally raised objections or expressed anxiety about the presence of psychotic or senile members, but they continued coming to the meetings anyway.

Some—especially those on the more closed units—were too agitated to attend. They were hostile and threatening and felt frightened and threatened. Typically, when they became more accustomed to the hospital setting—perhaps after two or three weeks—they would join the group and enjoy the meetings.

The following consistently proved to be core issues:

1. *Somatic complaints.* "Why can't I sleep?" "I just have no appetite." "My stomach is nervous."

2. *Memory loss.* "I can't remember like I used to. You shouldn't take your time to bother with me." "My memory's failing. I can't do my work. What's to become of me?"

3. *Social losses.* "My life changed when my husband passed away. Now most of my friends are dead too." "I lost my job, so now what?" "My children moved. That's why I'm in the hospital." "Nobody loves you when you're old and gray."

4. *Treatment.* "Does EST work?" "I don't understand how talking to my doctor is supposed to help me." "Isn't there a pill that can cure me?"

5. *Future placement.* "Where will I go when I leave here?" "I don't want to go to a nursing home. I want to go home, but my family doesn't want me."

6. *Independence vs. Dependence.* "I don't want anybody to take care of me. I can do fine myself." "I need help, but who's going to give it?" (same patient).

Other recurring issues were chronic infirmity, food, religion, and death.

DEVELOPMENT OF THE THERAPISTS' ATTITUDES

In the planning stage the therapists discussed their preconceived notions of the capacities and abilities of the aged. Group leaders were concerned that the patients might be reluctant to participate, slow to form a cohesive group, and adverse to discussing their problems with considerably younger staff members. On the contrary, patients were enthusiastic about meetings and were, in general, verbal. Certain issues, however, were not discussed initially due to the therapists' own anxiety. As the group therapists became more aware of their own feelings—as measured by postmeeting discussions—about such issues as memory loss, debility, sexuality, and death, these issues were discussed more openly at the meetings. It is postulated that any therapist who has not had to face the realities of aging—either because of his own youth or lack of experience with the aged—will undergo a major reorientation that will re-semble the phases listed below. Such a major reorientation seems inevitable, since there is very little in a youth-work-success-future-oriented culture that makes it necessary for one to view life from a different perspective. Reviewing developments and changes with the benefit of hindsight, our attitudes seemed to have evolved through three major phases.

Phase 1. Initially, the therapists' inexperience led them to view the patients as needy and empty individuals. They subsequently adopted an overprotective and unrealistically reassuring stance. The therapists, for example, provided tea and cookies for the patients at each meeting. Since the staff imagined that the patients were empty, we presented ourselves as concerned providers; since the patients were not expected to be verbal, and long periods of tensions and anxiety were anticipated, we thought the refreshments might provide some relief. What, in fact, happened was that the patients at first summarily rejected the cookies and tea. It was only when the patients prepared and served the refreshments that the group enjoyed them. Gradually, the discussion of important issues occu-pied so much of the meeting time that the group decided to discon-tinue serving. The refreshments were never missed nor mentioned again.

Another early error was responding to patients' concerns and complaints in an unrealistically reassuring manner. For example, one patient was just becoming aware of her memory loss. In an attempt to reassure her, the therapist proceeded to give a brief discourse on memory loss and concluded with the suggestion that the patient might think of writing things down. An older patient, with the wisdom that comes with age, then asked what good that was when she forgot where she had put the note or that she had ever written one.

In summary, the first phase was characterized by the therapists' attempts to "give" something to people perceived as needy indi-viduals. As the group members became more aware of the resources of both patients and therapists, it was no longer necessary to rely on refreshments and reassurances.

Phase 2. Increasingly, as the therapists became aware that aging involved *real* deficits and *real* losses that could not be replaced by well-meaning but unrealistic reassurances, they were less inclined to respond to every complaint or expression of frustration. On the other hand, they entered a phase characterized by a feeling of uselessness and sometimes mild depression. This period became one of self-questioning and inquiry. The therapists adopted a relatively nondirective stance. Patients' complaints were taken seriously, but rather than attempting to respond to every anxiety and concern, the therapists sought to clarify what the patients experienced. By this means the therapists were better able to empathize with the elderly patient and his emotional reactions to this situation. This technique helped patients to clarify their own concerns and feelings and later to begin to see how their feelings affected their decisions and actions.

Phase 3. The third phase was one of integration of learning and, of necessity, limitation of service. As the therapists better understood the aging process and the geriatric patient's deficits and resources, as they saw withdrawn and depressed patients reintegrated and symptomatically improve, and as they tested a variety of therapeutic techniques, they realized that most geriatric patients benefitted from the group. Group leaders became aware of other services that could profitably be provided for the aged—for example, placement, postdischarge therapy, and vocational planning. It is hoped that soon these services will supplement the group program.

EFFECTS OF THE GROUP ON HOSPITAL PERSONNEL

Preliminary indications reveal that this geriatric group has generated interest and affected the attitudes of those nurses and aides who work most closely with the geriatric patients. Seven of these nurses and aides were interviewed. They felt that the group had made them more aware of the problems of the geriatric patient. The number of lines written about the group members in the daily nursing report doubled between the time the group began and the reevaluation nine months later. Moreover, several nurses and aides requested and were granted permission to attend one or two group meetings.

Now that P&PI has an older adult program, as well as an adolescent and young adult (ages 18 to 25) program, the 25-to-65 year-old group feels neglected. Many women in their fifties have inquired about joining the geriatric group. The year 1970 has seen the beginning of a middle-aged group at P&PI.

Private psychiatrists initially were reluctant to refer their patients to the group. They questioned whether their patients could benefit from such an experience. The group sees increased cooperation and communication with several interested psychiatrists.

Finally, group staff members have found the older adult group so interesting and rewarding that all four plan to continue their work with older patients.

DIFFICULTIES IN EVALUATING THE GROUP

It is difficult, of course, to determine the degree to which the group was therapeutic. First, other forms of therapy were utilized contemporaneously—e.g., EST, drugs, individual psychotherapy, and adjunctive therapy. It is therefore impossible to determine the most important reason that a patient improves.

Second, many patients leave the hospital before group staff members feel they are ready. Often the patient's finances run out or his family insists that he leave the hospital for other reasons.

Third, to date we have not obtained a follow-up study. The private psychiatrist often does not see the patient after discharge, and reliable information is not given by family or nursing homes. Also, once a patient leaves the hospital, there is no outpatient group to support or aid him. At the present time, staff members are reviewing patients' charts with particular attention paid to modalities of treatment and prognostic evaluation at time of discharge. In addition, we are conducting a follow-up study by contacting each ex-patient directly and in the near future plan to start an outpatient group.

REFERENCES

Benaim, S. (1957), Group psychotherapy within a geriatric unit: an experiment. *Internat. J. Soc. Psychiat.*, 3:123-128.

Kalson, L. (1965), The therapy of discussion. *Geriat.* 20:397-401.

Klein, W., LeShan, E. & Furman, S. (1966), *Promoting Mental Health of Older People through Group Methods: A Practical Guide.* New York: Mental Health Materials Center.

Linden, M. (1953), Group therapy with institutionalized senile women: study in gerontologic human relations. *Internat. J. Group Psychother.*, 3:150-170.

—— (1955), Transference in gerontologic group psychotherapy. Studies in gerontologic human relations. *Internat. J. Group Psychother.*, 5:61-79.

Nodine, J., Shulkin, M., Slap, J., Levine, M. & Frieberg, K. (1967), A double-blind study of the effect of ribonucleic acid in senile brain disease. *Amer. J. Psychiat.*, 123:1257-1259.

Rechtschaffen, A. (1959), Psychotherapy with geriatric patients: a review of the literature. *J. Gerontol.*, 14:73-84.

Ross, M. (1959), A review of some recent treatment methods for elderly psychiatric patients. *Arch. Gen. Psychiat.*, 1:578-592.

Schwartz, E. & Goodman, J. (1952) Group therapy of obesity in elderly diabetics. *Geriat.*, 7:280-283.

Silver, A. (1950), Group psychotherapy with senile psychotic patients. *Geriat.*, 5:147-150.

Wolff, K. (1963), *Geriatric Psychiatry.* Springfield, Ill.: Charles C Thomas.

Wolk, R. & Goldfarb, A. (1967), The response to group psychotherapy of aged recent admissions compared with long-term mental hospital patients. *Amer. J. Psychiat.*, 123:1251-1257.

CHAPTER VI

GROUP PROCEDURES: A REVIEW OF THE LITERATURE

GROUP APPROACHES:
A REVIEW OF THE LITERATURE

Richard J. Malnati, Ph.D.
Assistant Professor
Temple University

Bach, G. R. Intensive group psychotherapy. New York: Ronald Press, 1954.

Back, K. W. Beyond words: The story of sensitivity training and the encounter movement. New York: Russel Sage Foundation, 1972.

Bales, R.F. Interaction process analysis: A method for the study of small groups.

Bany, M., & Johnson, L. Classroom group behavior: Group dynamics in classroom. New York: MacMillan, 1964.

Batchhelder, R. L., & Hardy, J. M. Using sensitivity training and the laboratory method: An organizational case study in the development of human resources. New York: Association Press, 1972.

Bates, M., & Johnson, C. D. Group leadership: A manual for group leaders. Denver, Colorado: Love Publishing, 1972.

Bennett, M. Guidance and counseling in groups. New York: McGraw-Hill, 1963.

Berkowitz, I. H. (Ed.) Adolescents grow in groups: Experiences in adolescent and group psychotherapy. New York: Banner, Mazel, 1972.

Berne, E. Transactional analysis in psychotherapy: A systematic individual and social psychiatry. New York: Grove Press, 1961.

Berne E. Principles of group treatment. New York: Oxford University Press, 1966.

Berne, E. What do you say after you say hello. New York: Grove Press, 1972.

Bion, W. R. Experiences in groups. New York: Basic Books, 1959.

ORIGINAL MANUSCRIPT, 1974.

Blake, L. R. Group training vs. group therapy. New York: Beacon House, 1958.

Blank, L., Gottsegan, G. B., & Gottsegan, M. G. (Eds.) Confrontation: Encounters in self and interpersonal awareness. New York: MacMillan, 1971.

Blatner, H. Psychodrama, role-playing and action methods: Theory and practice. Thetford, England: Howard A. Blatner, 1970.

Blumberg, A. Sensitivity training: Processes, problems, and applications. Syracuse: Syracuse University Publications in Continuing Education, 1971.

Bonner, H. Group dynamics. New York: Ronald Press, 1959.

Bradford, L. P. Group development. Washington, D. C.: National Training Laboratories, 1961.

Bradford, L. P. Gibb, J. R., & Benne, K. D. (Eds.) T-Group theory and laboratory method: Innovation in re-education. New York: Wiley, 1964.

Bugental, J. F. T. (Ed.) Challenges of humanistic psychology. New York: McGraw-Hill, 1967.

Burton, A. (Ed.) Encounter: The theory & practice of encounter groups. San Francisco: Jossey-Bass, 1969.

Cartwright, D., & Zander, A. (Eds) Group dynamics: Research and theory. Harper and Row, 1968.

Cohn, B. (Chm.) Guidelines for future research on group counseling in the public school. Washington, D. C.: American Personnel and Guidance Association, 1967.

Cooper, C. L., & Mangham, T. L. T-groups: A survey of research. New York: Wiley. 1971.

Corsini, R. J., & Putzey, L. J. Bibliography of group psychotherapy literature 1906-1956. Beacon, New York: Beacon House, 1957.

Corsini, R. J. Roleplaying in psychotherapy: A manual. Chicago: Aldine Publishing, 1966.

Davis, R. Reducing social tension and conflict through the group conversion method. New York: Association Press, 1971.

239

De Marie, P. B. Perspectives in group psychotherapy: A theoretical background. London: Allen & Unwin, 1972.

Diedrich, R. C., & Dye, H. A. (Eds.) Group procedures, purposes, processes, and outcomes. New York: Houghton-Mifflin, 1972.

Dinkmeyer, D., & Miro, J. J. Group counseling: Theory and practice. Itasca, Illinois: E. Peacok, 1971.

Dreikurs, R. Group psychotherapy and group approaches: Collected papers. Chicago: Alfred Adler Institute, 1960.

Driver, H. I. Multiple counseling: A small group discussion method for personal growth. Madison, Wisconsin: Monona Publications, 1954.

Driver, H. I. (Ed.) Counseling and learning through small group discussion. Madison, Wisconsin: Monona Publications, 1958.

Durkin, H. The group in depth. New York: International Universities Press, 1966.

Dye, H. A. Fundamental group procedures for school counselors. New York: Houghton-Mifflin, 1968.

Dyer, W. G. (Ed.) Modern theory and method in group training. New York: Van Nostrand Reinhold, 1972.

Eagan, G. Encounter: Group processes for interpersonal growth. Belmont, California: Brooks/Cole Publishing, 1970.

Edelson, M. Ego psychology, group dynamics, and the therapeutic community. New York: Grune and Stratton, 1964.

Edelson, M. The practice of sociotherapy: A case study. New Haven, Connecticut: Yale University Press, 1970.

Fagan, J., & Shepherd, I. R. Gestalt therapy now. Palo Alto, California: Science and Behavior Books, 1970.

Fast, J. Body language. Philadelphia: J. B. Lippencott, 1970.

Foulkes, S. H. Therapeutic group analysis. New York: Public Affairs Committee, 1959.

Foulkes, S. H. & Anthony, E. G. Group psychotherapy: The psychoanalytic approach.

Frank, J. D. Group methods in therapy. New York: Public Affairs Committee, 1959.

Freud, S. Group psychology and the analysis of the ego. London: International Psychological Press, 1922.

Fullmer, D. W., & Bernard, H. W. Family consultation. New York: Houghton-Mifflin, 1968.

Fullmer, D. W. Counseling: Group theory and system. Scranton, Pennsylvania: International Textbook, 1971.

Gazda, G. M., & Golds, J. H. Group guidance: A critical incident approach. Champaign, Illinois: Research Press, 1968.

Gazda, G. M. (Ed.) Group Counseling. Journal of Research and Development in Education, 1968, 1 (1), pp. 1-132.

Gazda, G. M. (Ed.) Basic approaches to group psychotherapy and group counseling. Springfield, Illinois: Charles C. Thomas, 1968. (a)

Gazda, G. M. (Ed.) Innovations to group psychotherapy. Springfield, Illinois: Charles C. Thomas, 1968. (b)

Gazda, G. M. (Ed.) Theories and methods of group counseling in the schools. Springfield, Illinois: Charles C. Thomas, 1969.

Gazda, G. M. (Ed.) Groups in guidance. Washington, D. C.: American Personnel and Guidance Association, 1970.

Gazda, G. M. (Ed.) Group counseling: A developmental approach. Boston: Allyn and Bacon, 1971.

Gibbard, G. S., Hartman, J. J., & Mann, R. D. (Eds.) Analysis of Groups. San Francisco, California: Jossey-Bass, 1973.

Ginott, H. Group psychotherapy with children. New York: McGraw-Hill, 1961.

Glass, S. D. The practical handbook of group counseling. Baltimore: BCS Publishing, 1969.

Glasser, W., & Iverson, N. Large group counseling. Los Angeles: Reality Press; 1966.

Glanz, F. C., & Hayes, R. W. Group in guidance (2nd Ed.) Boston: Allyn & Bacon 1967.

Goldberg, G. Encounter: Group sensitivity training experience. New York: Science and Behavior Books, 1970.

Golembiewski, R.T. The small group: An analysis of research concepts and operations. Chicago: University of Chicago Press, 1962.

Golombieski, R. T., & Blumberg, A. (Eds.) Sensitivity training and the laboratory approach: Readings about concepts and applications. Itasca, Illinois: F. E. Peacock, 1970.

Golombiewski, R. T., Renewing organizations: The laboratory approach to planned change. Itasca, Illinois, Peacock Publishers, 1972.

Gordon, T. Group-centered leadership. Boston: Houghton-Mifflin, 1955.

Gorlow, L., & Hoch, E. L. & Teleschow, E. G. The nature of non-directive group psychotherapy: An experimental investigation. New York: Columbia University Press, 1952.

Hass, R. B. Psychodrama and sociodrama in American education. Beacon, New York: Beacon House, 1955.

Hanson, J. C., & Cramer, S.H. Group guidance and counseling in the schools. New York: Appelton-Century-Crofts, 1971.

Hare, A. P. Handbook of small group research. New York: Free Press, 1962.

Hare, A. P. Borgatta, E. F., & Bales, (Eds.) Small group studies: Studies in social interaction. New York: Knoph, 1965.

Harris, T. A. I'm Ok, you're Ok; A practical guide to trans-actional analysis. New York: Harper & Row, 1969.

Hebst, P. G. Autonomous group functioning: An exploration in behavior theory and measurement. London: Tavistock Publications, 1962.

Hill, W. F. Hill Interaction Matrix: A method of studying interaction in psychotherapy groups. Beverly Hills, California: Sage Publications. 1965.

Hill, W. F. Learning through discussion. Beverly Hills, California: Sage Publications, 1969.

Hinckley, R. J., & Herman, L. Group treatment in psychotherapy: A report of experience. Minneapolis: University of Minnesota Press, 1951.

Howard, J. Please touch: A guided tour of the human potential movement. New York: McGraw-Hill, 1970.

Ivey, A. E., & Alschuler, A. S. (Eds.) Psychological education: A prime function of the counselor. Washington, D. C.: American Personnel and Guidance Association, 1973.

Johnson, J. A. Group therapy: A practical approach. New York: McGraw-Hill, 197, 1963.

Kadis, A. L., & Krasner, J. D. A practicum of group psychotherapy. New York: Harper & Row, 1963.

Kaplan, H. I., & Sadock, B. J., Comprehensive group psychotherapy. Baltimore: Williams and Wilkins, 1971.

Kemp, C. G. Perspectives on the group process: A foundation for counseling with groups. (2nd. Ed.) Boston: Houghton-Mifflin, 1970.

Kemp, C. G. Foundations of group counseling. New York: McGraw-Hill, 1970.

Klein, A. F Effective group work: An introduction to principle and method. New York: Association Press, 1972.

Klein, A. F. Role-playing in leadership training and group problem-solving. New York: Association Press, 1956.

Klapman, J. W. Group psychotherapy: Theory and practice. New York: Grune & Stratton, 1946.

Knowles, J. W. Group counseling. Englewood Cliffs, New Jersey: Prentice Hall, 1966.

Lakin, M. An encounter with sensitivity. New York: McGraw-Hill, 1970.

Lakin, M. Interpersonal encounter: Theory and practice in sensitivity training. New York: McGraw-Hill, 1972.

Levy, R. B. Human relations: A conceptual approach. Scranton: Pennsylvania.

Lewin, K. Field theory in social science. (Edited by D. Cartwright) New York: Harper and Bros., 1951.

Lieberman, M. A., Yalom, I. D., & Miles, M. B. Encounter groups: First facts. New York: Basic Books, 1973.

Lifton, W. M. Working with groups. (2nd ed.) New York: Wiley, 1966.

Lifton, W. M. Groups: Facilitating individual growth and societal change. New York: Wiley, 1972.

Locke, N. M. A decade of group psychotherapy: The bibliography for 1950-1959.

Lubin, B., & Lubin, A. Group psychotherapy: A bibliography of the literature from 1956 through 1964. East Lansing, Michigan: Michigan University Press, 1966.

Luchins, A. S. Group therapy: A guide. New York: Random House, 1964.

Luft, J. (Ed.) Group process: An introduction to group dynamics. Palo Alto, California: National Press, 1970.

Luft, J. Of human interaction. Palo Alto: National Press, 1969.

MacLennan, B. W., & Felsenfeld, N. Group counseling and psychotherapy with adolescents. New York: Columbia University Press, 1968.

Mahler, C. A. Group counseling in the schools. Boston: Houghton-Mifflin, 1969.

Malamud, D., & Machover, S. Toward self-understanding: Group techniques in self-confrontation. Springfield, Illinois: Charles C. Thomas, 1965.

Maliver, B. L. The encounter game. New York: Stein and Daly, 1973.

Mann, J. H. Encounter: A weekend with intimate strangers. New York: Grossman Publishers, 1970.

Marrow, A. The practical theorist: The life and work of Kurt Lewin. New York: Basic Books, 1969.

McCarty, T. It all has to do with identity: A handbook of group interaction. Salt Lake City: Institute for the Study of Interaction Systems, 1969.

McGrath, J. E., & Altman, I. Small group research: Asynthesis and critique of the field. New York: Holt, Rinehart, & Winston, 1966.

Miles, M. B. Learning to work in groups. New York: Teachers College Press, 1959.

Mintz, E. E. Marathon groups: Reality and symbol. New York: Appleton-Century-Crofts, 1971.

Moreno, J. L., & Moreno, Z. Psychodrama. New York: Bacon House, 1959.

Moreno, J. L. (Ed.) The international handbook of group pscyhotherapy. New York: Philosophical Library, 1966.

Mowrer, O. H. The new group therapy. Princeton: D. Van Nostrand, 1966.

Mullan, H., & Rosenboum, J. A group psychotherapy: Theory and practice. New York: Free Press, 1962.

Muro, J. J., & Freeman, S. L. (Eds.) Readings in group counseling. Scranton, Pennsylvania: International Textbook, 1968.

Noland, R. L. (Ed.) Counseling parents of the emotionally disturbed child. Springfield, Illinois: Charles C. Thomas, 1972.

Napier, R. W., & Gershenfeld, M. K. Groups: Theory and experience. Boston: Houghton-Mifflin, 1973.

O'Banion, T., & O'Connell, A. The shared journey: An introduction to encounter. Englewood Cliffs, New Jersey: Prentice-Hall, 1970.

Oden, T. C. The intensive group experience: The new pietism. Philadelphia: Westminister Press, 1972.

Ohlsen, M. M. Group counseling. New York: Holt, Rinehart, and Winston, 1970.

Ohlsen, M. M. Group counseling in the elementary school. New York: Holt, Rinehart, and Winston, 1972.

Ohlsen, M. M. Counseling children in groups: A forum. New York: Holt, Rinehart, and Winston, 1973.

Otto, H., & Mann, J. (Eds.) Ways of growth: Approaches to expanding awareness. New York: Grossman, 1968.

Otto, H. Group methods of actualize human potential: A handbook. Beverly Hills: California: Holistic Press, 1970.

Ottoway, A. K. Learning through the group experience. New York: Humanities Press, 1966.

Peck, H. B. Treatment of the delinquent adolescent: Group and individual therapy with parent and child. New York: Family Service Association of America, 1954.

Perls, F. S. Gestalt therapy verbatim. Lafayette, California: Real People Press, 1969.

Pesso, A. Movement in psychotherapy: Psychomotor techniques and training. New York: New York University Press, 1972.

Pfeiffer, J., & Jones, J. The annual handbook for group facilitators. Iowa City: University Associates Press 1972.

Pinney, E. L. A first group psychotherapy book. Springfield, Illinois: Charles C. Thomas, 1970.

Powdermaker, G., & Frank, J. Group psychotherapy: Studies in methodology of research and therapy. Cambridge: Harvard University Press, 1953.

Rogers, C. R. Carl Rogers on encounter groups. New York: Harper & Row, 1970.

Rose, S. D., Treating children in groups: A behavioral approach. San Francisco: Josey-Baas, 1972.

Rosenbaum, M., & Berger, M. (Eds.) Group psychotherapy and group function: Selected readings. New York: Basic Books, 1963.

Ruitenbeck, H. M. Group therapy today: Styles, methods, and techniques. New York: Atherton Press, 1969.

Ruitenbeck, H. M. The new group therapies. New York: Avon Books, 1970.

Sarger, C. J. & Kaplan, H. S. (Eds.) Progress in group and family therapy. New York: Bruney Mazel, 1972.

Satir, V. Conjoint family therapy. (Rev. Ed.) Palo Alto: Science and Behavior Books, 1967.

Schein, E. H. & Bennis, W. G. (Eds.) Personal and organizational change through group methods. New York: Wiley, 1965.

Schein, E. H. Process consultation: Its role in organizational development. Reading, Massachusetts: Addison-Wesley, 1969.

Sheppard, M., & Lee, M. Marathon 16. New York: Putnam, 1970.

Schmuk, R., & Schmuk, P. A. Group processes in the classroom. Dubuque, Iowa: W. C. Brown, 1971.

Schutz, W. C. Joy: Expanding human awareness. New York: Grove Press, 1967.

Schutz, W. C. Here come everybody. New York: Harper & Row, 1972.

Schaftel, F. R., & Shaftel, G. R. Role-playing for social values: Decision-making in the social studies. Englewood Cliffs, New Jersey: Prentice-Hall, 1967.

Shaffer, J. B., & Galinsky, M. D. Models of group therapy and sensitivity training. Englewood Cliffs, New Jersey: Prentice-Hall, 1973.

Shaw, M. E. Group dynamics: The psychology of small group behavior. New York: McGraw-Hill, 1971.

Siroka, R. W., Siroka, E. K., & Schloss, G. A. (Eds.) Sensitivity training and group encounter: An introduction. New York: Grossett and Dunlap, 1971.

Slavson, S. R. An introduction to group therapy. New York: International Universities Press, 1943.

Slavson, S. R. (Ed.) The practice of group psychotherapy. New York: International Universities Press, 1947.

Slavson, S. R. A textbook in analytic group psychotherapy. New York: International University Press, 1964.

Slavson, S. R. Reclaiming the delinquent by para-analytic group psychotherapy and the conversion technique. New York: Free Press, 1965.

Slavson, S. R. (Ed.) The fields of group psychotherapy. New York: Schocken Books, 1971.

Sigrell, B. Group psychotherapy. Studies of process in therapeutic groups. Stockholm, Sweden: Almqvist & Wiskell, 1968.

Simon, A., & Boyer, E. G. (Eds.) Mirrors for behavior: An anthology of observation instruments. (9vols.) Philadelphia: Research for Better Schools, 1970.

Simon, S., Howe, L., & Kirshenbaum, H. Values clarification: A practical handbook for teachers and students. New York: Hart, 1972.

Solomon, L. N., & Berzon, B. (Eds.) New perspectives on encounter groups. Washington, D. C.: Jossey-Bass, 1972.

Thompson, S., & Kahn, J. H. The group process as a helping technique. New York: Pergamon Press, 1970.

Vriend, J., & Dyer, W. W. Counseling effectively in groups. Englewood Cliffs, New Jersey: Educational Technology Publications, 1973.

Walton, H. J. (Eds.) Small group psychotherapy. Baltimore: Penquin Books, 1971.

Warters, J. Group guidance: Principles and practices. New York: McGraw-Hill, 1960.

Wassell, B., & Bohdan, E. Group psychoanalysis. New York: Philosophical Library, 1959.

Witaker, D. S., & Lieberman, M. A. Psychotherapy through the group process. New York: Atherton Press, 1964.

Whitely, J. M. (Ed.) Encounter groups. Washington University, Missouri: American Psychological Association, No. 2, 1970.

Whitely, J. M. (Ed.) Integrity group therapy. Washington University, Missouri: American Psychological Association, No. 2, 1972.

Willey, R., & Strong, W. M. Group procedures in guidance. New York: Harper & Row, 1957.

Winder, A. E., & Appley, D. G. T-groups and therapy groups in a changing society. San Francisco, California: Jossey-Bass, 1973.

Yalom, I. The theory and practice of group psychotherapy. New York: Basic Books, 1970.